FIELDWORK CONNECTIONS

FIELDWORK CONNECTIONS

THE FABRIC OF ETHNOGRAPHIC COLLABORATION
IN CHINA AND AMERICA

BAMO AYI • STEVAN HARRELL • MA LUNZY

WITH A CONTRIBUTION BY BAMO QUBUMO

UNIVERSITY OF WASHINGTON PRESS • SEATTLE & LONDON

University of Washington Press
P.O. Box 50096, Seattle, WA 98145, U.S.A.
www.washington.edu/uwpress

Library of Congress Cataloging-in-Publication Data
Bamo, Ayi.
Fieldwork connections : the fabric of ethnographic
collaboration in China and America / Bamo Ayi, Stevan
Harrell, Ma Lunzy with a contribution by Bamo Qubumo.
p.   cm.
Includes bibliographical references and index.
ISBN-13: 978-0-295-98668-5 (pbk. : alk. paper)
ISBN-10: 0-295-98668-9 (pbk. : alk. paper)
1. Ethnology—China—Sichuan Sheng—Field work.
2. Ethnology—Washington (State)—Seattle—Field work.
3. Ethnologists—China—Sichuan Sheng—Biography.
4. Ethnologists—Washington (State)—Seattle—Biography.
5. Bamo, Ayi.   6. Ma, Lunzy.   7. Harrell, Stevan.
I. Harrell, Stevan.   II. Ma, Lunzy.   III. Title.
GN635.C5B36   2007   306.0951—dc22   2007003438

CONTENTS

PREFACE TO THE ENGLISH EDITION

STEVAN HARRELL

E thnography is an odd science. Fieldworkers spend relatively short amounts of time in familiar or alien communities, and attempt to write about their experiences for an audience much less familiar with the communities than the authors are. In the process of data collection and writing, fieldworkers raise unique epistemological, rhetorical, emotional, and ethical questions. In order to illuminate the ethnographic process through a somewhat unusual set of examples, four ethnographers have written a book together, each telling his or her own story. This book is an account of the intertwined professional research history of three anthropologists—Bamo Ayi, Ma Lunzy, and me—between 1987 and 2000. The research described in the book took place both in Liangshan Yi Autonomous Prefecture, Sichuan, the home of the Nuosu and other ethnic groups, and in Seattle, Washington. One of the researchers was a complete outsider to the Liangshan Nuosu research context; one is a Nuosu "native" who grew up outside the native cultural context; and one is a Nuosu who grew up within the native cultural context.

The book begins with short accounts by the principal authors of the process by which each became involved in anthropological field research, and then proceeds to accounts of the research itself, beginning with

Bamo's dissertation work and Harrell's initial fieldwork in China, both in 1987–88. In 1991, the stories of the authors begin to connect, as Harrell and Ma, then Harrell and Bamo, and eventually Harrell, Ma, and Bamo's younger sister, Bamo Qubumo, become active collaborators. The scene shifts in the course of the narrative from China to America, and the relationship between the authors shifts from distant, wary, and somewhat hierarchical to close, egalitarian, and reciprocal. The book ends with a brief essay by Harrell that relates the narrative to theoretical concerns about anthropological research. There is no structure, no argument, to the body of this book; the arrangement of material is chronological and not expository. Each author wrote his or her own field research history in several chapters, and then the chapters were interwoven to create a chronologically ordered account.

Our ethnographic histories begin in the late 1980s, but the book as a book began in 1997, when I wrote a draft introduction to the more conventional ethnographic work later published as *Ways of Being Ethnic in Southwest China* (Harrell 2001), pointing out some of the ways that I had encountered and dealt with the perpetual problems of doing ethnography. At the time, Bamo Ayi was living in Seattle as a scholarly exchange fellow of the Committee on Scholarly Communication with China, doing the field research on the Free Methodist Church described in chapter 16, and giving me intermediate-level lessons in the Nuosu language. On a snowy weekend, she had begun translating some of the substantive chapters of my book draft, and I asked both her and my then graduate student Ren Hai to read and comment on the introduction. Ren Hai, who had been very involved in an early episode of the story (see chapter 5), said that he would like to write a parallel story of his own, and soon Ayi had signed on to a three-way project. Since I had collaborated more closely with Ma Lunzy than with anyone else, and since he was also a friend of Ayi's, we quickly enlisted him in the project, each of us intending to write a single narrative, to be combined between the covers of a book. Ren Hai later became busy with other projects, and decided not to contribute, though we salute him as the originator of the concept of the project.

The original idea for the book encompassed only our work in Liang-shan (chapters 4 through 14), and included three separate narratives, overlapping in some but not all of the stories told from the different authorial perspectives. But Ayi expressed an interest in writing about her Seattle fieldwork, and, as the book continued to take shape, it became clear that it would be even more interesting if it were not just about our interactions in China, where Bamo Ayi and Ma Lunzy were natives, and I an outsider, but also about our work in America, where the roles were reversed. This meant that we needed to deal not only with Ma Lunzy's first impressions of America (chapter 15) and with Bamo Ayi's Seattle field research (chapter 16) but also with the exhibit "Mountain Patterns: Survival of Nuosu Culture in China," which Ma Lunzy, Bamo Qubumo (Ayi's younger sister), and I curated at the Burke Museum. This meant bringing in accounts of the exhibit process by Ma Lunzy and me, and including one chapter by Bamo Qubumo, who otherwise hovers outside the authorship but by no means outside the story of the book. Chapters 17 through 19 (originally published as a joint account of the exhibit in *Asian Ethnicity* in 2001) thus present three perspectives on another project that is part of the overall story.

Eventually, it became clear that separating the various authors' contributions into three big chunks and one little chunk was rather awkward, and that we ought to present the material in chronological order, giving rise to the current arrangement of interthreaded chapters. And, since readers were not likely to be familiar with our backgrounds, we added short biographies of our early years (chapters 1 through 3) to give readers an idea of where each of the three principal authors came from.

Finally, the more technical or theoretical treatment of ethnographic problems, originally the introduction to my section, then the preface to the chronologically arranged book, has seemed to us less and less central to the overall project; we are, quite frankly, more interested in telling an interesting story that will help readers think about ethnography than we are in making theoretical hay out of the story's context and contents. We have thus relegated this discussion to an epilogue (chapter 20), which readers should consider distinctly optional.

We also decided to try to publish this book in an English-language edition in the United States, and in a Chinese-language edition in China. I translated all of the chapters by Bamo Ayi and Bamo Qubumo; they commented on the translations, which were revised accordingly. Ma

Lunzy knows no English and has to rely on my goodwill for the accuracy of my renderings of his prose. For the forthcoming Chinese edition, my chapters were translated by Zhang Haiyang; I made comments on his translations.

As far as we know, this book is unique in the literature on anthropological field research. Our stories involve personal history, professional ambition, scholarly pursuit, cultural conflict, cooperation, and friendship. As our stories overlap and connect to each other, the book becomes like a piece of Nuosu needlework. Bright threads of four different colors, combined in unequal proportions, have been twisted together into a series of intricate and symbolically meaningful designs, but no single thread has meaning until it is sewn together with the others. All of us enjoy writing; none is any good at actual needlework; and each of us hopes to tell a story that not only entertains but also concretely addresses the process of ethnography and the dynamics of international and intercultural communication. We have worked together for almost fifteen years now, and the stories in this volume do not even bring us up to the present, let alone predict anything about a collaborative future whose end is nowhere in sight.

ACKNOWLEDGMENTS

All of us wish to thank the many people, too numerous to mention, who helped and encouraged us in our research and writing. In addition, each of us has the following special thanks:

I am extremely grateful to Amber M. D. Joy and Solveig Arnold, who opened another wonderful world for me. I would very much like to dedicate this book to my dear friend Mr. Edwin E. Williams.

BAMO AYI

I want to thank Ren Hai, who first had the idea for this book, as well as those who read and commented on the manuscript—Gail Hershatter, Robert Weller, and Hill Gates. My Chinese mentors—Tong Enzheng and Deng Yaozong—are gone now, but my gratitude and my memory of them continue to hover over the project. In addition, I want to give special thanks to my wife Barbara Harrell, who not only materially improved the book by her careful and critical reading but supported me in so many ways while I was doing both the fieldwork and the writing.

STEVAN HARRELL

I first want to thank my friend Meiguo Muga, from whom I have learned so much since we first met in 1991. Seeing him on his visits to Yangjuan, I often think that if the strong and weak of the world, the poor and rich, the educated and the uneducated could live together like this, "I," "you," and "he" would merge, and we would have peace and harmony. I also want to thank Muga's wife Barbara, who took such pains to make sure that I, "blind in English," ate well and felt at home during my time in Seattle. Finally, I want to thank Professors Bamo Ayi and Bamo Qubumo, scholars of deep learning who were so considerate to me during our fieldwork together; one is indeed fortunate to have teachers like them.

MA LUNZY

FIELDWORK CONNECTIONS

PART I ORIGINS

GROWING UP HALF YI

BAMO AYI

" **A**nthropological field research" usually refers to participant observation in a culture different from one's own. But in my mind,
Yi culture is not some kind of "other" culture. In terms of identity, I have a lifelong natural identification with it; it is my own culture;
but in terms of knowledge, it is somewhat distant from me. Because I
have a certain but not completely familiar understanding of it, I am a
long way from being able to give a perfect explanation. Maybe it was
the contradiction between the strong emotional attachment and the considerable intellectual distance that pulled me onto that path over mountains and across valleys, that road of no return that is fieldwork.

I come from a half-Yi household. My father is a Yi; my mother is
from Inner Mongolia, a land distant from the Southwest, where we,
along with most Yi, lived. This kind of household, although made up
of people from different ethnic groups, didn't eliminate the ethnic consciousness of its members; on the contrary, unlike those "wholly" Yi
households, a bell sounding out "Yi" often rang in our ears. In my childhood memories, what rang this bell was when we wore our beautiful
Yi clothing on holidays or special days, when we learned from our father
to sing Yi children's songs, or when Father taught me to recite the twelve
calendrical animals in the Yi language.

When I was about five years old, because my widowed grandaunt (my father's paternal aunt) needed a companion, I went from our house in Zhaojue County Town to the seat of a Yi district in Puge County, called Tumugou. Grandaunt was a worker in the district supply and marketing cooperative, and had always been in charge of selling agricultural tools and chemicals. Half of the salespeople in the cooperative were Yi, and half were Han; the Yi could speak not-too-fluent Chinese, while the Han could use Yi to discuss the worth and the prices of their goods. In the local central primary school, in addition to children of workers in the various offices of the district and the children of nearby farming families, there were quite a few boys who had come down from high mountain villages to board and study at the school. Most of them were older and taller. All of the teachers were Han, and they used Chinese in class; some also explained things in Yi. Outside of class, if I wasn't in the store helping Grandaunt lift hoes, fetch 66 pesticide powder, or greet and send off Yi farmers, I was going up to the mountains with the mountain children to pick wild fruit or bathe and catch fish in the rivers. The days I looked forward to most every year were the night of the Fire Festival, when I played with torches with the village children and prayed for a rich harvest, and the Nuosu[1] New Year, when we went to nearby farmers' houses to ask for meat frozen in sour soup. My most visceral memory is of lying in bed while everyone else was asleep, hearing Grandaunt's loud, drunken Nuosu laments for her deceased elder brothers, or during a fierce storm hearing Grandaunt in a hushed voice and a secretive manner discussing the glorious history of the Bamo clan.

When I think of it now, though I was only a little companion, I was nevertheless the receptor for Grandaunt's unburdenings, and without understanding what I was doing, I helped her rid herself of her feelings of loneliness and pain.

At the beginning of 1972, when I was eleven, because Mother found

---

1. "Yi" is a Chinese-language term for one of the fifty-six officially designated *minzu*, or "nationalities" into which the population of China is divided. There are about eight million Yi in China. "Nuosu" is a native-language name for the largest ethnic group among the Yi, who live in Liangshan, Sichuan, and number about two million. All the Yi referred to in this book, including the coauthors, are Nuosu. We use the terms almost interchangeably, though we tend to use Yi in official and Nuosu in less official contexts.

several wrong characters in a letter I had sent her, she felt strongly that the level of my country education was just too low, and had me return to Zhaojue. Even though Zhaojue was a Yi county, its county seat was the capital of the prefecture, and the majority of the people in the offices and bureaus were Han from outside. My school, East Is Red Elementary, was a school for prefectural and county cadres' children, and of over forty students in my class, only a few were Yi. In school and out, I lacked a Yi linguistic environment.

The Nuosu language that I had spoken in Tumugou came on the scene only when relatives visited from the country. There were no Yi language classes in school, and at home Mother couldn't speak Yi. Father had written a conversational Nuosu book to teach us children, and sometimes even Mother was hauled in by Father to be a student. But Father was often away in the villages doing his social education work, and it was difficult for him to carry on his household Yi education. My Nuosu language deteriorated, and at the same time my schoolwork improved greatly; from being the worst student in my class when I transferred into the school, a year and a half later when I graduated, I tested fourth. During my junior-high and high-school years, aside from a few songs and dances such as "Song of the Slaves,"[2] which was performed by the prefectural song and dance troupe, and a few other Yi songs, in school and out I rarely heard mention of topics related to the Yi. At that time, there was only a government-sponsored movement encouraging us to sing the praises of the new Chinese Communist society by "recalling bitterness and thinking about sweetness," for the purpose of which we went to the sanitarium to interview ill and crippled former slaves who had suffered the abuse of the horribly evil slave lords. We also went to villages to debate or even throw rocks at the Bbaqie clan slave lords who, we were taught, wanted to reverse the tide of history. Only these experiences gave me any new knowledge about the past of the Nuosu.

I contrasted my impression of the Bamo clan that I had learned when

---

2. The events referred to here happened during the period known as the Great Proletarian Cultural Revolution (1966–76), when "class struggle" was the basis of social and political mobilization everywhere in China. Since the Nuosu society in Liangshan was classified as a slaveholding society rather than a feudal society like that of Han China, the targets of class struggle were not landlords but slave lords.

I was with Grandaunt with what I had heard about the slave lords, and doubtfully asked Father, "Was his dad also . . . ?" Father told me that, before the Democratic Reforms in 1955, because of fights with enemy clans, Grandfather's opium smoking, and Grandmother's early death, our family's wealth was exhausted and its people scattered, and so our class had been designated as "semi-slave." But because Grandfather had once been local village head for the Kuomintang regime, he was attacked as a historical counterrevolutionary, and died in a prison at Leibo. During the Cultural Revolution, when class origin was emphasized, from the Democratic Reforms until about 1980, because of Grandfather's counterrevolutionary status, Father had also been implicated. Even in my own dossier there was a note about my grandfather being a historical counterrevolutionary. During my second year of college, the organization department of the prefectural Chinese Communist Party Committee notified my academic department that they had corrected a mistake in my dossier, and had thereby "taken off the hat" of my grandfather's historical counterrevolutionary status, removing a blot from my record.

When I was in school in Zhaojue, there were often country relatives who came to visit, and Father encouraged us to go to the country to see relatives and visit friends. Many times, as soon as vacation began, I took my younger brother and sisters, either on the bus or hitching a ride on a Liberation-brand truck, to our old family home in Yuexi County or to Grandaunt's place in Tumugou. At the old home, our second uncle took us to see the stone mill or the watchtowers from the time of the flourishing of the Bamo clan, or our youngest uncle organized all of us cousins to go to the cemetery to worship the ancestors, or our grandmothers would tell us stories of when our fathers and uncles were little. We went to pay respects at the battlefield where the Bamo clan had fought its enemies. We went together with village children to herd pigs or to climb around the valleys and haystacks. But as soon as I returned to Zhaojue, even though the majority of the people coming to market were Yi men in their *vala*[3] or Yi women in their flowery clothing, these people didn't seem to have much connection with the little world of us children.

---

3. Fringed capes.

In 1977 the national educational reform meant that students would be admitted to universities according to their scores on university examinations. At that time, I had just entered the second year of high school, and our school recommended six students from the class of 1978 to take the college exam a year early. I was fortunately selected to take the exam, and was admitted to the philosophy major in the politics department of the Central Nationalities Institute. When the list of admitted students was posted, my name, Bamo Ayi Shybbumo, was the longest—seven syllables—and listed on the last line. This quickly became news in all the prefectural offices and throughout the county. To this day, people still joke with me that I not only switched from a Han name to a Yi name but switched to the longest name in Liangshan Prefecture.

The name I had previously used at school was a Han name, An Lan, but when I registered for the exam, Father said that we Yi ought to use Yi names, and that I should use my formal Nuosu name from our old home, Bamo Ayi Shybbumo. Bamo is a surname; Ayi is the sibling-order name for the oldest among a group of sisters; Shybbu is a personal name; and "-mo" is a suffix indicating a female. I happily accepted the idea of changing to a Yi name, but to go from using my original two-syllable name to the formal seven-syllable name that Father suggested was a little unfamiliar at first. But I thought Father's suggestion had merit, so I bravely registered my seven-syllable Yi name. Most of the Nuosu children born in the 1960s and '70s used Han names, but in the '80s and '90s, the number of people using Yi names increased steadily, including those of us in the younger generations. In addition, using seven-syllable formal names became a kind of fashion, to the point that Nuosu children born in places like Beijing or Chengdu, far removed from the Nuosu homeland, to my knowledge still mostly use Yi names. After this, my younger brother and sisters changed over to using Yi names (fig. 1.1).

During four years of college, Marxist philosophical theory, the history of Chinese and foreign philosophy, and original philosophical works were part of my basic course of study. At the same time, I learned about another topic that wasn't on the official class schedule: ethnic identity and ethnic feelings. The Central Nationalities Institute was a great multiethnic family; there people of different ethnic groups interacted, and also made comparisons to each other. Every ethnic group celebrated its own holidays, had its own gatherings, and people of the same ethnic group helped and supported each other. People of the same ethnic group from different areas increased their knowledge of each other, and deepened their fellow feelings. Because there were more sources of information, we learned that although the government stressed ethnic equality, instances of inequality in fact still existed. Before college my ethnic consciousness was a seeking after my own clan-mates and ancestors, a physical identification with close relatives in our own villages, and an enthusiasm for beautiful clothes and interesting customs. But what began in college was a concern for the survival and develop-

1.1 Bamo Lurhxa with his daugthers, Ayi (left) and Qubumo (right), Tian'-anmen, Beijing, 1978.

ment of our own ethnic group, a concern for the position of our ethnic group within the politics, economy, culture, and life of the multicultural nation.

At the beginning of 1982, I returned to Liangshan, to the new prefectural capital, Xichang, as a member of the first university graduating class after the revival of the university examinations, with a job assignment as a propaganda worker at the propaganda department of the Xichang City Communist Party Committee. Father, who was then mayor and later City Party Secretary, was actively pursuing his agenda of reviving and developing Yi culture. He made a decision to have two of his daughters—my sister Bamo Aga Qubumo and me—take the examinations for graduate school in order to put us on the road toward becoming researchers in Yi studies. In his words, if we wanted to inherit and cultivate our ethnic culture, we first had to understand it. For a Yi who had devoted himself wholeheartedly to the career path of a government official since the time of the Democratic Reforms,[4] this was no ordinary move; children of officials usually do not move into academic careers. In addition, people who cared about me thought at that time that I had a great prospect to develop along the official path myself because I was one of the first minority university students. Thinking about it now, Father was making a choice for us between fish and bear paws—we couldn't have it both ways.

In Autumn 1983, I again went to the Central Nationalities Institute—in the daytime auditing classes on Yi historiographic sources and Yi writing systems in the program on Yi-language documents, and in the evening inviting the elder Leng Guangdian to teach me the famous Nuosu classic *Hnewo Abu* and a work that he had compiled and recorded, "A Collection of Yi Women's Proverbs." The old man often complimented my quick progress, and my confidence increased. In the spring of 1984, I took the test for admission to the master's program in the Tibeto-Burman languages major, with a concentration in collation and research of Yi-language documents, and I was accepted. I was

---

4. The revolutionary reforms carried out in Liangshan and other minority areas beginning in 1956, roughly corresponding to the land reform carried out in Han areas between 1947 and 1951.

the first Yi from Liangshan to pass the test for graduate study, and to focus on Yi historical documents.

I spent seven years as a graduate student, going all the way through the master's and doctorate programs. My advisor, Professor Ma Xueliang, designed a class for me: documentary and field research in Yi studies. Document research and field research may at first sound like apples and oranges. The former consists of sitting in front of a pile of papers and interacting with books; the latter is investigation on the spot, interacting with people. But Professor Ma was always bringing the two together. In his opinion, "If you want to understand Yi-language classics, you have to first understand Yi rituals and customs. You need to understand the meaning of the texts through rituals and customs; and, conversely, if you understand the basis of rituals through the texts, you can better understand the origins of the rituals." As early as the late '30s and the early '40s, Professor Ma had lived in Yi villages around Wuding and Luquan in Yunnan, observing the local people's lives, participating in their rituals, investigating and recording Yi spoken and written language, and collecting, collating, translating, and annotating Yi-language scriptures. At that time, Ma had already combined mastery of scriptures with field research; he later enriched his work on documents by incorporating anthropological theory and field research. He introduced me to a book by Chen Guojun from Taiwan, *A Summary of Anthropology*, as well as other anthropological works, and recommended that I read Ling Shun-sheng's *The Hezhe of the Lower Sungari River* and other anthropological field studies. He lectured on the importance of field research for understanding texts, as well as teaching the field techniques, processes, and sequences used to approach Yi-language texts. It was the first time I had had any contact with field research or known about the field of anthropology. Later on, many more translated anthropology books, such as Roger Keesing's *Introduction to Contemporary Cultural Anthropology*, William Haviland's *Cultural Anthropology*, and others, found their way to my bookshelves. Of course, my advisor's motive in teaching me field research was not to train me as an anthropologist but rather to give me one more weapon to master Yi-language scriptures. And my own purpose in studying anthropology was to become better able to understand and describe my own people and culture.

2

IN THE SHADOW OF THE HAN

MA LUNZY

M y Nuosu name is Mgebbu Vurryr Lunzy, and I was born in 1957. Nuosu people ordinarily don't celebrate birthdays, and often ignore what month and day they were born. My month and day of birth were similarly ignored, but Father and Mother both said that it was the third day after the Nuosu New Year in the fall of 1957. In 1957, the Nuosu New Year was in December, but nobody can say anymore just what day it was.[1] So when I went to study at Baiwu Elementary School in 1963, the uncle who took me to register said I was born on September 1, 1958, and from then on that has been my official birthday, even though I was actually born at the end of 1957.

I was born and raised in Yangjuan, an exclusively Nuosu village, so when I was little I lived far from people of other ethnic groups, and had no opportunity to understand them. But I have a lasting impression that when we were naughty or wouldn't stop crying, adults used the threat of tigers or Han people to scare us. They had but to say "A tiger has come" or "A Han has come," and children would stop cry-

---

1. To this day, *bimo* priests in each local area divine the particular day each year when the Nuosu New Year (*kurshyr*) should be celebrated. This explains why no one could recall the particular date in 1957.

ing and cling motionlessly to some adult. In the evening, adults would tell children stories about tigers eating people or Han cutting off people's ears. There were a lot of us the same age in the village, and we would get together and play happily every day. But if anyone said loudly "Hxiemga la o" (A Han has come), everybody would startle immediately. My grandmother was the eldest daughter of a prominent local leader, Hxiesse Bata Syly, and, under the benevolent influence of her father and husband, she was less prejudiced toward the Han than many. But, like other Nuosu people, if someone behaved in an ill-mannered or clumsy fashion, she described them as "Hxiemga su"—like a Han person. In this kind of environment, one who had never had any contact with the Han would feel that Han were as fierce as tigers and as dumb as oxen.

In 1963, when I was sent to school, I saw Han teachers and Han classmates with my own eyes. I also got to know Ozzu,[2] who spoke to us in broken Nuosu. In the first grade, I always had a kind of inarticulable fear of Han teachers and classmates; because of the language barrier, I could not talk with the teachers directly, so I tried to understand Han teachers and classmates from their behavior and attitudes. Perhaps for both linguistic and psychological reasons, as soon as we were let out of class, each group immediately went to play separately—Nuosu with Nuosu, and Han with Han—and we had little to do with each other. Our Han teacher was very friendly—in class she took our hands in hers to show us how to write; on the playground she took our hands and showed us how to play fun games; on rainy days she carried an umbrella and put on her raincoat in order to help us cross the river. We thus gradually extinguished many of our prejudices.

In the first grade, we Nuosu pupils understood virtually nothing of what the teacher was saying, but mumblingly imitated the sounds of her speech. Our test scores were naturally very poor—mine were almost negative—so I, along with many other classmates, had to repeat the first grade. By the second grade, most of us could guess at or understand the gist of most of what the teacher said in class, and by the third grade,

---

2. Ozzu is the Nuosu name for Tibetans, Prmi, Na, and other Buddhist Tibeto-Burman-speaking groups living in the western parts of Liangshan.

the scores of the Nuosu pupils gradually began to improve, and a few students advanced toward the head of the class. The Han students, especially the children of the cadres in state units, began to lose their natural linguistic advantage, and a few lazy or unintelligent Han students asked us for help with their homework.

At this time, actual contact between Nuosu and Han classmates began. Two completely different streams flowed into one, and there developed collective feelings of the school as a unit that cut across classes and grade levels. But, from another angle, feelings of ethnic identity (which are really feelings of difference) became even stronger, and the struggles between Nuosu and Han became even more acute. Conversations opened up space for debates and quarrels, and each side emphasized its own advantages and found it hard to understand many of each other's customs. For example, Han classmates thought that the Nuosu and Prmi customs of cremation were just too cruel, while Nuosu students thought that leaving the body in the ground to slowly rot, stink, and become food for worms was just too improper. Han students said that the skirts of the Nuosu and Prmi women were inconvenient for walking, and Nuosu would retort that it was better than bound feet. In general, the debates were wide-ranging, unceasing, and extreme. When they quarreled, each had a set of sayings. The Han would say:

Luoluo luo ganzi	Lolo naked sticks
Shao huo dian qiaozi	Light a fire and plant buckwheat
Qiaozi bu jie zi	The buckwheat won't bear seeds
E si ni jia er ye zi.	Grandpa and grandson will all starve to death.

The Nuosu would say:

Lubi Shuo ju hlie	The pestle pokes the Han in the waist
Dinie Shuo uo zu	The mortar bops the Han on the head
Liggu Shuo lie hxie	The rattan strip binds the Han in the sinews
Mge li Shuo mge che	Buckwheat is the Han's funeral food
Chy njy Shuo mge hmu	Goatskin is his funeral clothes
Mge bie Shuo sha ka.	The Han corpse we throw into a deep cave.

The meaning of this is that the Han is a slave, and when he disobeys his master, he is prodded, beaten, and bound, and is too poor to have anything fitting for his food, for his clothes, or for his grave after he dies. The students didn't make these verses up; verses of mutual deprecation are common in the folklore of both sides and they would curse each other all over heaven and earth.

Starting in the third grade, my grades gradually got better, but my relations with Han classmates were just ordinary. I was very envious of the Han cadres' children, who often brought colored pencils and comic books. Driven by an intense curiosity, many Nuosu classmates would hang around the cadres' children, in order to be able to use the colored pencils or look at the cartoons. There at school we heard stories of how the guerrillas had fought the Japanese, of how Zhou Bapi, Liu Wencai, and others had lived lives of exploitation in Han areas before the Liberation, and from sources outside the textbooks we understood more about the deeds of Mao Zedong, Zhou Enlai, Zhu De, Chiang Kai-shek, and others. Later on, trading favors strengthened our contact: There were a few Han who would lend us books to read if we would do their homework for them, or would lend us their colored pencils if we would catch birds for them.

Before we finished third grade, we suffered the attacks of the Cultural Revolution, and the campaign to criticize and struggle against landlords, rich peasants, counterrevolutionaries, and "bad elements" picked up strength. There were calls for people of all social levels to criticize the factions within the Party that were taking the capitalist road, and the schools turned into clubs for the rebel factions—the tables, benches, and blackboards becoming their improvised beds. In 1967 the situation in many areas escalated to violent struggle, and the schools became places the "soldiers" had to fight over, so that schools didn't begin accepting students again until 1969. But the schools had already fallen into disrepair, and had no tables, benches, or blackboards, so that people just set down some planks for tables and benches. Not enough teachers had been assigned, so two classes were combined into one. Classes were conducted in a very informal way, with students and teachers "fishing for three days and drying the nets for two." We read *Quotations from Chairman Mao*, sang *Quotations* songs, and all learned to recite "The

Foolish Old Man Who Moved Mountains," "In Memory of Dr. Norman Bethune," and "Serve the People" by heart.[3] Not until I was in the fifth grade, the graduating class, did the school revive any real curriculum. Naturally, the relative weight of *Quotations* was still quite large, but at the same time a simplified examination system was revived, and I worried that I wouldn't be able to test into middle school. But I quietly put a lot of effort into studying, my grades quickly improved, and I easily made it into middle school.

From the beginning of the Cultural Revolution, the local government had made everything associated with Nuosu traditional culture and customs into targets for reform; they emphasized wearing Han-style clothes, cooking on a stove, making dry land into paddy fields, and propagandized, "There is boundless joy in struggling against heaven, struggling against earth, struggling against people."[4] Though they dared not openly oppose the changes, Nuosu people secretly all said that the Han policy was strange: A people has its own lifestyle; why do we have to do everything the same way the Han do it? What was really difficult to understand was how the Han couldn't get their boundless joy unless they turned us into a gaggle of motherless chicks butting heads and pecking at each other, the daughter pecking at the mother's mouth and the son biting at the father's comb. The adults' way of thinking penetrated deeply into ours, and so we began to hate Han people and Han people's society. Because everybody had these feelings, our relations with our Han classmates were very unstable. When things were going well, we called each other brothers, but when there were disagreements, Nuosu cursed the Han *shuo* (slaves), while the Han cursed the Nuosu *manzi* (barbarians).

A lot of disputes that began as individual grievances could expand to become grounds for group disputes. People who could ordinarily discuss ethnic questions in a rather neutral and sensible way would take the side of their own ethnic group no matter what once conflicts between the two sides heated up. Many of the disputes and quarrels

---

3. These "old three articles" by Mao Zedong were required reading and memorization for everyone in China during the Cultural Revolution.

4. In Chinese, *Yu tian dou, yu di dou, yu ren dou, qi le wu qiong.*

between ethnic groups on the school grounds happened behind the teachers' backs, and the teachers often didn't know about them. People did things without thinking beforehand that they had anything to do with ethnic factors, but when something unpleasant happened, the side that had suffered couldn't help wondering whether it was because of being part of a particular ethnic group.

When I was in the fourth grade, I was a skinny kid, and I developed some sores on my lips, which was very unpleasant. A local Han classmate named Duan often used to make fun of me, and said that "the barbarian" was eating and drinking all sorts of awful things that gave him sores on his lips. He was three years older than I was, and quite tall, so there was no way I could fight with him. One weekend, all the students gathered on the school grounds to listen to the principal speak, as was the custom. As everybody was happily running over to the schoolyard, Duan started kicking and hitting me, as he had done before, and hit me so hard that my lips bled. I was very hurt, and a felt that I had to confront him in order to stop picking on me because of my bad family background. I knew that I was not his equal in a frontal fight, so I waited until Teacher Zhou called everyone to stand at attention, and when Duan was standing with his feet together and his eyes to the front, right at the front of our row, I snuck up behind him, taking advantage of his not paying attention to me, grabbed him around the legs, and pulled backward. I heard a "Huh!" as he fell to the earth, and his whole face was bloodied. After I kicked him hard, I bolted for the road home. I figured I was done with school. Because I had become the greatest example of someone poisoning ethnic relations among the teachers and students, when I got home I told Father the story from beginning to end, and asked permission to quit school. Father said, "If you act this way, the school won't want you either, and, anyway, we have hoes and plows here for you to shoulder" (fig. 2.1).

After I had skipped two days of classes, the head teacher, a Han teacher, came to visit our house. He pulled me to his side, and after criticizing Duan's behavior, said told me that if something like that happened again, not to hide it from the teacher, and not to use such a crude method to try to solve it, and to be sure to go to school the next day. The next day I went back to school, but it was difficult; I felt very unglori-

2.1 *Mgebbu Ashy and his son, Mgebbu (Ma) Lunzy, Yangjuan, 1993.*

ous in front of my classmates, and at the same time was afraid that Duan would take his revenge. Han students said among themselves, "If the Nuosu don't change, they will suffer," and the Nuosu and Prmi said about the Han, "If you don't hit them, they won't respect you." After giving the class a speech full of political slogans about how every ethnic group should strive to strengthen unity, the teacher called on Duan and me to shake hands and make up. After that, Duan was not only friendly toward me, but changed his behavior toward other students as well, and the teacher praised him for it in front of the class. Unfortunately, Duan had to quit school out of poverty before he graduated from elementary school. We became good friends as adults, and now when we bring up the fight in elementary school, we have a good laugh, and jokingly call each other "ethnically prejudiced" and "poisoner of relations."

In the spring of 1971, I graduated to Yuanbao Middle School; at that time they were taking students for spring semester. To advance to middle school, all you had to do was to have graduated from elementary school and want to continue studying. At that time the pedagogical level of the teachers at Yuanbao was quite high; most of them were 1960s graduates of teaching colleges. In 1971 the quality of teaching was taken relatively seriously; because of this we made fast progress. But the good situation didn't last long, and in 1973, before we graduated, the wind of campus revolutions blew all over the country. Schools constantly had to organize political activities, and we had to take part in all kinds of struggle meetings. It was emphasized that we were taking the road of "politics first, study second." Yuanbao was a basic-level unit, and when it came under poor and lower-middle peasant management, the teaching system became noticeably more chaotic. Everything the students read or wrote were essays attacking people. The content did not reach beyond recalling the myriad evils of the old society, singing the praises of the beautiful new society, and lauding the wonderful current situation. When we graduated in 1974, there were very few places for students continuing to high school (in the whole county, there was only one high school, in the county town). Yuanbao Middle School received a quota of only four places, two of which were already reserved for the children of cadres. Judging by grades and behavior, I should have been one of the top choices, but although I was recommended to the township government several times by teachers and students alike, the recommendation bounced back every time. Finally, the poor and lower-middle peasant representatives who were in charge of the school came to the school to choose students, and said that I was a descendant of the exploiting classes, not suitable to be recommended for further study, and after that my name was definitively wiped off of the recommendation lists.

At the graduation dinner, students and teachers were laughing and talking; some even cried for the end of the camaraderie of the schoolground. I had a hard time restraining myself, and occasionally looked at the poor and lower-middle peasant representative with an angry eye; I felt pained and hopeless at the loss of the opportunity to go to high school. After the banquet was over, a very popular language teacher (an ethnic Tibetan) called me to his dormitory, advised me sympathetically not to give up hope, and expressed his desire that I would soon have an opportunity to study further. When I was about to leave, he took two small bundles of tobacco leaves and told me to give them to my father, whom he didn't know, and to the head of the production brigade. When I understood his purpose, I took the unwieldy tobacco leaves and actually did give them to those two. When I woke up the next day, I was an "educated youth returning to his home," a production brigade member who could eat only by relying on work points.

After I returned to the agricultural collective production team, the brigade was organizing a short-term propaganda team and a basketball team. I was chosen; it was just a political make-work job, and we loafed our way through it for two months. After that, the elementary school needed a teacher for a three-month temporary position. Yi, Han, and Tibetan teachers all recommended me, and I taught three months of language and math classes, for a monthly teaching stipend of twenty-four yuan; I was quite pleased. Through taking on these classes, I discovered, however, that my basic knowledge level was still quite low—well below the level needed to teach elementary school; I had none of the feelings of a gifted middle-school student. I began studying quietly, but there was very, very little to read at that time other than the *Selected Works of Mao Zedong;* all I could do was tediously choose a few vocabulary words from the text to memorize every day. When I returned to the village for farm labor, more of my time was taken up by "specialized team" assignments from the production team leader. "Specialized teams" were teams of peasants chosen from a brigade or commune, mostly to do public-works construction labor such as building roads, dams, or dikes, or converting farmland. Most commune members did not want to take part in "specialized teams"; I couldn't refuse. During that time I had contact with a lot of Yi, Han, and Tibetan villagers and cadres; everyone was working hard and our relations were pretty good; there were no disputes that turned into ethnic conflicts.

In the fall of 1975, through the joint recommendation of friends, relatives, and militia representatives that I had come to know well in the brigade, production team, and village, I received a letter of admission to the Yanyuan Normal School as a worker-peasant-soldier student; I would study there for two years, and when I graduated I would become a people's teacher. When I looked at the admissions notice, I felt like I was in clouds and fog, and I suspected it wasn't genuine. Not until I had finished filling out the paperwork did it feel real, and I was elated.

When I graduated from normal school in 1977, I was assigned to the Meiyu middle school in our own county as a teacher. Meiyu is a Han district. At that time, there were only a few minorities in that area as salaried employees, and among us, only another Nuosu and I were bilingual. While I was there, I discovered how deep the feelings of prejudice between Han and Nuosu were; the mantras that Han people used to scare their children were almost exactly the same as those the Nuosu used: "The *manzi* are capturing people; the *manzi* have descended from the mountains." Old people called everyone but the Han *manzi* (barbarians), and middle-school students who had never had anything to do with minorities were full of talk that was hurtful to the Nuosu. In high school, every class in every grade had a few minority students, and since the minority students were bigger and stronger than the local Han, the Han were generally able to hold their tongues in public situations, because if they let their anger rise, the minority students would resort to their fists. Not only were village Han and students at school sometimes careless in this way but even local Han who had received secondary and higher educations would run off at the mouth. Many times I found myself in the situation where Han colleagues who wanted to get along well with me talked nonsense to my face about Nuosu and other minorities, and only felt ashamed when they found out that I was Nuosu. Nuosu students at the high school in Meiyu would also insult the Han as *shuo* (slaves), "water buffaloes,"[5] or "donkeys" in the Nuosu language; the only difference was that the local Han people didn't understand. I myself try to overcome this prejudice and not speak in ethnic slurs, but there are times when I too have unintentionally let them slip. Nobody living in contact with other ethnic groups, whether Nuosu, Ozzu, or Han, has completely conquered this mutual prejudice; some people just have a lesser degree of prejudice.

---

5. One way to classify local people in the Nuosu language is according to their affinity for various bovine species. Thus Han are *yynyi* or "water buffaloes," Nuosu are *nuonyi* or "oxen," and Ozzu are *bbunyi* or "yaks."

3

A WHITE GUY DISCOVERS ANTHROPOLOGY

STEVAN HARRELL

To begin with, I knew little about the subject of ethnic identity, and never intended to do research on it. I had grown up very, very white, in the segregated San Fernando Valley section of Los Angeles. We had African American servants when I was little, and when I was in high school, our church was heavily involved in the civil rights movement, which meant exchange visits and summer-camp retreats with kids from black churches, but it never occurred to me that identity was a question. We all agreed that Negroes didn't get a fair shake, and we agreed that this was wrong. But the identity question—the idea that group membership was problematical, or that one might not know what group one identified with—never crossed our minds. There were a lot of Jewish kids in my high school, but I always thought of that as a religious difference, not an ethnic one; in fact, I don't think I knew what "ethnic" meant.

Even when I went off to college at Stanford, I was not particularly interested in languages and cultures. Astronomy had been my passion through childhood and adolescence, and I intended to major in the physical sciences. But I got stuck hard on calculus (I could set up the equations just fine, but then I couldn't solve them because my arithmetic was so bad), and began to think that my early ability for foreign languages (I had been at the top of my high school Spanish and German classes) was more an indication of my career direction than was my fascination with the universe. By the middle of my freshman year, I was a German language and literature major, and had been accepted into the Stanford-in-Germany program for the following winter and spring.

But something happened during the summer between my freshman and sophomore years. Sometime around late winter quarter 1965, a man named Dwight Clark came to the freshman dorms, recruiting. Two years before, he had started a program to take Stanford students to Hong Kong to teach English to refugees from Communist China. I was entranced with the idea, and managed to talk my mother out of the thousand dollars necessary to go on the program. My father had just died, and I think she wanted me to have the opportunity to do something interesting that summer.

First Japan, then Taiwan, then Hong Kong captivated me. Four of us American students taught English in a missionary middle school on a steep hillside crisscrossed with concrete paths in Rennie's Mill, or Tiu-keng-leng, a small settlement in the New Territories of Hong Kong that was populated mostly by die-hard Guomindang partisans who had settled there after 1949 (fig. 3.1). I began to learn a little Cantonese (I can

3.1 *Stevan Harrell working on a construction project, Tiu-keng-leng (Rennie's Mill), 1965.*

still order food in restaurants and converse with taxi drivers and bank guards when I go to Hong Kong or Guangzhou), but, more importantly, I was hooked on China and on Chinese culture. We went to the border, where we could overlook the Communist mainland—I took a picture (which I can no longer lay my hands on) from the top of a hill showing people working together in a collective field—and I vowed in my journal that someday, somehow, I too would visit the Forbidden City.

That did not happen, however, until 1980. In the meantime, my interest in China had to be deflected to some area or other where Americans could go, since we were uniformly excluded from the People's Republic as imperialists, a prohibition that grew even more stringent with the coming of the Great Proletarian Cultural Revolution in the late 1960s. In 1966, after returning from a grand time studying and traveling in Germany, Europe, Russia, and Israel, I changed my major to Chinese language and literature, with only a vague idea that I wanted to pursue some career where I could help the poor people of Hong Kong, and maybe someday be in a position to visit Mainland China.

Up to that time, I had never studied anthropology. I learned of Professor G. William Skinner from a classmate who had taken one of his classes, and talked my way into his Contemporary Chinese Society class for winter 1967. I also signed up for Lyman Van Slyke's two courses in modern and contemporary Chinese history, and a graduate seminar in politics taught by a brand-new assistant professor named Michel Oksenberg. Mr. Skinner, as we always addressed him, had a fearsome reputation with students—his standards were high and his temper notoriously short, but I somehow survived two of his classes that year and the next, and I was very interested in his ideas, even if he did scare me as much as he scared everyone else, including the junior faculty.

During that same year, I met and fell in love with Barbara Blain, and by spring we were engaged to be married, at the very tender ages of nineteen and seventeen, so our plans needed to be coordinated. When I graduated in June 1968, I was still not sure what I wanted to do for a career, and anthropology had still not occurred to me, even though I had taken the introductory course from Professor James Gibbs in my final quarter as a senior, and received a B. So that I could remain at Stanford while Barbara finished her degree, I had gotten myself admitted to the M.A. program in East Asian Studies to start the following fall. Then Barbara went off to Vienna for overseas study in March 1968, and I took off for a year's language study at the Stanford Center in Taipei beginning in June. When she came to visit me for Christmas vacation, we decided to get married then and there, so I returned ahead of schedule to Stanford in March of 1969, newly married and in need of a summer job.

The only person I could turn to for a job related to my academic interests was the dreaded Mr. Skinner, because I knew that he was hiring many graduate assistants for his massive bibliography project, to catalogue hundreds of sources and enter them into the primitive forerunner of a database. But for some reason, he decided to use another budget for me, and instead gave me a position that determined my future intellectual direction: He put me to work locating market towns in the Ningbo-Shaoxing region of central Zhejiang, finding the names and schedules of the various market gatherings, and plotting them on a clear plastic map with a black Rapidograph pen. And, even more surprisingly, he didn't chew me out once all summer but in fact kept praising my work. About a month into the job, I told Barbara that maybe I would like to go for a Ph.D. in anthropology. Intervention on Mr. Skinner's part got me admitted to the program in early September, even though the class had been officially closed the previous March.

This led me back to Taiwan, where I conducted field research in 1970, 1972–73, and again in 1978. At that time, what I did was much more like traditional fieldwork than what I did later on in Liangshan; this was especially true during 1972–73, when I was collecting material on folk religion and family structure for my doctoral dissertation. Barbara and I, together with our infant daughter, Cynthia, settled into a village in the hills at the southern tip of Taipei County in July, intending to stay a year and a quarter. Our daughter, however, was stricken with repeated respiratory infections, so Barbara took her home in November, and I cut short my stay, returning after a little less than a year.

During that year, however, we lived like real fieldworkers. Barbara bought food at the village market and cooked it in our makeshift kitchen; we hung out in the evening with our village neighbors; Barbara washed the clothes by hand in a local spring. After she left, I took over the marketing and cooking for myself, but paid a neighbor woman to do my laundry. Barbara, a lactating mother at the time, was interviewing village women about their own breastfeeding experiences, and ended up publishing an article about it in *American Anthropologist* (B. Harrell 1981). I originally had a local assistant to help me translate from my Standard Chinese (Mandarin) into the Taiwanese spoken by the villagers, but he left after a month of fieldwork, and from then on I did all my interviewing by myself, more and more of it in Taiwanese as the time went on. One dark and misty evening in February, I had finished writing up my day's notes, and went for my accustomed walk around the village, just to see what was going on and who might be there. I wandered into a neighbor's house (in those days, you didn't knock) and sat down among a crowd of older and middle-aged men, who were gossiping about village affairs. I joined in. And after a few minutes, I realized that I was understanding absolutely everything they said, even though the language was Taiwanese and the subject was local gossip, some of it going back two or three generations. Though I never did improve my language to the extent that I could understand all the puns and classical allusions in the Taiwanese-language puppet shows presented on local holidays, I had arrived as a fieldworker. My Nuosu language has never reached that level, and it almost certainly never will.

That night I became a "real" anthropologist. Like many anthropologists of my generation who were interested in China, I had conducted my dissertation fieldwork in Taiwan not because I was interested in Taiwan (that happened while I was there) but because we couldn't go to China. When it did become possible for Americans to begin field research in China, in the early 1980s, I missed the brief pre-Mosher opening[1] that produced the first wave of field studies (such as Potter

---

1. Immediately after the announcement of the policy of "Reform and Opening" (Gaige Kaifang) in late 1978, the Chinese Academy of Social Sciences agreed to allow a few American researchers to conduct fieldwork in China. This brief "honeymoon" was cut short when Stephen Mosher, a Stanford graduate student, was expelled from China on allegations of unethical conduct in 1981; fieldwork by foreigners was thereafter severely restricted to three weeks in any one place.

and Potter 1990; Siu 1989; Wolf 1985). Barbara was in medical school, and then in residency, and our two daughters were small, and I didn't even think of getting away long-term. Throughout the early '80s, I retained a potential interest in doing fieldwork in China, but certainly not in minority areas, and not on the topic of ethnic identity.

PART II CHINA

4

YINCHANG: MY FIRST FIELDWORK, 1987–88

BAMO AYI

W hen I was a graduate student, I traveled many times to Yi areas in the outskirts of Kunming, in Wuding, and in my own homeland of Liangshan to conduct field research. Of these trips, the longest was from September 1987 to January 1988 in Kaiyuan and Yinchang townships of Xichang City—in order to research and gain an understanding of the ritual life and texts of the Yi in the mountain villages there, and at the same time to make preparations for my upcoming doctoral dissertation.

In mid-September 1987, my father, who was then serving as Party Secretary for Xichang City, arranged for Ma Zhengfa, a culture and education cadre who was familiar with the local situation, to take me to Kaiyuan Township to begin my research. Ma Zhengfa thought that I had returned from Beijing to do nothing more than come to the countryside to experience what it was like. When he saw that I really wanted to do research, he proposed that I go to Yinchang, which was sixty some kilometers farther to the northwest. He said he couldn't come with me, and I didn't much want to let him come either; because of his sense of responsibility to my father, he was more concerned with my health and safety than with my fieldwork, and could have become an impediment to my research. Ma Zhengfa notified Jjike Hoqie, a teacher in a locally

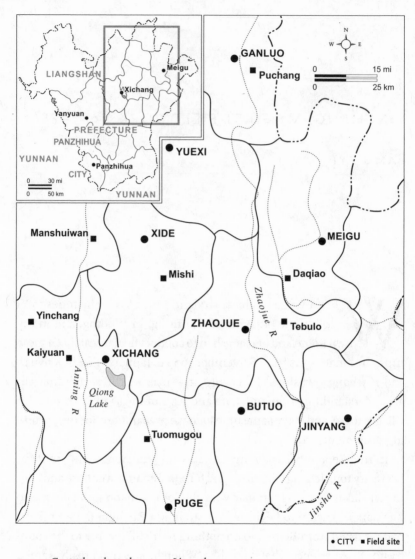

MAP I. *Central and northeastern Liangshan*

sponsored literacy class in Yinchang, to come get me and take me up to the mountains. The two of them earnestly informed me of the difficulties I would face doing research in Yinchang—there was no road, you couldn't get vegetables, you'd have to eat potatoes all the time, there was no place to bathe, and so on.

My time in Tumugou had made me no stranger to any of these things, and I had worked in Xichang for two years, but had never been to Yinchang. I knew that Yinchang was the remotest, poorest, most purely Yi place in Xichang Municipality. I was very determined not to go to Yinchang for a few days and then pull out. I went home and announced that this time I was going to "fight a protracted war" in the mountains, and that I wouldn't return home until after the Nuosu New Year. Mother complained up and down about my picking such a distant, roadless, high, mountainous place. She was afraid that if I fell ill there would be no clinic, and gave me more medicine than I had ever taken in my life; she was also afraid I would freeze, and got me a little padded jacket, an army overcoat, sweaters, and wool long underwear. Father said that going to the villages was just like going home, and that nothing would be particularly shocking. He pulled about ten bottles from his liquor cabinet and got some cigarettes and candy, just as if I were actually going home to visit relatives. So, weighted down with big and little packages and feeling full of pride and enthusiasm, I embarked on the tall country bus—a Liberation-brand truck exposed to the searing sun—with Jjike Hoqie, heading for Yinchang.

We alighted at the headquarters of Baru District, in which Yinchang was located. Because of the flying yellow dust on the dirt road, we were coated with dust from our eyes to our hair. From there to Yinchang it was still over fifteen kilometers, and the villagers who had come down the mountains to go to market jostled to be the first to help us carry our luggage. After eating something at a roadside restaurant and taking a short rest, our procession of people and horses advanced gloriously toward Yinchang. Yinchang is in the high mountains eighty-two kilometers from the urban center of Xichang. In this high-mountain cold zone, there is frost every year in summer and fall, and every winter the snowflakes fly. Aside from one young Han cadre in the township government, the people and officials—even the teachers in the elementary school—were all Nuosu. Aside from a few Chinese phrases inserted into their daily speech, they used the Nuosu language almost exclusively. This was a Yi world, and it gave one the feeling that "the mountains are high and the emperor is far away." My father's name, Bamo Lurhxa, was a household word even there, but in the local people's eyes, it was more important that he was a Nuosu headman than that he was secretary of the City Party Committee. So I was the daughter of this headman. The night I got to Yinchang, the local government organized a big dance party on a flat space to welcome me.

Most of my research was conducted with the support and help of Jjike Hoqie, who was a villager of Ajju Kedde ("the place where the fox makes its den") in the seventh production team[1] of Ganbian Village. Descended from a *bimo* priestly lineage of the Jjike clan,[2] he had apprenticed with his father as a *bimo* since he was small, and had a relatively good grounding in written Nuosu. When the city Education Committee was promoting Standard Yi writing and carrying out literacy work in that script, because Hoqie had studied and been a *bimo*, he quickly gained a thorough knowledge of the new script, and was very enthusiastic about the work of spreading literacy in that script, so that he was made an official teacher of the locally run program to eliminate illiteracy in Yi. Hoqie knew Nuosu customs and rituals like his own hands and fingers; he had memorized much of Nuosu *kerre* (verbal dueling) and *lurby* (proverbial couplets), and was also very familiar with *bimo* ritual texts. You could really call him a village intellectual. At any wedding, funeral, celebration, or gathering within several neighboring villages, his shadow and voice were present. He was resourceful and capable, liked to help people, and was good at explaining what people meant. On the one hand, because he had traveled everywhere doing rituals and disseminating Standard Yi writing, he was extraordinarily

---

1. During the period of socialist collective agriculture, farming was organized by production teams of twenty to forty households. Even though collective agriculture was abolished in the early 1980s, the groups continued to exist under such names as "village people's small group" and were still informally called "production teams."

2. A *bimo* is a Nuosu priest, usually from a hereditary priestly lineage, who is schooled in traditional books and performs rituals. See chapters 6 and 14 for detailed descriptions of *bimo* and their world.

4.1 *Bamo Ayi with Jjike Hoqie and Jjike Xojy in Ajju Kedde Village, Yinchang, Xichang, 1986*

familiar with every village, even every household, in Yinchang; on the other hand, because he was able to understand my motivations and comprehend my questions, he was the best collaborator and informant I have encountered to this day.

Another important collaborator and informant was Jjike Hoqie's father, Jjike Vudda, a famous *nimu bimo*,[3] who did rituals for the ancestors in the area, at that time active in Yinchang and its neighboring townships of Baima and Zhangmu. He was very open-minded and cheerful. When he saw that I was studying his *bimo* knowledge very diligently, whenever he ran into people, he would say I was his *bisse*, or apprentice. Whenever people would ask him, "How can a woman study to be

---

3. *Bimo* can be classified according to the rituals they command as *gahxa bimo* and *gajji bimo*, or "high-road" and "low-road" *bimo*—first- and second-rate. High-road *bimo* command the rituals of *nimu cobi*, including the *nra nimu* for people with children who died of old age or illness, the *ssy nimu* for those who died untimely deaths, the *cu nimu* for those who died of leprosy, and the *nyu ni re nimu* for people who have died of consumptive tuberculosis and other lingering diseases. The high-road *bimo* are all also called *nimu bimo*.

a *bimo*?" he would answer, "What do you mean, there can't be one? Wasn't Bi Ashy Lazze's daughter a famous *bimo*?"[4] Whenever a family arranged for him to do a ritual at their house, he would always notify me and Hoqie ahead of time, and we would go. If the way to the host's house was long, then along the way he would give me his seat and let me ride the horse for a while. In a Nuosu ritual arena, there is a special place set aside for the *bimo*, and when an animal is sacrificed, the *bimo* eats first by himself. Whenever I joined a ritual, I would sit with Vudda in the *bimo*'s place, and eat the *bimo*'s food with him. If the host family happened to complain about my sitting in the *bimo*'s place, Vudda Bimo would usually cleverly persuade them, and not allow me and the host family to get into an awkward situation. He taught me some Nuosu characters and helped me to familiarize myself with some of his ritual texts. During the rituals, he supervised me in placing the "sacred sticks" in the ground, in reading the ritual text, making "straw ghosts," and painting ghost boards. Jjike Vudda was the first *bimo* who ever made me feel like an apprentice, and of all the tens of *bimo* that I have interviewed over the years, he is one of the ones I have liked the best.

Even though I was very lucky to have two people who developed into ideal collaborators and informants, nevertheless, from the start, my research in Yinchang couldn't be considered completely successful. The most critical challenge involved ritual language and the way I recorded my notes on my research. My Nuosu language was basically confined to everyday speech. Rituals went by as if in a dream, in clouds and fog. Even ordinary villagers, those who did not act as *xymu lomu*, or ritual helpers, did not understand the ritual instruments or processes in any detail, and I was like a semi-deaf person. Jjike Hoqie could only explain to me in Nuosu, and, as this ritual knowledge was almost entirely new to me, I could not accumulate information in a hurry.

An even more daunting challenge was that I discovered that it was impossible to record either Nuosu rituals or Nuosu scriptural verses

---

4. The tradition holds that Bi Ashy Lazze, the most famous *bimo* in history, had no sons, and thus trained his daughter Shyse in the priestly vocation. She was exceptionally accomplished, but had to perform rituals disguised as a man. After someone found her out (because she had both ears pierced, while men pierced only the left ear), there were no more female *bimo* in Nuosu history.

using Chinese characters. There were many names of spirits, books, rituals, famous persons, concepts, and so on for which I could find no corresponding concepts in Chinese. After several rituals, and after several sleepless nights worrying about it, completely frustrated, I decided to put aside my research and learn to use Standard Yi writing, to take the path of using Yi language to record my research.[5] What I had learned in school from my professors was the Yi writing of areas in Yunnan around Wuding and Luquan, and the shape, sound, and meaning of those letters was very different from the Nuosu writing of Liangshan. In addition, professors approached Yi writing as a kind of epigraphic or philological exercise, and themselves couldn't use it to write field notes. Luckily, I had studied a little of Liangshan's Standard Yi writing with Ma Ming, a specialist in Yi linguistics, and could read reports and books with some effort. I sat down and remained in the township seat, and had Jjike Hoqie recite to me his wedding ritual text, the *Hnewo amo* (which deals with the origin of weddings, among other things), while I wrote it down in Yi, looking up the words I didn't know in a chart I kept at my side. Jjike Hoqie was a Yi-language literacy teacher, and because of this, while I was recording the text, he helped me learn and remember letters. Ten days or so later, when I had finished writing down this text, I was able to record things using Standard Yi writing with some facility. I remember that when I was just about done with my research there, Teacher Jjike said to me that I could take notes in Yi faster than he could. Thinking back on it, if I hadn't rigidly determined to spend those ten days tackling Yi writing, I don't know how I could have continued that period of research. Using Standard Yi to take notes on rituals and to translate ritual texts not only made this period of research possible, it also had unlimited benefits for my future research.

With the problem of the script used for taking notes solved, my research could proceed. Even though quite a bit of ritual language and

---

5. *Bimo* texts are recorded in the traditional Nuosu script, which is one of a family of Yi syllabic scripts used by several Yi peoples in Sichuan, Yunnan, and Guizhou. In the 1970s, a modern script, known as Standard Yi writing, was developed on the basis of the traditional *bimo* script. Most of the syllabic symbols are the same; the biggest difference is that the Standard Yi Writing reads from left to right, while *bimo* script reads from right to left. See Bradley 2001 for a fuller account of Yi writing.

orally recited texts remained difficult to understand, I could at least write them down first in Yi. Before a planned ritual, I would question Hoqie or sometimes Vudda Bimo himself and take notes about the selection of the auspicious date, the steps and sequences of the ritual, what kinds of "sacred sticks" were used, what animal sacrifices were required, and what texts would be read, as well as the meaning of the ritual, so that I would have a general understanding of that ritual. When we arrived at the ritual arena, I observed the layout, figured out the method of placing the sacred sticks, interviewed the client about the reasons for performing the ritual, and compared these with the notes I had made before the ritual, found problems that I didn't understand, and asked the *bimo*. After the ritual was finished, I would return to the township government and record and supplement my account of the entire ritual sequence in detail with Jjike Hoqie. Using this method, I recorded sixteen different major and minor rituals that I observed.

In Yinchang, I was fortunate enough to participate twice in the most solemn and important ritual of the Nuosu: the seven-day-long *nimu cobi*, sending off the soul and worshipping the ancestor; just this one ritual took up fourteen notebooks and nearly 200,000 characters. The process of the *nimu cobi* rituals that I observed, the richness of the ritual content, the profundity of the ritual meaning, the bewildering array of ritual symbols, and the obscurity of the ritual texts all drew my attention to the area of Yi ancestral spirit beliefs. One could say that this period of research in Yinchang rang the bell that led me later on to write *Yi Ancestral Spirit Beliefs: A Discussion of Yi Language Ritual Scriptures and an Investigation of Yi People's Ancestral Rituals* for my doctoral thesis (Bamo 1994).

The research in Yinchang was not just a period of scholarly investigation, it was also a return to and a baptism into my own culture. There I renewed my familiarity with things that I already knew, evaluated customs that I had not previously taken to heart or thought about carefully, and made contact with rituals and celebrations that I had never heard of or seen before. I think I could fairly have been suspected of "not paying attention to familiar things" and of "refusing to recognize when I had been enlightened," but I also experienced the "culture shock" that anthropologists often speak about. One day in November, I went with more than ten men and women, young and old, from the village of Ajju Kedde to the village of Gabie across the way to attend a wedding. I knew that Nuosu take liquor or sacrificial animals only when they go to funerals, and arrive empty-handed as wedding guests. But, in order to express my feelings, just before we left I specially prepared a necklace. When, along the way, I happily announced to the group that I wanted to give a necklace as a bridal gift, the laughing chatter on the mountain path halted, and everybody looked at each other in astonished silence. Hoqie immediately told me the reason: He said that Nuosu women in that area never give their own jewelry to anybody else, because women's "birthing spirit" or *gefi* prefers to attach herself to jewelry more than anything else. If you give your jewelry away, your birthing spirit will readily attach herself to the other person, and you will be barren or your children will die young. He continued to say that it didn't really matter, that even if I had given the necklace away, afterwards he could have done the ritual of "calling the birthing spirit" for me; but I felt the necklace in my hand, and, even though it was light in weight, its significance was weighty. Imagining that there was a spirit on this necklace, and that she could determine my future ability to give birth and whether I would be able to raise a son or daughter to maturity, made me tremble. Later on, I did take part in a ritual to "call the birthing spirit," making drawings and taking notes on the complex arrangement of "sacred sticks" and the process of the ritual, but this ritual was not done for me.

This shocking episode reminded me to pay attention and investigate a lot of customs that I had seen or known about, as well as ritual details that I was witnessing for the first time. For example, when choosing a young man to carry the bride into her husband's house, the first condition is that the young man's wife not be pregnant, or else the bride's birthing spirit will follow the young man and run off to his wife, because the birthing spirits of pregnant women have a particularly strong spiritual power. Nuosu even go so far as to prohibit pregnant women from coming into contact with brides, and strictly prohibit them from combing or braiding a bride's hair. From taking part in rituals of engagement (*vussa mu*), marriage (*xyxy*), and moving to the husband's house (*oli ggu*), as well as observing the rituals of asking for fertility (*zhyzuo*) and sex (*bo*) as part of the *nimu cobi* ritual complex, I came to under-

stand the extent of the Nuosu people's thirst and striving for prolifer-
ation of the clan and growth of its membership. I saw the unhappiness
and tragedy in the lives of infertile women, and understood just how
important childbearing was for Nuosu women. I finally understood the
meaning of that proverb that I had learned from Grandpa Leng Guangdian: The most important thing for a man is the *chusi* protective spirit;
the most important thing for a woman is the *gefi* fertility spirit.

At the end of November, I made contact with a famous *bimo* named
Shama who lived at a place called Malu, over ten kilometers from the
township seat, and Hoqie and I decided to go visit him. Over hill and
valley, we proceeded to Malu, but how could we have known that just
the day before Shama Bimo had left home to go do a ritual? His house
looked deserted and lonely; the walls on three sides ran along a slope;
a river ran rapidly along the fourth, and there were no other houses
around. We ducked our heads and stepped in over the threshold, and
when we looked up the first thing that caught our eyes was a group of
more than ten pig heads hanging from the beams with their mouths
open. Jjike Hoqie saw my surprise, and when we sat down by the fire
he told me that these were the *kaba*, offerings from Shama Bimo's *disi*,
clients on contract with Shama Bimo to take care of all their ritual needs.

After being sumptuously entertained by Shama Bimo's family and
engaging in lively conversation with them, it was late evening. I men-
tally counted the number of people in the room and measured the space
around the fire in the rather small house, and figured I would have no
choice but to sleep upstairs, using one of the pig heads as a pillow. But
with the banging sound of a door closing, the hostess, carrying a flashlight, asked me to sleep in the loft of the sheep barn several tens of meters
away from the house. The hosts' house was made of mud daubed onto
a bamboo frame, like a fence; the sheep barn was nothing more than
a simple shed made from a few pieces of wood framing wrapped in bamboo matting. It would probably be cool and pleasant there in the summer, but this was winter, when the cold wind bites your bones. I
whispered to Hoqie that I was likely to freeze out there; couldn't we
sleep upstairs inside the house? He said that he could sleep there, but
I couldn't. A guest follows the host's wishes, so I didn't say anything
more, and, following the sound of Hoqie's footsteps, I climbed the lad-

der and stepped into the loft. The sheep below probably thought we were rustlers, and let out great bleats. I told Hoqie, "You go back and sleep in the house; I'm not afraid." He joked that if he weren't there to stop them, people might come to carry me off as a bride in the middle of the night. So we each took our own side of the loft. I dug out a big hole in the pine needles that were stored in the loft to line the sheep fold, fit my big army overcoat into it, stuck my pant cuffs into my socks, and wrapped my big square scarf tightly around my head. I put gloves on, crawled into the overcoat, put my hands into the sleeves, buttoned up the coat, and used my hands to gather more pine needles around me; except for my head, I was completely buried in the pine needles. Hey, it was okay, actually quite comfortable. Even though the winter wind was whistling, blowing into the shed through the bamboo matting, I didn't feel too cold; only my exposed nose and eyes were a bit cool, so I snuggled down further so that my head was also inside the overcoat, even though the rushing of the river and the whistling of the wind still reached my ears. I held my breath, wanting to find out if Hoqie was already in the land of dreams. But I discovered that he wasn't, so I started up a conversation and asked him why it was that he could sleep upstairs in the house but I couldn't.

What came up in this conversation was a bucket of customs and habits dealing with taboos concerning women. Hoqie said *Sihni bboasho*, "Women are unclean." Because of this, women are not allowed to be physically above men or other "clean" things. A mature woman who has undergone the skirt-changing ceremony[6] is not allowed to go upstairs in someone else's house. A woman cannot pass behind the hearth on the upper side. A woman cannot touch a man's weapons. A woman can't pass over her husband's head, and isn't allowed to touch any man's hair braid "horn," including her own husband's, or to touch a *bimo*'s ritual tools or books, and so on. If any of these taboos is violated, a household will usually carry out the *lurca su* cleansing ritual, and particularly strict households will want to hire a *bimo* to perform the ritual of *zhonyie*

---

6. Nuosu girls traditionally wore skirts somewhat different in design from those of adult women; at age thirteen, fifteen, or seventeen a girl underwent a skirt-changing ceremony that initiated her into adult womanhood.

sho to get rid of pollution and expelling dirtiness. Unconvinced, I told Hoqie, "This isn't right; it's you men who are unclean; isn't it we women, who clean up after you everywhere around the house and yard, and you still suspect us." He said, "These are customs that have come down from our ancestors." "These aren't good customs," I replied. Looking at it, it was still better that I slept in the loft of the sheep barn. Besides, I quickly got used to the whistling of the wind, the rushing of the water, and even the sudden bleating of the sheep below.

Doing fieldwork in Yi mountain areas, if you are afraid of hardships, you won't have special experiences. Hoqie and I spent six days in Malu, setting personal records for me by sleeping for six days in the loft of the sheep barn and for six days not washing our faces. Shama Bimo's wife told me that at that point in the winter, all the water in the river came from the mountain snows, and if you washed your hands or face in it, your skin would crack. She wouldn't let me go to the river to wash my hands or face, and I didn't. Mountain Nuosu don't boil water for drinking, so their hydration, other than the pickled turnip-top soup served at each meal, consists of cold water; they wash and rinse everything in cold water also. Even though I didn't really believe that washing in the cold river water would make my skin crack, it was best to follow local customs. Besides, the water in the river was cold enough to pain one's bones. When I went to the village, I had forgotten to take the little mirror I usually used, so I didn't look at myself for six days. Because it was cold, we spent most of each day warming ourselves by the fire; I knew that after all that smoke and coal dust, I certainly must have looked odd.

I remember that when I returned from the field to the university, my female classmates asked me whether I had been able to accustom myself to the food and the living conditions, and whether I had been lonely and depressed, while my male classmates asked me whether any young fellows had been after me or had taken advantage of me. Actually, what I had been unable to accustom myself to or what I had been afraid of was two kinds of "dogs": the big, barking kind that bit people, and the small, silent kind that bit people—fleas (the Nuosu word for "fleas" sounds just like the word for "dog"). When I was little and living in Tumugou, I had gone to Deyu Township to take part in a wedding, and had been bitten by a dog. The scar is still visible on my leg to this day. It's probably a case of "Once bitten by a snake, ten years afraid of the winch rope," but every time I go to a village, I make sure to have a stick ready to hit dogs with, to give myself a little courage. There is a Nuosu proverb, "*Ssevo vo jie; sihni ke jie*" (Men fear pigs; women fear dogs). Being afraid of dogs is part of women's nature.

In fact, though, the hardest things to get used to were the swarms of fleas. On the first of December, 1987, I had gone with Vudda Bimo to the home of Jjivo Vazha in Jjivo Village for a *xuo bbur* ritual to protect against curses and a *kepo tegge* ritual to harmonize the fortunes of a husband and wife. That evening, the *xuo bbur* finished very early; we sat around the fire with the hosts and talked about ordinary affairs. Before long, fleas started to attack me. At the start, when they had bitten in one or two places, I had been determined not to do any unsightly scratching, but they itched more than anything, and I couldn't stand it. From my neck to my body to my four limbs—so many places started to itch. The hateful fleas didn't spare even the soles of my feet or the spaces between my toes. First I tried spit to stop the itching, and after that I tried the liquor still left in my cup. I scratched at my pant legs for a while and then clawed at my collar, and then scratched at the small of my back. When the hostess noticed this, she started to make fun of me. She said I had come from a Han area, so the fleas were curious about me, and wanted to see what a Han tasted like. She showed me how to hold my breath and squash fleas quickly. She said that she had been sitting one day chatting with some old ladies from the village. She was just chatting and squishing the fleas that were biting her, and after she squished them she threaded them onto a needle. After she had strung a long string of them, she counted them the next day—twenty-eight altogether. I don't have that kind of native ability.

That night I was attacked by fleas the whole night long. The host family had given me the only little bed in the house; the bed was not sturdy, and squeaked every time I moved. The host and the *bimo* were both sleeping around the fire to the side of the bed, so I was embarrassed to move very much, and could only lightly turn over, slowly turn back, and scratch those places where I had been bitten. That was the longest and hardest night of my life. Early the next day, during the *kepo tegge* ritual,

as the *bimo* had just begun to recite the *mugu cy* ("lighting a fire to welcome the spirits") text, I began to fall asleep to the rhythm of the chant.
Hoqie knew exactly what was going on; he knew that I had been suffering all night long at the hands of the fleas, and told me to go out to the
pine needles in the loft of the sheep barn and sleep for a while. When
I woke up, the sunshine was streaking in between the wooden framing of the sheep barn, and when I focused my eyes and looked around,
I could see four or five small children staring at me through the open-
ings of the wooden rails. I smiled at them and made faces, but didn't
dare say anything, because Hoqie had warned me that if I saw anyone
not to speak to them, since, prior to the *zzazze,* the ritual meal, if anyone who had been at the ritual spoke to anyone who had not been at
the ritual, the ritual would *mo hlur,* it would fail. In my village fieldwork, fleas have always been my biggest enemy, but the fleas in Jjivo
village were unusually fierce.

On the eighteenth of December, I went in a group of about eight or
nine leaders and cadres of Yinchang Township to take part in Mahxie
Ama's funeral. Mahxie Ama was Hoqie's mother-in-law, a nice old lady
of few words. A few days earlier, I had eaten tofu that she had pressed,
and at the time I had thought that it was the best thing in the world to
eat. I had had no idea that robust and healthy Ama would so suddenly
be gone. Once again, I thought about how fragile people's lives were
there, because not long before, I had been to another funeral. The
deceased had been Keggu, a young fellow who had often line-danced
with us. That day he had been working on the land, and had lain down
below an embankment to rest. The embankment had collapsed and
crushed him to death while he slept. Keggu's house was close by the
township government, and he had graduated from elementary school
and spoke quite fluent Chinese. He had been one of the lively young
people of the township, often asking me about this or that. When the
news of his death came, I was crushed but incredulous, unable to connect this young man, so talented and full of life, with death and anni-
hilation. When I saw his twisted face, a shock, an incomprehension,
and unbearableness welled up in the depths of my heart.

Ama's death was not like the horrible death of Keggu. It was a good
death. Ama was old, and she died on an auspicious day: the third day

of the Nuosu New Year, when the ancestors who have returned to pass the New Year go back to their ancestral resting place. The people in the village told me that Ama had gone back to carry the cutting board for the ancestors.[7] People didn't seem that sad; I was just wooden. Before we set out for Ama's funeral, everybody took shares, with each person putting in 2.40 yuan, and with one share we bought a jug of distilled liquor, while Township Head Lu prepared his pistol and bullets. When we approached the village, with the township head leading the way shooting, following him was Dr. Mujy, who was the best at wailing. Because I didn't know how to wail, I walked in the middle, a fish eye pretending to be a pearl. In the midst of the shooting and wailing, we were welcomed into the host's house by the *vazy hli,* the singing and dancing team that welcomes visitors to the funeral. Death happens often, and in the villages I had been to many funerals, but I didn't know much about the funeral songs and dances that were part of the ritual. I thought I should note down the relevant points. Accompanied by Yoqiemo, an unmarried woman who had come to the funeral from Ajju Kedde village, I assumed the role of a researcher, watching the young men of the deceased's clan and its affinal clans performing the *vazy hli.* I recorded everything, from the songs they sang about the origins of things, such as "The Origin of Death and Illness," "The Origin of the Funeral Sacrificial Sheep," "The Origins of the Crow" (the crow is the ambassador of the spirit of death), to the genealogies they recited in competition, such as "The Genealogy of Heaven and Earth," "The Genealogy of Gguhxo," and "The Genealogy of Qoni,"[8] to the genealogies of the Nzymo, Nuoho, Quho,[9] and finally to the singers' own clan genealogies.

Afterward, I don't recall exactly how, Yoqiemo and I found ourselves in the line of more than ten girls standing in front of the corpse rack singing the Aggu Gge (a lament), their bodies rocking back and forth with the rhythm of the chant, chanting to the deceased soul, "Don't take the black road, the black road is the road of the ghosts; don't take the

---

7. The cutting board is used for slaughtering a pig to offer to the ancestors.

8. Gguhxo and Qoni are the common ancestors of all the Nuosu of Liangshan; everyone is descended from one or the other according to traditional genealogies.

9. The three "good" or "respectable" castes in Nuosu society.

yellow road, the yellow road is the road of the victims of rheumatism; take the white road, the white road is the road to back to the ancestors." We somehow got seated to the side of the rack, and were listening to the daughters and granddaughters of the deceased singing the moving laments—"The little birds in the mountains sang today; tomorrow they won't sing; our dear mama will never speak again. The sun is running around in the clouds; he ran today; tomorrow he won't be able to run; our dear mama will never run again"—when I suddenly thought that I should learn to sing those laments. When my Ama died, who but I and the other Bamo Ayi that she had raised (the eldest daughter of my father's second brother) would come to sing for her? I followed along with the rhythm, "When Ama was alive, she got up early every day, when beads of dew still hung on the tips of the grass, and Ama told the children to go do their chores. The grandchildren's clothes were sewn by Ama; the clothes that Ama sewed were the sturdiest; now that Ama has left us, who will sew the grandchildren's clothes? The grandchildren's clothes were put on by Ama; the clothes that Ama put on you were the warmest; now that Ama has left us, who will put the grandchildren's clothes on for them?" Without realizing it, I was singing along in unison. I started to cry. I wasn't sure whether I was crying for my own Ama or for Mahxie Ama, or for both at the same time.

One day in the middle of December, Gao Feng, a director from China Central Television Station, went to my university in Beijing to look for me, and then placed a telephone call to our house in Xichang inviting me to be a host of the 1988 Spring Festival Eve Gala.[10] I had taken part in the hosting of the 1985 Lunar New Year's Eve "Everybody Celebrating Together" program that he had directed, and later on had been the sole host for another of his programs. In order to inform me, Mama dialed the phone for over two hours; township telephones in those days were not easy to connect to. When I took the call, after a few seconds of excitement, I firmly told Mama that I wasn't going. I knew my mother, and knew that she wanted me to go back to Beijing to be on television.

---

10. The TV gala for Spring Festival (the Han New Year, or Chinese New Year, as it is known in Western Chinatowns and in Taiwan) is a several-hour-long extravaganza watched by hundreds of millions of Chinese every year.

But I told her that at that time, I was like a country girl from a high mountain village, both dark and rustic, and even if I were to go, they wouldn't want me.

Actually, I didn't want to leave the research or the people. There were rituals that I hadn't finished going over my notes on, and scriptures that I hadn't finished copying, and I had arranged to study *syyi mu*, wood-carving divination, with Mahxie Kepo a few days later. I had also already agreed to spend New Year with Hoqie's wife and daughter. I was planning to buy white rice, something hard to get in a high-altitude place like Yinchang, for Old Man Vudda for New Year. The township Communist Youth League Committee wanted to arrange a class in line dancing, and I had volunteered to help with the teaching. With so many plans, how could I just say I was going and go? I wanted to stay, continue my research in Yinchang, finish what I had planned. I suddenly thought that I was no longer an outsider, that I had entered the lives of people there, and that the people had become part of my life. Even though I planned to return eventually to Beijing, and people knew that I wasn't planning to get married and settle down there, still, when I thought about leaving, I felt disturbed, unquiet. When I went back to my room, Lama Bimo, who was helping me to learn the *Zhamo* divination text, asked me what the phone call had been about. Hoqie said, "If your mother tells you to go back to Beijing, then go, and come back to our Yinchang sometime later." My nose started to run, and tears started to fall down my face. Hoqie immediately said, "Well, if you don't want to go, then don't go; just settle down here. I know you like *bimo*; I'll find you a *bimo* to marry." I saw that Hoqie's eyes were getting moist also. We had spent almost three months working together. Afterwards, my classmates and my younger sisters and brother all thought that it was really strange that I had given up a rare opportunity, and asked me what it was about old high-mountain Yinchang that attracted me more than being a host of the Central TV New Year's gala.

Until the end of January 1988, when I left Yinchang, the whole township didn't have a single television, and, aside from a few township cadres who had taken the opportunity to go to the city for meetings, very few people in the villages knew what a TV was, much less a TV host. Every time the township projectionist backpacked films all the way up from

Xichang, people would rush about informing each other, and come from ten or fifteen kilometers away to watch them. But most of the films were in Chinese, and their content was far removed from the local people's lives of farming and herding, rising and retiring with the sun, so the audience really didn't understand much of what they were seeing—in particular a few foreign films; the embarrassed unmarried girls gasped and scattered. What the young people liked to watch the most were the action movies, war movies, because they could generally use their eyes and not their ears.

It would be less accurate to say that people came to see the movies than to say that they came to see the social excitement and to exchange gossip. People had a thirst to know about the world outside the mountains, and the occasional movies that were shown, the things that the caravan traders brought, the Han people who came to pan for gold, and my experience in the city all began to bring a little outside content and urban flavor to the place. But still the traditional way of life and the established customs and habits prevailed. When I first arrived in Yinchang, I thought that everything was new and curious: When we got thirsty while traveling to rituals, we pulled up *vama* turnips to slake our thirst; if we were hungry, we would shout to a householder to hold the dog, and would go in and roast a few potatoes to satisfy our hunger; at a wedding or funeral banquet, whoever showed up would get a portion—even strangers were welcomed. If one family was building a house, everyone in the village had to help; if a calamity befell a family, the whole clan would contribute money and goods. I felt very warm and moved by this simple folksy atmosphere. Even though the research was difficult, there often welled up in me a kind of gladness and spontaneity.

In the beginning, in order to enable me to win the good feelings of my hosts and to thank them for their hospitality, Hoqie encouraged me, or, better said, egged me on or even forced me to sing. My "Ayi Jyjy," "Asu Badi," and "Ploughing Song" were soon sung all over many mountain villages. Some young people also asked me to sing Han-language songs for them. I became a "highlight." Whenever I visited a village, people would come from households that I had never been to before, and before I was even settled in they would make requests for me to sing; whatever house I was in, people from the village would gather in that house to see what I was doing, and wait for me to be entertained by the hosts, listen to me sing, and ask me to lead them in line dances. I was very happy to use my singing voice and the dances I knew to bring some happiness to them and also to myself. There was a long period of time when Hoqie and I, whenever we went to a village, took with us a big tape recorder. Its purpose was not only to make recordings for my research, but to play tapes to accompany the line dances. My time in Yinchang was the time in my life when I did the most singing and the best singing, because there I had an enthusiastic audience, and I really found a feeling for singing; when I found out that I actually sang so well, I often moved others and moved myself to sing. This was a kind of feeling that I had never had before, and have never had since. I remember that at that time there were a lot of villagers who wanted me to record tapes to leave with them, but, because I was short on tapes, I probably only recorded one or two.

My days were long, the villages I visited were many, and gradually I developed in my mind a kind of worry, or, more incisively, a kind of anxiety. This anxiety sometimes clutches my mind to this day; it is about children going to school. Teacher Hoqie had two sons and a daughter. At that time, the elder son was eleven, and the daughter eight, both school-age, and their house was only a twenty-minute walk from the township elementary school. Hoqie himself was a Nuosu-language teacher, and stayed in a room at the school. But he didn't send his two elder children to school. This was something about which I was always nagging him and expressing my dissatisfaction. He assured me that he would send his younger son to school. The school-entrance rate for children was low, especially for girls. The township central elementary school was less than 150 meters from my room, and among the children who came and went there were no more than three to five girls. The students in the village schools that I passed on my ritual travels with Vudda Bimo were also almost entirely boys; it was rare to see a girl. "An egg is meat and not meat; a daughter is a family member and not a family member." A lot of Nuosu girls are promised to other families very early on, and could a parent be expected to invest in schooling for someone else's daughter-in-law? Girls became even less likely to get schooling after the privatization of farming; there are never enough hands around the house, and daughters are naturally the ones sacrificed. Marriages arranged by parents for their children are the rule in Yinchang; the price of a bride is a measure of the social position and wealth of the two households, and an indication of the ability and beauty of the bride. When I was doing research in Kaiyuan, a Ddisse Bimo told me that my "brideprice" would be at least four or five thousand yuan. I asked him why this estimate was higher than for the majority of girls, and he said that it was because I had been to school for so many years. I joked that the *bimo* respect knowledge, otherwise I would not be worth a penny, since I couldn't do embroidery, carry water on my back, or raise pigs. Nobody at all would want me as a wife.

Poverty was something else that made one hurt and worry. That year in particular was a bad one for Yinchang. Because of a drought, the grain harvests were short, and not long after the festival of the bountiful harvest, many families already began to lack grain. In order to be able to afford to buy grain and salt, they had to sell the pigs with which they had planned to celebrate the New Year. The pigs that they did raise became skinnier and skinnier; without good feed, the pigs could not grow any fat. The township government anxiously decided to ask the old *munyi sico*, the chooser of auspicious days, to select an auspicious day on which to celebrate New Year early. At New Year, I joined the pig-slaughtering team of Ajju Kedde village, and the biggest New Year pigs were not over 100 kilograms, and the little ones were not much over 50. The households that didn't have a pig to slaughter just killed a white chicken to worship the ancestors and had done with it; any pork was sent by neighbors or relatives. Hoqie calculated for me that ordinary households that year had a per capita cash income of around 150 yuan.

To say that Yinchang was short of doctors and lacked medicines would not be an exaggeration. Mujy, the only doctor in the township, was basically unemployed. In the first place, the township clinic did not have any commonly used medicines or basic equipment, and in the second place, the people believed in spirits and worshipped ghosts, and if they were sick or in pain they usually asked a *bimo* to exorcise the ghosts and cure the disease; very few people visited Mujy's crude, ten-square-meter clinic. Once, out of curiosity, I went to check out what medications the clinic had, and what surprised me was that they were almost all expired. The villagers believed in spirits and ghosts, but they were also practical, and interested in real results. I gave out just about all of the medicine Mama had given me to bring, in small increments. Some of them were given out when I was traveling to do rituals with Vudda Bimo, right in front of him. I discovered that Vudda was in no way opposed to medications; sometimes he himself asked me for a pill or two. Later on, when villagers got sick, they sometimes came to the township center to ask me for medicine. I became a "doctor," often giving out medicines free of charge to people. The medicines that Mama had given me were for common illnesses such as colds and fevers, headaches, and intestinal troubles. I just had to ask what was ailing the person and give some medicine, and usually it would work. But, unluckily, just after the secular New Year of 1988, I came down with a bad flu, with fever and headaches, and felt generally awful. By that time my medicine bag was totally empty. As evening approached, I got two aspirin from Mujy's clinic, and the fever went down for a while. But it rose again in the middle of the night. I lay by myself in the office of the old township headquarters, and, with the winter wind whistling outside, I began to shiver at the core and my fever boiled. That night I thought that I might just die there. The outside world was so distant from me; I was so alone and without help. I suddenly realized why people there needed their *bimo* to exorcise ghosts and cure illnesses, why they need the rituals that mobilize the collective strength to fight disease. I awoke the next morning from my stupor; I hadn't died. The winter sun outside the window was so bright.

There didn't seem to be a time when the research really concluded; several religious activities are cyclical and can only happen at a certain time; illness and disaster return regularly; new rituals keep being carried out. But because the term was about to start at the university, I had to leave Yinchang. What I carried away from Yinchang was not just a heavy bag of field notes, but also a heavy heart.

"When the wild goose has flown away, his sky-splitting honk remains behind him; when the tiger and leopard have run by, the pattern of their stripes and spots remains behind them; when Little Sister Ayi has gone far away, her voice, her face, her smile remain behind." It's sad that, having moved several times, I lost the letters that Teacher Hoqie wrote for me in Yi. But I still remember distinctly these words that were writ-ten in the first letter he sent me, because I can't forget how beautiful a feeling I had when I read these words. After I returned to Beijing, the first research report that I compiled and published was "The *Xuo Bbur* Counter-curse Ritual of the Liangshan Yi" and the authors were listed as Bamo Ayi and Jjike Hoqie, because I wanted to use that article to commemorate the help he had given me and the friendship that we had developed.

5

GETTING STARTED IN SOUTHWEST CHINA, 1987–88

STEVAN HARRELL

M y idea that fieldwork in China was a distant dream changed dramatically when my graduate student Dru C. Gladney would not take "no" for an answer. In summer 1982, at the height of the chill induced by the Mosher affair, Gladney traveled to China to study language, and talked to professors at the Central Nationalities Institute, a college for minority students in Beijing, about conducting ethnological studies among the minorities. They encouraged him to contact them when he received funding. Less than a year later, against my advice to be sensible and go do something in Taiwan, he was a visiting graduate student at the Institute, spending most of his time in Beijing but conducting two field swings around practically every province of China, checking out the situation of the Hui Muslim minority in each place. The following year, he received permission to be a visiting graduate student at the Ningxia Hui Autonomous Region Academy of Social Sciences, conducting further forays into the field in Ningxia and neighboring provinces.

When Gladney returned from his two years in China, he arranged for a delegation of bureaucrats from the Guojia Minwei, or Central

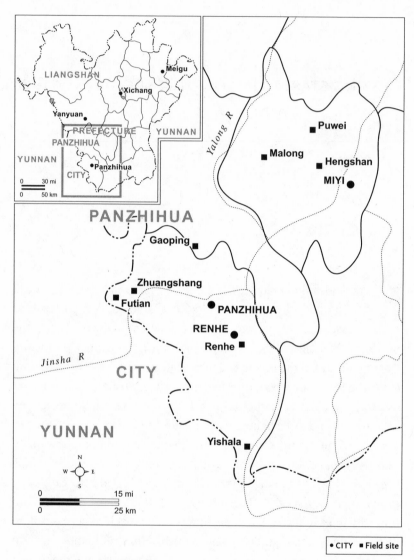

MAP 2. *Panzihua Municipality*

Nationalities Affairs Commission,[1] to visit the University of Washington, and they then invited us for a return tour in 1986, visiting nationalities institutes in Beijing, Chengdu, and Kunming. Six or seven of us spent three weeks on this junket, and in addition to meeting scholars young and old eager to exchange stories with foreign colleagues, many of us gave lectures to audiences of faculty and students. One member of our delegation was Professor Charles Keyes, an expert on the theory and political economy of ethnic identity and ethnic relations, who works in Thailand and Vietnam. While translating his talks and his conversations with local scholars, I was beginning to develop an interest in the topic of identity, but felt far from competent to conduct research on it. Each of these institutes ended up hosting University of Washington anthropology faculty or graduate students for their field research.

I never conducted field research under the auspices of any of these institutes, however. Not long before our tour in September 1986, Dr. Kathleen Tomlonovic arranged a visit to Seattle by Professor Tong Enzheng, a polymathic archaeologist, ethnologist, novelist, designer, and general visionary who taught at Sichuan University in Chengdu (fig. 5.1). When I met him, I had already been thinking about doing fieldwork in minority regions, not because I was interested in minorities, but because it seemed clear that the Nationalities bureaucracy was more open than others to fieldwork by foreigners, never having been officially placed under the three-week post-Mosher ban (see chapter 3). Realizing that not every approach to an institution in China would result in a research affiliation, I explored with Professor Tong, then director of the Sichuan University Museum, the possibility of conducting field research under his auspices. He invited me to come to Sichuan in March 1987 to talk about details.

By the time I was ready to spend my spring break in Sichuan and Yunnan, I was already assured of funding for a project to study the effects of economic modernization on family structure in a series of Chinese

---

1. The Central Nationalities Affairs Commission, or Guojia Minwei, as it is known informally, is a cabinet-level agency that manages the system of minority autonomous areas. There are also *minwei* at provincial and prefectural levels of government.

5.1 *Tong Enzheng and Stevan Harrell, Sichuan 1987.*

villages. Like a general preparing to fight the previous war, I wanted to test in China some of the ideas I had formed in Taiwan throughout a decade of intermittent fieldwork on industrialization and the family. I would find an area where there were both Han and minority people, and choose two Han villages and two minority villages—one close to and one remote from a nearby industrializing center—and control for the two variables of industrialization and ethnicity in observing family change. I had somehow managed to convince the Committee on Scholarly Communication with the People's Republic of China that I knew something about the family structure of the Yi and Naxi minorities of Southwest China (I didn't, but they knew even less, making the deception fairly easy to pull off), so my visit to Sichuan and Yunnan was mainly for the dual purposes of picking a field site (Professor Tong suggested the Panzhihua area) and convincing local officials to allow me and my Chinese collaborators (whoever they might eventually be) to conduct household surveys there.

After a few days and a few lectures in Chengdu and its environs, and after cadging a Nuosu conversational grammar and some tapes from people at the Southwest Nationalities Institute, Professor Tong and I caught a soft-sleeper train for Panzhihua, a city on the southern border of Sichuan. Overnight we emerged from the miasmic dankness of early spring on the Chengdu Plain into the full searing vernality of the Panxi Rift Valley. When we reached the Panzhihua station and stood up in our compartment to haul our luggage off, a short, semi-toothless figure on the platform shouted at us in that Sichuanese way that reverses the third and fourth tones of Standard Chinese, "Lao Tong! Lao Tong!" This was my first meeting with Deng Yaozong, head of the Artifacts Preservation Office of the Panzhihua City People's Government.

I could barely understand Lao Deng's rapid-fire, heavily accented speech at first. We caught the waiting jeep for the half-hour ride to the middle of town, where we attempted a quick morning nap in the Silk-cotton Hotel, the only place in town for foreigners. I was too nervous, however, to sleep much, knowing that my opportunity to do actual field-work in Mainland China might just rest on what happened that after-noon. I have no recollection of lunch, but after lunch we met with local officials, including Li Chaoshen, head of the municipal *minwei* and a Yi himself, and Lao Deng's boss, Lao Xiang, the vice-head of the city Cultural Bureau and my future bridge-tournament partner. Professor Tong had obviously done the spadework. Lao Deng told me, with his nominal superiors looking on approvingly, that he had already selected three sites for our village household surveys, and was working on the fourth. He also told me that Panzhihua was an excellent place to study the Yi, since there were at least three kinds. The Liangshan Yi, in the northern part of the municipality, were still at the "slave society" stage (as of the 1956 democratic reforms), while the Yunnan Yi to the south (much of the municipality was carved from what were formerly Yon-gren and Huaping counties in Yunnan) had long since entered the stage of "feudal society." In addition, there were the so-called Shuitian ("rice-field") Yi, who lived in the western part of the city, whom nobody knew too much about.[2] Lao Deng said that he could find a village for us to study in each area, and, yes, if we wanted to include a Han village for comparison, that would also be easy to arrange.

There was a big banquet that night, during which *minwei* chair Li Chaoshen disappeared for a few minutes and came back with a curi-ous artifact: a red, yellow, and black lacquered wooden drinking vessel, with a thin pipe protruding diagonally from one side. One poured the

---

2. According to the orthodox Stalinist ethnology still taught in the PRC, all human societies progress from a primitive society to a slave society, then on to feudalism, cap-italism, and, finally, socialism.

liquor in the bottom, Tong explained to me, and when the vessel was turned right side up, the liquor would not spill out, because of the tube that extended well into the upper part of the opening. The liquor was then sipped through the straw. This was my first acquaintance with Nuosu lacquerware, and since then I have seen many of these drinking vessels, but until I was in Meigu on a museum collecting trip in 1999, I never saw anyone drink out of one. To my astonishment, Director Li was not just showing the vessel to me, he was giving it to me.

Afterward, as Professor Tong and I sat recovering in our hotel room, a small, crew-cut figure in a natty pale blue sports jacket and tie appeared at the door and nodded slightly. Tong sprang to his feet, and I, sensing the importance of the visitor, did the same. This was Party Secretary Zhang Boxi, number two in the local hierarchy, and a Sichuan University *xiaoyou*, or fellow alumnus, of Professor Tong. He spoke quickly, but with less of a Sichuan accent than the people I had been listening to all afternoon, and had come to pay respects to his friend the professor and to welcome me to do research in Panzhihua. Perhaps we would like to go dancing? We followed the secretary to the upstairs ballroom of the Panzhihua Hotel, where the Cultural Bureau was having a dance. Tong glided around the floor with a succession of pretty young women, from Deng's and the Secretary's daughters to the hotel help, and I fumbled my way through the steps with some of the same ladies, cursing to myself the fact that, vainly striving to be cool, I had purposely forgotten in high school the elegant steps I had once learned when my mother had sent me to that stupid cotillion. The first Party Secretary, the boss of Panzhihua, the tall, suave, and imposing Han Guobin, also stopped by to say hello and wish us well. I went to bed reeling.

There was no time to reflect, however, as the next morning I was leaving for Kunming. Tong had asked the culture bureau people to get me a train ticket, but they either couldn't get one or had another agenda, and I found myself back in the previous day's jeep with Lao Deng, his wife (whom I came to call Zeng Saosao, or "sister-in-law"), a young researcher named Ma, and the driver, Dai Wanping, later to become a trusted friend (fig. 5.2). We were driving to Kunming, eleven hours over four mountain ranges away. We stopped to take pictures at a breath-

5.2 *Steve's mentor Deng Yaozong, his wife Zeng Qiansu, researcher Li Miao, and Driver Dai Wanping, Ertan Dam, 1996.*

taking overlook of the Jinsha River, passed by *tulin* or earthen-forest formations reminiscent of Red Rock Canyon in my native California, had lunch in a little café in Yuanmou (the liver was so delicious, Lao Deng ordered another serving), picked red rhododendrons growing wild on one of the higher ranges, and munched cucumbers in the back seat, throwing the peels out the window. On reaching Kunming, I found housing at the Nationalities College, but there wasn't room for the others, so they went elsewhere for the night. I flew to Hong Kong and eventually to Seattle the next morning.

So I became implicated with the Chinese Communist Party (they seemed like nice guys, those secretaries on the dance floor), with the Chinese ethnological discourse (I thought it incredible that anybody actually believed that "five stages of society" stuff), and with the Panzhihua establishment (which was very solicitous), all at once. Already, the predicament of the field worker, with conflicting loyalties to his research mission, the safety and welfare of his subjects, the well-being and safety of his collaborators, and the demands of his funding agency (see Hsieh

1987) was upon me, and I had yet to spend more than an hour or two in a minority village. I set to work trying to learn conversational Nuosu from books and tapes.

On January 5, 1988, I left a warm Hong Kong winter to fly into the mists, and was met at the Chengdu airport by Professor Tong's young research assistant, Ren Hai. In Chengdu in January the temperature hovers just above freezing, and the overcast hovers just above the building tops. In 1988, the buildings didn't have any heat (this was not cold country, after all), and electricity was often interrupted for a day or two by shortages. In this thick atmosphere I met my research collaborators around an antique table in the Sichuan University Museum. Ren Hai—tall, thin, and intellectual—would be part of the team, and there would be two graduate students from the sociology program in the philosophy department, Liu Xin and Lan Mingchun. And up from Panzhihua were Li Mingxi, a forty-two-year-old female researcher from Lao Deng's artifacts office, along with two younger men, Li Miao and Wang Chengxiao. We would spend a week in Chengdu paying respects to all the right officials at Sichuan University and working on the questionnaire.

We sat in that cold if elegant meeting room for days on end, arguing about what to put in the questionnaire, which would be administered to about 300 households in the four villages Lao Deng had chosen for us. The questionnaire covered the educational, occupational, and reproductive life histories of every household member, including detailed sections about the history of the household and its economy for the last three years. The two young sociologists, along with their professor, Yuan Yayu, who occasionally joined us, were methodologists to a fault. Their concerns were with the codability of variables, the replicability of results, the randomness of sampling. Li Miao and I argued the anthropological perspective, while Li Mingxi (the most senior member of the team), continually supplied common sense.

Between the questionnaire sessions, the lectures I gave, and the banquets, at some point I got sick. I had been walking around the city, and stopped at a Muslim noodle restaurant where the chefs twirl and stretch the dough. Later on, Ren Hai told me that place was not too clean. That night, I lay in bed groaning, bloated, nauseated, and sleepless, and, of course, the diarrhea started. There was an important meeting the next day at noon and a banquet that night, and by lying in bed until late morning, taking large amounts of Pepto-Bismol (I didn't want to waste my precious Lomotil[3]—after all, I was not in the field yet), and eating judiciously, I made it through. But the ailment—later diagnosed as giardiasis—would recur every few days for the next month, and, after a February respite, come back again in March. It caused me as much anxiety as actual physical distress throughout my whole 1988 stay in China. When we were done with all our preliminaries, the Panzhihua people went home, and we followed them a few days later—not only the four-person research team, but also Professor Wu Jialun, the head of the Chuanda research office,[4] and his assistant, Mr. Zhou Jian.

Nine days more days passed in Panzhihua before I could get permission to reside and do research in a village. Lao Deng must have pulled every mid-level *guanxi*, or connection, he had from his eighteen years in Panzhihua, where he had been in charge of pork rationing (Fatty Deng the Meat King, they called him) before he took over the artifacts office. I didn't know it at the time, but he and Ren Hai had been required to sign a personal guarantee of my good conduct and safety to the Foreign Affairs Bureau, the police, and the City Office for the Preservation of State Secrets. Ren Hai showed me the document later, when we had been in the field for weeks and I seemed less like a foreigner.

So it was the end of January before we started our actual research in Yishala, a Lipuo (or Central Yi) village in the pine-covered, red-soil mountains to the south of the city. When we first visited the village to arrange things with the local cadres, the Chuanda students were all terribly disappointed: These minorities were too *han hua* (Hanified) to be interesting at all. They lived in four-sided houses around courtyards, wore the same clothes as any other poor Chinese peasants, worshipped the ancestors and the earth god on altars in their front rooms, and married according to distressingly familiar ceremonies. Only their Libie language, of which none of us could understand a word, distinguished them from Han peasants; it turned out, in fact, that some of them were Han peasants.

---

3. A common drug for diarrhea, in the days before Immodium.
4. Chuanda is a short way of referring to Sichuan Daxue, or Sichuan University.

But this was the place that had been chosen for us (it was a model village), and a blackboard overlooking a reservoir at the entrance to the village was inscribed, in English, "Wellcome [sic] to our Village." I never found out if it had been put there for me, or had been there earlier—maybe other foreigners had been there, too. Certainly Li Mingxi had been there while doing a previous survey with the provincial Nationalities Research Institute.

We were put up in three offices in the four-story concrete workers' dormitory of the Panzhihua cement plant, which was started in the village as a minority enterprise. Somebody cooked for us, giving us two basins of fried dish, along with rice, on the two-meal-a-day schedule common to most of the Southwest. Lao Deng's boss, Lao Xiang, visited once, and was very solicitous of me, making sure I had enough covers and a thick-enough pillow. And one day two fellows from the Foreign Affairs Office came out, but didn't want to hear much about how our research was going, or even walk around the village. Later on, I found out that they were from the police, and were worried that I might be able to see a military radar station from the village, but by climbing all over the roofs and balconies they convinced themselves that I wouldn't be able to see anything.

Interviewing went smoothly; each of the five team members besides me, the foreigner and team leader, hired a local guide, and I accompanied the researchers on some of their interviews and collated and corrected their questionnaires. Only one morning was I too sick to go out with everybody else. In between interviews we had four weddings, a funeral, and lots of invitations to people's houses. We copied old documents—genealogies, land deeds, and an intervillage treaty from the early Qing—and interviewed old people. We collected kin terms and basic vocabulary, and learned to speak a few sentences of the Libie language, or at least I did. The students thought the repetitious questionnaire interviewing was boring, but they were good sports about it.

Between interviews and visits, we climbed around the nearby hills and talked incessantly about social science, modernization, Westernization, democracy, America, and the village we were living in. Ren Hai and I shared a room, so we talked the most, but Liu Xin, a brilliant sociological theorist, was always ready with a question about functionalism or structural Marxism or some other school of thought. This was like months of fieldwork packed into a two-week span; when we were done, we had interviewed 100 households and had reams of other material. I remember returning to the city a little sick, extremely exhausted, unbelievably dusty, and quite elated—Professor Tong had told me not to expect too much, but what more could one expect than what we had done in only two weeks?

We had three more villages to survey. First we went to a Han village called Renhe, where we stayed in a nice little government guest house for about four days, and I took my place as an ordinary interviewer along with the others. In the evenings, I read Tom Wolfe's *Bonfire of the Vanities*. Then it was New Year, and all three Chuanda researchers disappeared back to Chengdu for a week. Lao Deng thought I might be lonely—I was the only guest in the 400–room Panzhihua Hotel on New Year's Eve—so I had lunch or dinner at eight different people's houses over the first four days of the new year. I was lonely anyway. But there was more important business to attend to. So far, the municipal Foreign Affairs Office, having worked out permission for me to go to Yishala, Renhe, and the Shuitian village of Zhuangshang, was still balking at letting me go to any village in Panzhihua inhabited by Nuosu people, or Liangshan Yi, who spoke a strange language and wore "ethnic costumes." They were in Yanbian, which was a closed county. Lao Deng, however, had a plan. On the second day of the new year, we would go to the home of the vice-mayor who oversaw the Foreign Affairs Office. We would take no presents—we don't do that when we *bai nian*, or pay New Year courtesies. And I was to let Lao Deng do the talking.

The apartment was lavish, with two balconies and several rooms, and Vice-Mayor Tan Huizhang listened carefully to Lao Deng's recitations (in slightly edited form) of what I had told him about our first two village experiences. Tan didn't say anything, so imagine my surprise when, on the way back down the stairs from his apartment, Lao Deng cracked a big smile and said, "Success." Responding to my puzzlement, he said, "Didn't you see him nod? You can go to Gaoping." For good measure, we then went to visit Vice-Mayor Li Zhixia, in charge of education and culture, but he wasn't home. His wife, however, somehow knew that I liked Fujian Oolong tea, and served me some of that naturally sweet

5.3 *Sports Day at the Panzhi-hua Culture Bureau, 1988. Stevan Harrell is flanked by Liu Xin (left) and Wang Chengxiao (right).*

brew, which I much prefer to the artificially enhanced jasmine tea so beloved of the Sichuanese. I had never laid eyes on the woman before, and began to wonder how thick my dossier really was, and how many people had memorized it.

After four or five more days of interviewing in Renhe, we returned to the city with another thick pile of completed questionnaires, and were eager to proceed to our third field site, the Shuitian Yi village of Zhuangshang. But it was Yuanxiao, the Lantern Festival, and time for the Culture Bureau's sports fest. Tug-of-war (fig. 5.3), bridge, and a game consisting of blowing a feather over a net were featured, but I was seeing my time grow short, and was eager to proceed. Lao Deng kept counseling patience—"Lao di, ni bie ji" (Little brother, don't fret), he kept saying—and, sure enough, after the sports fest was over, we took Driver Dai's jeep to the village of Jingtang, where there was a Catholic church, founded by French missionaries in the 1870s, that had been converted into a village grain depot during the Maoist period and only in the 1980s restored to its congregation. It loomed over the dry, hot plain by the Jinsha River like Cinderella's castle loomed over Anaheim before the skyscrapers were built (there's now a huge electric power plant dominating the view on that plain, too), with Chinese-style upswept tile roofs, painted red beams, and a six-sided tower that might have been the top of a pagoda except for the gilded cross on top (fig. 5.4). We would stay in the church's guest rooms, and walk daily to Zhuangshang, about a forty-minute trek each way.

Because there was nobody to cook for us at the church, we took our own equipment, including a kerosene stove, and bought fresh vegetables in abundance from the local villagers. Every night after we returned from interviewing in Zhuangshang, we would sit at a square wooden table on the slightly tilted plank balcony of the church, shelling peas, chopping vegetables, and mixing sauces (fig. 5.5). We started talking about each other as family. We all cooked, except Li Mingxi, the "elder sister," who resented the fact that women were supposed to cook all the time (nevertheless, she professed to be happy to do the dishes). Lan Mingchun was the "daughter-in-law": He had learned cooking from his mother, who was an expert, and his own skills were admirable. I even chipped in with eggs-and-tomatoes a couple of times, and when the story got back to Lao Deng that I was kneeling on the floor stir-frying, it became his favorite example of how foreigners didn't have to be coddled.

The people of Zhuangshang were poor, but the local cadres acted all the more generously for that. Every day they killed chickens for our lunch, and always shared what little they had when we visited their run-down homes. Toward the Han in general, however, they expressed considerable resentment, especially since a government coal mine had diverted part of their irrigation water. They were not even happy with their designation as Yi, even though it gave them minority status; they spent a lot of their time with us trying to convince us that the Shuitian were a separate *minzu*.[5] As an American, all out for the underdog, and a critic of *minzu shibie*, I tended to sympathize. *Minwei* Director Li Chaoshen told me that it was silly; everybody knew they were Yizu.

Then there was Gaoping, at the top of the pass leading from the city to Yanbian County. Finally—the anthropologist's dream. I had been studying Chinese society since my first fieldwork in Taiwan in 1970,

---

5. *Minzu* is a Chinese word that has a lot of meanings: "ethnic group," "nationality," "nation," "minority." In this instance, it refers to the fifty-six *minzu* into which the State divided the population of China beginning with the process of *minzu shibie*, or "ethnic identification," in the 1950s (see Gladney 1991, Harrell 2001).

5.4 *The Catholic church at Jingtang, near Zhuangshang, where the research team stayed for a week in 1988.*

5.5 *Cooking at the Catholic church, Jing-tang, 1988. Left to right: Lan Mingchun, Liu Xin, Wang Chengxiao, Li Mingxi, and Stevan Harrell.*

but in Gaoping I felt like a real anthropologist. The people wore funny hats, spoke a language few outsiders understood, and even practiced bilateral cross-cousin marriage. From the students' standpoint, these minorities were almost not Hanified: people living in the mountains, practicing subsistence agriculture, and not very involved in the market. Here was the "true" anthropological aspect of our fieldwork.

There were problems, however. In the first place, the only public housing was in the Red Flag Logging Camp (nobody had yet thought of our living in people's homes). It was headed by a nice-enough Han veteran cadre who offered the six of us a standard, eight-bunk room, but he himself had never, in twenty years in the mountains, brought himself to try the Yi style of food known in the Han language as *tuotuo rou*, or "chunk-chunk meat." He was sure that it would make him sick. Because we were in new and different territory, we were also accompanied by a local researcher on the staff of the Yanbian County Cultural Office, Mr. Fu. Mr. Fu had written two books of Yanbian "local color" that included a lot of quaint minority customs; he gave us a list of taboos in Nuosu culture that included farting in front of your father-in-law, which he said would compel the offender to commit suicide. Or so he said.

These people, we were told, were not like the Hanified villagers in the other minority areas. They were deeply suspicious of outsiders, and we would have to interview whatever families our local guides took us to, not take a random sample as we had done so faithfully in the other villages. And they were poor, living in one-room houses without furniture or electricity. I was terrified of the dogs, who would bark, snarl, and growl when you passed their houses—especially since Ren Hai had already been bitten by what seemed like a much gentler animal in Renhe. This would be real fieldwork.

It only got better when we found out that we could be guests at a wedding the second day we were there. We watched the bride, covered from head to foot in a massive headdress and a big wool cape, walk with her male relatives to her husband's house; we watched the bride's party received around bonfires with liquor and cigarettes; and we watched the bride have her hair combed and braided by her future sisters-in-law before being carried piggyback by her cousin into her husband's house. We ate the notorious *tuotuo rou*, pork chunks boiled and then roasted in the coals. And I got sick—so sick that I stayed behind one morning while the others went out interviewing. That afternoon and for the next two days, I took my Lomotil and my chances, not wanting to miss this adventure in exoticism. I was so sick that I thought of nothing but home; so exhilarated that I wanted to stay longer. I made friends with a young villager named Nyite, who had me over to his house a couple of times, helped me with kin terms and conversation practice in Nuosu, and later even corresponded with me.

The visit to Gaoping was only a week, and we actually had very little "data." Our household questionnaires were basically useless when we tried to analyze them, and even my notebook from that time is very sparse. My field journal says:

> I also emerged from the whole field experience with a feeling of considerable frustration: of course, in a week you can only scratch the surface of a culture. And I realized that the satisfaction gained in Yishala, Renhe, and Zhuangshang was the satisfaction of adding some more data, some more places, some different or even off-beat cases, to the same store and lore of sino-anthropology. Yishala people, Yi or otherwise, are recognizably Chinese in the sense that they make use of much of the core of culture elements common to all Han Chinese and those on Han society's near-fringes. They may have a fierce sense of being separate from and different from the Han, but they understand each other's cultures (or each other's variants of Chinese culture) because the cultures really share so much in common. This both makes the problem of ethnic consciousness more interesting and makes the whole culture easily accessible to an ethnographer with twenty years' experience in studying Chinese and a couple of intensive weeks to interview in.

> But a place like Gaoping is a different story. One should, in a funny sense, pay more attention to the fact that the young ladies wear those incredible getups. The surfaces of the culture are as like as the clothes of Yi and Han men, but the way the society actually works is as different as a Han woman's slacks and jacket are from a Nuosu girl's ruffled skirt, appliquéd jacket, and square black headdress with beads hanging down. You learn the basics in a week; you can learn the kin terms and the clan system and the difference between Black Yi aristocrats and White Yi commoners. But to learn who is

who and why it matters would take months or years of fieldwork, as well as a more than "eating food and drinking water," as the Nuosu say, knowledge of the language.

And so I became interested in the study of ethnic identity. The six of us researchers planned a compendium of articles on various aspects of the household survey and related research, but it never happened; I'm not sure exactly why, but the renewed ideological pressures after June 4, 1989,[6] combined with the data having gone cold by the time things had loosened up again, basically made people lose interest. I did publish two articles based on analysis of the household survey materials (Harrell 1992, 1993), but most of the data sat, one copy in Panzhihua, probably one in Chengdu, and one in my office, waiting for the restudy, which was finally funded by the National Science Foundation in 2005. But most of what I wrote and thought about concerned the problems of ethnic identity, and I composed a series of arguments based on the premise that the idea of Yi was nothing but an artificial category to begin with, perhaps becoming more naturalized among the population now that people were living as part of a political unit called the Yi *minzu* (Harrell 1990, 1995). Like a good American, I favored the local over the national, the popular over the state-determined, the little guy over the bureaucracy.

Before I left Panzhihua at the end of March, I hosted two dinners. One was a three-table banquet to which I invited everyone important in Panzhihua who had contributed to our project. First Secretary Han Guobin didn't show up, but many other dignitaries did, and I made sure to toast them all. Second Party Secretary Zhang Boxi was hosting an official dinner in another room in the same hotel, and after I had met most of my obligations at my own banquet, I went to find and toast him. A few minutes later, he came back and found me, plunked three glasses of liquor down on the table in front of me, and challenged me to finish them off. From that point forward, I lost control, got the drunkest I have ever been since college, and felt quite sick for the next two days.

---

6. The night when the People's Liberation Army killed over 1,000 protestors in and around Tian'anmen Square in Beijing.

The other dinner was just for the six of us in the research team, plus Lao Deng and Lao Yan, and, of course, Driver Dai. We agreed ahead of time that there would be no drinking contests, and I got Wang Cheng-xiao to write two characters in his distinctive calligraphy for each of the other members. Ren Hai's said *peng tou,* or "bump head," since he kept hitting his head on low doorways (fig. 5.6). Liu Xin, who was always getting sick and missing out on research, got *liaoyang,* or "convalescence." Li Mingxi's said *pa po,* or "climb the hill," because we had to wait for her at the top of every uphill climb. And Lan Mingchun got his nickname, *xifu,* or "daughter-in-law." I wanted to surprise everyone, so I didn't tell Wang to write his own *banye,* "midnight" (because he always stayed up so late finishing his questionnaires); instead I wrote it for him in what was probably the crudest calligraphy with a traditional brush that he had ever seen. I passed these out at the dinner, and, of course, Wang had one for me: *kai men,* or "open the door," because of the way the door in the logging camp dormitory at Gaoping had creaked and woken everyone up when had I gotten up to race to the outhouse in the middle of the night while I had giardiasis. Wang also composed a celebratory poem incorporating all of the two-character phrases; we sent the original to Tong Enzheng, the "midwife" of all this, but a nice framed photocopy hangs on my office wall, and Wang's two characters "open the door" adorn my office door.

5.6 Ren Hai, who kept bumping into doorways, under an improvised sign reading "Watch your head!" Jingtang, 1988.

Of our research group, Wang Chengxiao worked in Panzhihua for another seventeen years, gaining a reputation as a prominent calligrapher; he moved to Chengdu in 2004. Lan Mingchun has been an editor with Sichuan University Press, Southwest Financial University Press, and now Tiandi Press, in

Chengdu. Liu Xin is chair of the sociology department at Fudan University in Shanghai. And Li Mingxi moved to Chengdu with her husband when he took up a job in the provincial Foreign Affairs Office, retiring not long afterward. Ren Hai finished his dissertation in anthropology at the University of Washington in 1999, and has claimed off-and-on that he no longer feels Chinese. He teaches popular culture in the Asian Studies program at the University of Arizona. Tong Enzheng died of liver failure in 1997. Deng Yaozong died of heart disease in 2002, with Zeng Saosao following him less than two years later; my friend Li Xingxing said that "they had the fate of mandarin ducks."

6

CHASING AFTER *BIMO*, 1992–93

BAMO AYI

At the end of 1991, at Father's urging, we three sisters formed the "Bamo Sisters' Yi Studies Research Group." In October 1992, I arranged to return to Liangshan from Beijing to do fieldwork with my sister, Bamo Qubumo, who was working at the Institute for Ethnic Literatures in the Chinese Academy of Social Sciences (fig. 6.1). With her background in literature, my sister would concentrate on the literary analysis of *bimo* texts and the artistic aspects of *bimo* rituals. My own focus was to be the core personnel of traditional Yi religion: the *bimo* (fig. 6.2).

At that time, Father, who was the vice-chair of the local People's Consultative Conference, arranged for an official trip to accompany his two daughters to Ganluo County to look for a field site. In the late '50s, Father had been a vice-magistrate in Ganluo. As soon as the word got around that he had returned with his two daughters, friends and relatives there began to slaughter pigs, sheep, and cattle to entertain us. When he heard that my sister and I were there to do research, a private entrepreneur of our uncles' generation, Ahxo Vuli, lent us two suites in the local People's Congress office building. Keddi, a distant nephew of ours and a farmer-entrepreneur in Jimi Township, and Luo Xiaobo, an uncle who

6.1 Bamo Qubumo (left) and Bamo Ayi (right) with schoolchildren and slaughtered animals, Meigu, 1991.

worked in Ganluo Town, contributed 2000 and 1000 yuan to help us with our fieldwork. Friends and relatives enthusiastically recommended field sites and introduced us to prospective informants. We quickly chose our principal informant: Ganluo's most famous *bimo*, Jjike Sadda. Sadda Bimo was the principal *bimo* for the family of Leng Guangdian's wife, Quhxamo, who had arranged the blood-liquor oath between the Yi elites of Ganluo and the People's Liberation Army in 1935.[1] Fieldwork this time was going to be different from going to the village and living in the households in Yinchang. We were preparing to make our headquarters in the county town; our informants would come into the town

---

1. When the Workers' and Peasants' Red Army was on its long march in 1935–36, it passed through parts of Liangshan. At one point, Red Army commander Liu Bocheng and local Nuosu leader Xihmi Asho signed a pact guaranteeing the Red Army safe passage in territories where he had influence, sealing the bargain by drinking cups of liquor with a drop of blood from each of the signatories.

6.2 Bamo Ayi unscrambling a ritual scripture with Bimo Qubi Nuomo, Qise Village, Meigu, 1991.

to meet us, and we would go to villages only when there were rituals or other activities. With respect to such a resoundingly famous *bimo* as Sadda, the first thing I was interested in was his life history.

"There's no fir that's not evergreen; there's no boy from the Jjike who isn't a *bimo.* . . . " The starting point for Sadda's story wasn't himself; it was his clan and his *bimo* genealogy. "A monkey can't be without a forest; a Nuosu can't be without a clan." Embedded in this net, I understood, a Yi person, as an individual, must establish his own place in his clan, and affirm his position in his genealogy.

A few days later, in the People's Congress office building, Qubumo and I listened to Grandpa Sadda tell stories of the history and glories of an old *bimo*'s lifetime of work. We recorded the Jjike genealogy, the names and deeds of famous *bimo* that the Jjike clan had produced, and tales of Sadda's training and practice as a *bimo*. Our data collection was going smoothly, but in order to keep up the interviews, Sadda needed several pain pills every day. The old man himself couldn't say when the pain pills had become a habit, but if he didn't have his medicine daily, he couldn't summon up any energy. We bought one bottle of pain pills after another, and put them on the interview table for the old man to use. The old man joked that the fiercest illness spirits in other people's bodies all feared him, and that he could drive away any spirit that caused illness, other than this little ghost that had brought to his own body the addiction to pain pills. The two rituals at which Sadda Bimo was reputedly most skilled were the *cur nimu* and the *nyu nimu*. *Cur nimu* is a ritual to halt the disease and send off the soul when someone dies of leprosy; *nyu nimu* does the same for someone who has died of tuberculosis. The spirits that cause these diseases are the ghosts most feared by the Nuosu.

Sadda Bimo loved to eat peanuts; sometimes he would polish off a half-pound bag a day. Watching Sadda chew peanuts, my sister and I couldn't resist sticking our hand in the plastic bag once in a while and taking out a few to much on, so a snack of peanuts became a requirement for our interviews. Strolling the streets was the old man's other favorite leisure activity. He must have been very happy walking down the street with two young women like us on his arms. He would stop unconsciously and call enthusiastically whenever he saw someone he knew, and he introduced us to all of them and told them which family's daughters we were, where we came from, and that we were there as his disciples to "learn to be *bimo*," exaggerating how much of the *bimo* script we could understand and how much we knew about *bimo* knowledge. Sadda's young disciple, Mofu, who had not undergone the formal *bijjie* ceremony of certification but who was often asked to do rituals for people, also took part in our interviews when he wasn't out doing ceremonies.

It was in this friendly and intimate atmosphere that Grandpa rolled out his life story, his successes and failures, one by one, including at least one story of a not entirely flattering thing he had once done. In order to stop passersby from stealing fruit from his family's garden, he had once gotten the idea to put a hex on some of the unripe fruits that would give the thieves stomach aches; he secretly watched and enjoyed the spectacle. After he finished telling us, he childishly and frankly exhorted me and my sister, whatever we did, not to tell people in and around Ganluo about this, for how could a *bimo* as famous as Jjike Sadda do such a dirty little deed?

One day, early in the morning, Uncle Shen Zhitie, former magistrate of Ganluo, knocked at our door, saying that he was there to see "what these two women were really doing hanging out with an old *bimo* all day long." He hadn't sat down but he had stayed from morning to night for several days, reading and explaining *bimo* books and expressing his own opinions of *bimo*. From Uncle Zhitie, we took down the orally transmitted legend of the Flood as well as the legend about why Yi people sacrifice animals to cure diseases. Uncle Zhitie was moved by the sincerity and enthusiasm of our research, saying that it was no easy task, and forcing us to accept a thousand yuan to print *bimo* texts. The most valuable thing that he did was to give us two *bimo* books in his own possession: One of them was *Nyundi Amo* (The Book of Exorcism of the Monkey Ghost Who Causes Tuberculosis), and the other was *Vasa Laqie Rre* (The Vasa Clan's Book of Curses), the original of which was said to be a book written in the blood of women from the Vasa clan, which the clan used to curse their enemies, the Azhe. *Bimo* books are usually hand copied, and many of them are of very poor quality, but Sadda Bimo confirmed to us that the *Vasa Laqie Rre* that Uncle Zhitie gave us was a very good edition.

During a pause in our interviews, we asked Sadda Bimo to tell our fortunes. After consulting his *Zhamo Teyy* book of divinations, he very solemnly told me and my sister that we should have a *uoqie hxie* ritual of pacification performed very soon. *Uoqie hxie* means "turning the head," and during the ritual, the sacrificed animal is swung around the head of the client in a clockwise direction (signifying "toward the outside") nine times in order to extract all evil ghosts and spirits, and then swung around in a counterclockwise direction (signifying "toward the inside") seven times in order to call back the client's own spirit and bring peace and good fortune. According to the book of divinations, both my sister and I had some ghosts blocking the way of our *xidde* (yearly fortune). Sadda explained that this was not difficult to understand, since we two sisters had been away from home for a long time, not only riding in cars and walking, crossing rivers and climbing mountains in the wind and rain, but talking all day about spirits and ancestors, taking notes all day about evil spirits and ghosts. He thought we should have a ritual performed, otherwise, at the least we would be susceptible to diseases, and at worst we might lose our souls and be in mortal danger. Before the old man could finish talking, my sister and I blurted out our agreement in unison. For a long time, I had wanted to have a *bimo* do a ritual for me and to experience firsthand being a *bimo*'s client.

Sadda Bimo picked an auspicious day for the ritual to be performed for us at his house in Sipu Village. On the eleventh of November, a particularly clear and bright day, one of our friends, Qufu, and my sister and I, after riding a minibus to Puchang Township, set out on the trail to Sipu Village. Not more than a quarter of an hour after leaving the town, we came to a particularly steep and narrow stretch of trail, where if we were not careful we risked falling into a deep canyon. My sister cursed at Qufu, calling the trail "life-threatening," but he answered that for mountain people it was just like walking on flat ground, that even drunks returning at night had never slipped there. When we were just about to the village, I suddenly got a feeling of dejection and my heart started to race, I felt like I was suffocating, and couldn't control my footsteps. When my sister saw me in this condition, she held me up and shouted to Qufu. After leaning on my sister for quite a while, I felt recovered and sat down on a boulder. Gasping, I said, half seriously and half jokingly, "If I'm 'sacrificed' here, it has to be because of a sudden heart attack. I'm afraid it's just like Sadda Bimo said, 'Ghosts are after you.'" My sister didn't believe it. "When have you ever had a heart defect?" As soon as we entered Sadda Bimo's house, he told someone to go to a neighbor's house and get a chicken to use in the ritual, and they prepared to do the *uoqie hxie* ritual of pacification. They lit a fire outside the door, and Sadda and his nephew Gaga began to recite the text of *Lighting a Fire to Welcome the Spirits*, asking spirits to come and help, and exorcising the spirits of violent death, rheumatism ghosts, river ghosts, leprosy ghosts, and *xiggu xijji* (ghosts from the bones of the deceased)—all of which are ghosts that one is likely to encounter when one is traveling. I still felt as if I had no strength in my body, like a wooden chicken. I, who had eagerly awaited this ritual for several days could now not summon up the least bit of energy to experience the feeling of a ritual client. My sister, on the contrary, was extremely animated, telling me that I would feel better when the ritual was over, and leading me to follow the *bimo,* sitting above hearth for a while, squatting below the hearth for a while, now shouting the curses against the spirits along with the *bimo,* now busy writing in her notebook. My own notes from that day, Nuosu mixed with Han, didn't amount to more than 200 words for a three-hour ritual. But among them I did record a few sentences of the very beautiful verse that the *bimo* chanted to praise the sacrificed rooster:

> The rooster's blood roils like a spring,
> Rinsing away all the ghosts and evil sprits.
> The rooster's feathers are like fog and clouds,
> Rolling away the ghosts and evil sprits.
> The rooster spreads his wings and flies,
> Flapping away all the ghosts and evil spirits.

The rooster that was used for the sacrifice was a mottled rooster, bought for sixteen yuan. As the ritual entered its final phase, just as the sound of the chant sending back the *bimo*'s helper spirit had faded away, my sister asked me if I felt better or not. "Grandpa's ritual seems to have worked," I told her. I felt a lot better.

On the sixth of December, my sister went back to Beijing to take part in the design planning for the China Nationalities Park[2] there, but I stayed behind in Ganluo to continue research. *Bimos'* primary activities are conducting rituals, and they organize their professional lives around these rituals. This period of my research was concentrated around understanding such aspects of *bimos'* professional activities as the training of *bimo* apprentices, *bimo* retiring from practice, destroying old ritual texts, and the adjustment of relationships between *bimo* and their helper spirits. Father asked Jjike Hoqie, my former field assistant from Yinchang, to come to Ganluo to accompany me in my work. Hoqie was, after all, a son of a *bimo* household, and had an enthusiasm for interviewing famous teachers. He had long ago known the great fame of Sadda Bimo, and to boot he and Sadda both belonged to the Jjibu branch, one of the seven great branches of the Jjike clan. After Hoqie arrived, our room was never free of the excited atmosphere created by members of the Jjibu branch from two different areas reciting their genealogies and figuring out their kin relationships. Even though our interview time was shortened by Hoqie's and Sadda's chatting, I was quite happy

---

2. A minority-culture theme park on the outskirts of Beijing. It includes a Liangshan Nuosu house in the Yi section.

to sit quietly listening to their intimate conversations and laughing talk. On the fourth of January, Hoqie and I finished our research in Ganluo and caught a ride back to Xichang. Before I left, I made a special shopping trip to buy a few bottles of painkillers and two or three *jin*[3] of peanuts to give to Sadda to take home with him. I remember that when I said good-bye to Grandpa Sadda, I told him to take care of himself and that I would soon return to Ganluo with peanuts and aspirin for him. But it turned out to be a last good-bye. Grandpa has been gone for many years, but I will always remember his modesty, his warmth, his breadth of knowledge, his generosity, and his childlike candor.

> Go see, ah, go see. . . .
> If you want to go see a specialist in curing leprosy,
> Then go see Jjike Nyieddu of Yanyuan.

> Go see, ah, go see. . . .
> If you want to see a specialist in curing tuberculosis
> Then go see Jjike Nyieddu of Yanyuan.

In Nuosu mountain villages, there is an oral literature that is chanted in unison at weddings, called *hxe bbo mi*, or "Go see, ah," that talks especially about which places have produced famous Nuosu people or heroes. But most of the famous people mentioned in *hxe bbo mi* are dead. At the time of the Han New Year in 1993, when relatives from Yanyuan came to pay New Year respects to Father and Mother, the fact came up in conversation that Jjike Nyieddu, the famous *bimo* from Yanyuan who could cure leprosy and tuberculosis, was still alive and well, and I immediately decided that right after New Year I would go to Yanyuan to look for him and interview him. There is a Nuosu saying, "When an old person dies, he takes with him a burlap sack [of knowledge]." If a *bimo* like Nyieddu were to die, he might take with him even more.

In February 1993, Yyhxo Aga and Shen Jun, both of whom worked in the Yanyuan County Language and Translation Office, accompanied me to Yousuo District in Yanyuan, where Nyieddu was always travel-

---

3. A *jin* is 500 grams.

ing around practicing rituals. Yyhxo Aga was a *bimo* himself, and had been invited to lecture on *bimo* documents to the Yi documents class at the Central Nationalities Institute. Because of this stroke of luck, his household registration had changed from "peasant" to "urban," and he had risen from being a peasant to being a government cadre. Shen Jun was a student in the Yi documents class of our university, and had taken my classes in theory of comparative religion and in Yi religion. Because Nyieddu Bimo was often away from home conducting rituals, we hadn't risked making the day-long trek to his home village of Honghua, but instead remained in the market and asked people from different villages to spread the word for Nyieddu to come to Yousuo. Aga jokingly told the messengers to say that a leader of the central government had come to see him (the university for which we worked has the word "central" in it's title, and is located in Beijing).

One day, two days, three days went by. We had not seen even the shadow of Nyieddu Bimo, and I was beginning to get worried. On the afternoon of the twenty-seventh, as I was standing on the balcony of the district government building in Yousuo discussing with Aga and Shen Jun what to do, we saw an old man with a *vala* tied around his waist, wearing leggings and the traditional sky-blue wide-cuffed pants, with a spirit quiver[4] over his shoulder, excitedly leading a prize chestnut-colored horse into the courtyard. As soon as we saw someone gotten up like that, we knew without asking that it was Jjike Nyieddu. But he was much younger and more spirited than I had imagined.

As soon as Nyieddu Bimo arrived, the first thing he did was to arrange for hay for that precious horse of his. Only when the horse was safely stabled did he ask where the person from Beijing was, and what business she had with him. After Aga Bimo had made a simple introduction, I nervously and respectfully told Nyieddu Bimo that I had come all the way from Beijing to study the *bimo* arts with him. Nyieddu Bimo measured me up and down, and said seriously, "What are you doing studying *bimo* arts? There is no such practice as a woman being a *bimo*." I was immediately confused, and didn't know the best way to reply. In fact, in order to save the trouble of explaining, express respect for *bimo*,

---

4. One of a *bimo*'s principal ritual tools, made from a thick section of bamboo.

and increase the impression of my closeness to *bimo,* or to ingratiate myself with them, wherever I went I told *bimo* and other people that I had come to be a *bimo*'s apprentice, to learn the *bimo* arts. But my status as an apprentice had received a challenge.

The worst part of it was that the challenger was just the *bimo* master that I admired and wanted to interview, the one that I had come to take as a mentor. I suddenly thought of how both Vudda Bimo and Sadda Bimo had told other people that I was their apprentice. But perhaps they had never really thought of me as an actual apprentice. If one day I actually had taken up ritual implements on my back and put a *kuhlevo*[5] on my head and a spirit quiver on my shoulder, I'm afraid that they would have been the first to jump out and oppose it. Among the principles of transmission of *bimo* knowledge, the most important is that females are not allowed to perform rituals. *Bimo* is a male profession. Even though everyone says that Bi Ashy Lazze's daughter Lazze Shyse performed rituals as a *bimo,* no one can forget that the only way she could do so was to dress as a man. In addition, neither my own Bamo clan nor my husband's Qumo clan had a history of producing *bimo,* as Shyse's clan had. Nyieddu Bimo had asked a good question: What was I doing wanting to study *bimo* arts? In fact, my studying these arts was different from a disciple studying them. An apprentice studied so that he could become a *bimo*; it was a kind of professional preparation. I was doing it in order to research *bimo.* Maybe it was precisely because I would never and could never be a *bimo* that *bimo* referred to me as their disciple and that people didn't mind calling me a "*bimo* disciple."

Jjike Nyieddu Bimo belonged to the Pig year, and was seventy-one that year. He had originally been a *nbobi,* a *bimo* who performed happy rituals like ancestor worship and calling back souls. But when he was young he had killed a man in a clan fight. According to *bimo* custom, a *bimo* who has killed someone cannot do ancestor worship rituals. Nyieddu's only choice was to become a *ddibi,* that is a *bimo* who specializes in rituals that cure leprosy and tuberculosis, and that curse evil ghosts and enemies. In my imagination, a *ddibi bimo,* who spent all day trafficking with ghosts and enemies, certainly wouldn't be nice to people.

---

5. A *bimo*'s conical hat.

But, on the contrary, even though Nyieddu made me feel a bit uneasy, I quickly discovered that he was a cheerful, funny person, very different from those proper *nbobi bimo* that I had previously known, who were always paying attention to their own behavior. When Aga Bimo said to Nyieddu's face, unflatteringly, that Nyieddu had three wives, two of whom he got as compensation for doing rituals at people's houses, Nyieddu joked back that three was nothing; if it hadn't been for the Democratic Reforms, he could have had at least two or three more. Aga, given an inch, took an ell, continuing to tell stories about Nyieddu Bimo. One time, when Nyieddu had been resting on the road on the way to perform a ritual, he stopped for the time it took to smoke two or three bags of tobacco and counted a small pile of stones. When the disciple who was traveling with him asked him how many he had counted, he said only 103, and when the disciple questioned what it was that was only 103, he said that in his life traveling around performing rituals, he had been with 103 girls. When Aga finished, everyone competed to ask Nyieddu Bimo if it had happened or not, and I thought that Nyieddu would deny it. I should have known; he didn't blush a bit, and said that, yes, it had actually happened, but that 103 were too many, there were probably only 20 or 30. I think that a *bimo*, traveling around to the four directions, having seen a lot and learned much, good at making friends, strong in appropriate speech, and paying attention to self-cultivation could indeed incite the admiration of a lot of young girls, so a libertine *bimo* didn't seem strange.

In the field, plans are always slower than changes in plans. On the third day of our research, as we were in the middle of an interview in the district government office, the family of Ayur Lurhxo of the eleventh production team of the second brigade of Pingchuan came to ask Nyieddu Bimo to conduct a ritual. Nyieddu looked at us, troubled, and Shen Jun quickly expressed his opposition: We had waited several days for the *bimo;* he should turn down the invitation with thanks and stay to be interviewed. I knew, however, that there was no customary way for a *bimo* to decline an invitation, so I jumped to the rescue and stated that I would like to go along, and we could take part in the ritual and do interviews at the same time. That afternoon, Shen Jun and I followed Nyieddu Bimo to the client's house to conduct the ritual. The host,

6.3 Bamo Ayi
tying straw ghost
effigies with Bimo
Jjike Nyieddu,
Pingchuan,
Yanyuan, 1993.

Lurhxo, had abdominal pains, and had lain in bed for several days without getting up. Divination had revealed that he had encountered a chronic
gastritis ghost called a *ddeni*. That evening, as Nyieddu Bimo performed
the *nyicy ssy* ritual of cursing ghosts, I ventured to ask him if he would
let me tie the straw ghost effigies.

Ghosts are formless, so using tied bundles of straw to give them form
not only gives the ritual to expel them a visible result but, more importantly, has a psychologically reassuring effect. Nyieddu, half believing
and half suspicious, had me sit right below him, in the place of the *bisse*
disciple, and piled a bunch of *ryry* grass and raw hempen cord in front
of me. I quickly arranged a bundle of grass, tied a hemp string around
its head, and before long had tied a grass ghost, even though it wasn't
exactly exquisitely made (fig. 6.3). As soon as Nyieddu saw that I was okay
at this, he delegated the task of tying straw ghosts to me. In this way, I
was once again permitted to assume the role of disciple in a ritual, even
though Nyieddu Bimo had not proclaimed to everyone that I was his
apprentice. As Nyieddu had arranged, the object of expulsion in the next
day's ritual was a transformation of Lurhxo's father's spirit. But Lurhxo's
mother was still alive, sitting below the hearth, and the leaping flames
from the hearth illuminated her sad face. In the middle of the ritual, I

moved over to sit by her and struck up a conversation. She said, "Lurhxo's father died of tuberculosis, and in order to break off the roots of the disease, the *bimo* has to treat him as a ghost and send him away. I don't care; what has to be sent off or what has to be driven out is for the *bimo* to decide. I can't let my son die before me. I'd rather die myself in his place." The old lady took up the front of her shirt to wipe her tears. I couldn't stand it; I started sniffling and crying myself.

The ritual didn't finish until very late, and Nyieddu Bimo, Shen Jun, and I went to sleep by the hearth with our clothes on. Before dawn, I was awakened by the "bada-bada" noise of Nyieddu Bimo smoking a tobacco pipe. I couldn't sleep, so began talking with the old man. He opined that the most powerful *bimo*s in Liangshan at the time were himself and Yoga Hlumo of Gguli Ladda in Zhaojue County. He admitted that Yoga Hlumo's knowledge was richer than his own, but he also felt that his own *bilu asa* (protective spirit) was stronger than Yoga Hlumo's. Nyieddu Bimo said that in his life, he had cured more than 200 leprosy patients, and that his most effective ritual had been the leprosy-curing ritual that he had performed for the Ayur family of Vaggelieto in Ninglang County in Yunnan. The Ayur family had leprous roots, and it was said that even their dogs and chickens were lepers. When Nyieddu had done the ritual for the family, he had ritually extracted from the mouths of the sick people the leprosy ghosts that had manifested themselves as wasps, frogs, and snakes. When the ritual was completed, the leprous roots of the Ayur family had been cut off. For this one ritual, Nyieddu Bimo had received compensation of over 100 ingots of silver. Gradually, rays of light began filtering in through the gaps between the wooden roof shingles; dawn had come. The room became lively again; everyone was preparing for the *ddeni bi* ritual of expelling the ghosts of abdominal pain.

The previous evening, someone had come from the Axi family in a neighboring village, waiting to take Nyieddu Bimo back to their house to conduct a *bbyssy ggakie* ritual of breaking the path of the ghosts who had died violently. Axi was a cadre in the Pingchuan judicial court; his father had been shot to death at the time of the democratic reforms. Recently Axi had gotten into a lot of conflicts and arguments with his wife and others. Divination had shown that *bbyssy* ghosts who had died violent deaths were blocking his way. So Axi had returned to his younger brother's house in the village to do the ritual of cutting off the path of the ghosts who died by violence. In addition to blaming illness and disasters on ghosts and spirits, Yi people also attribute disputes, animosity, and enmity among living people to the agency of ghosts and spirits. They use ritual methods to expel such ghosts and spirits; to patch up contradictions between spouses, siblings, neighbors, clan-mates, or affines; and to achieve the goal of peaceful relationships.

After the road-cutting ritual, the *bimo* changes from the director of the ritual to a symbol of bad luck, and has to be driven out. When the ritual at Axi's house was nearing its final phase, people began to shout and fire off guns to terrorize and drive away the *bimo*. As Nyieddu Bimo's *biqo* (directly translated as "ritual companions"), Shen Jun and I were also the objects of expulsion. As soon as I saw Nyieddu Bimo put on his felt cape upside down and drive a goat in front of him, I picked up the big rooster and Shen Jun led the horse, and we were chaotically "driven" from the client's house. As we left the client's house, Nyieddu Bimo told me not to look back or else the ghosts of the violent deaths would return to the client's house and the ritual would be *mohly*, or ineffective. The most fearsome thing was that we were not allowed to take the trails that people ordinarily walk on, but instead had to pick our way through grass and forests. In the end, we came to the ridge of the mountains, where we couldn't see the smoke from any fires or the shadows of any people. Nyieddu asked us to stop and do the *uoqie hxie* head-turning ritual for expelling ghosts and pollution, using the rooster given to us by the ritual client to expel any ghosts or evil spirits that might have remained in our bodies as a result of doing the ritual, and to cleanse away any pollution we might have acquired. After Nyieddu Bimo had recited a bunch of curses, he used his knife to slaughter the rooster, and after it was dead, Shen Jun and I collected some firewood nearby and lit a fire, upon which we put the chicken to roast. After a while we plucked the scorched feathers with our hands and cut open and cleaned out the insides, then put the rooster back on the fire until it was done, and divided it up and ate it. I originally thought it wouldn't be good to eat because there was no salt, but the roasted chicken had a particularly enticing flavor. In one hand I held the chicken and gnawed at it; in the other I took the liquor bottle that was being passed and drank a great mouthful. I felt a satisfaction that is difficult to put into words. In just a short period of effort, the three of us had completely annihilated a big rooster.

After we performed the *uoqie hxie*, we could then take a regular trail again without worry. On the mountain slope there was no water to wash with, so we proceeded toward the next client's house with black faces and greasy hands. The rooster that I had been responsible for having been eaten, I helped Shen Jun shout at the goat and drive it along. We walked and walked, and then Nyieddu, who was riding his horse in front of us, suddenly turned around and looked at Shen Jun and me driving the goat along behind the horse's tail and then turned back around and started laughing wildly. I felt that Nyieddu was laughing oddly, and that it had something to do with me, so I ran up to ask him what he was laughing at, and he began laughing even more merrily, tossing his head back and forth. Shen Jun and I were totally puzzled. When we stopped to rest in a meadow full of blooming wild peas, I couldn't keep myself from asking Nyieddu Bimo what, after all, he had been laughing at, and finally he said to me, "What I'm laughing at is you, laughing at this woman chasing behind the backside of this old *bimo*. Why are you doing this?"

After we had followed Nyieddu Bimo to Shama Buji's house in the eleventh production group in Pingchuan to conduct a ritual to cure his five-year-old son of a skin condition by expelling a *cur*, or leprosy ghost, three more households from that village came to *bimbo* (engage) Nyieddu Bimo. It looked like it would be impossible to ever get him to come back to the district headquarters to be interviewed. I took advantage of the rest periods between rituals to question Nyieddu about *bifu*, or *bimo* chants. I had noticed that when Nyieddu was chanting during rituals, he was extraordinarily occupied with and conscientious of them, very concerned over whether people had heard him or not, and not like some *bimo*, who, when they have come to the end of a particular chant, just finish chanting the words and that's that. He not only had a very good singing voice, but, more importantly, was very concerned with tonal changes and uses of prosody. Aside from the occasional sounding of his brass bell, most of the time he sang or chanted unaccompa-

6.4 Bamo Ayi learning ritual paper cutting, Leibo County, 1993.

nied, and listening to him chant was an aesthetic experience. When the ritual at the Shama house came to the section where the meat of the sacrificial animals was roasted or boiled, Nyieddu Bimo gave me a lovely lesson in *bimo* chanting. He said that different rituals and different sections of rituals had different objects: Some of them were ancestors, some spirits, and some ghosts and demons, and because of this, the rhythms of chanting that one used were different; otherwise the object would not hear them. The chanting styles taken from animals or from the natural world, such as those used in the *nbobi,* or happy rituals, would imitate the sound of cicadas or the songs of a kind of bird called *hxo-hxo,* depending on which text was being read; in rituals sending off souls, the style mimicked the sound of cicadas or of sheep braying; when performing rituals to curse people or exorcise evil ghosts, a cow's voice is mimicked; and in rituals such as those for pacification, the sound should imitate that of a pig. Nyieddu Bimo said that learning these chanting voices was an important part of learning to be a *bimo.* His son Yojiesse learned texts and rituals very well, but he was no good at *bifuqi,* or chanting *bimo* voices, so he was unable to perform rituals. In my previous research, I had paid attention to paper cutting (fig. 6.4), clay modeling, straw tying, painting, and calligraphy, but had never reflected on chanting voices and rhythms. A *bimo* ritual can in fact be seen as a *Gesamtkunstwerk,* or integrated artistic performance. Nobody had researched voices and rhythms, so I began to.

After a ritual of *cur ji,* or expelling the *cur* ghost, at the Shama household, Shen Jun and I said good-bye to Nyieddu Bimo and caught a ride on a big Dongfeng truck back to Yanyuan. When we were on the highway waiting for a ride, we saw Lurhxo going to market at the district headquarters, and even though he looked skinny and weak, he seemed to be in much better spirits than he had been before the ritual. I asked him, curiously, whether he had recovered or not. He said, "You can see that I can get down the mountain to market."

Today, Nyieddu Bimo is gone, with his net bag on his back. And the sound of his laughter out in the wilds, the question he asked, still comes to my ears now and then: "What I'm laughing at is you, laughing at this woman chasing behind the backside of this old *bimo*. Why are you doing this? Why?"

7

GETTING STARTED AGAIN, 1991

STEVAN HARRELL

I n the *Sichuan Ribao* in February 1992, there appeared the following piece by one Zhou Jifen, a single mother, former ballerina, and
feminist fiction writer:

Hello, Harrell!
By Zhou Jifen
    The rugged Southern Silk Road, endlessly rising and falling through
remote country, an ancient and mysterious route through the passes. You
came striding and swinging with your two long legs, part of the "Southern
Silk Road Household Economy and Composition Research Team."[1]
    The phoenix trees with their caplike canopies have outlined your tall
shadow; the nakedly exposed sandstone of the mountain trails has heard
your hurried footsteps; the blazing, brilliantly scarlet sun and the crazy wind
that whips the dust both know you, because you repeatedly stride over the
Southern Silk Road, over the old pass route, over the hot soil of Panzhihua.
    In the countryside, you have slept on short, small plank beds; you have
knelt and squatted on the muddy earth around a little kerosene stove and

---

    1. This was the official designation of our 1988 Panzhihua research, which was part
of Professor Tong Enzheng's Southern Silk Road research program.

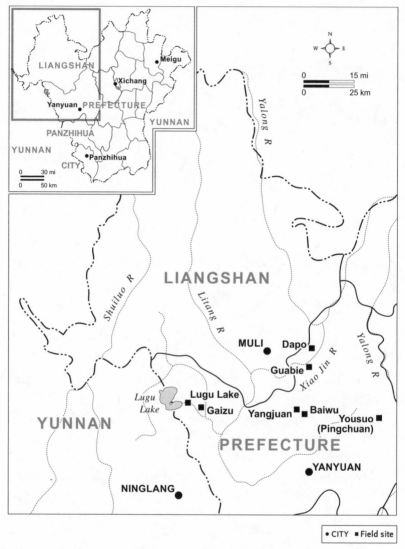

MAP 3. *Yanyuan County, Northwestern Liangshan and environs*

fried "Chinese food." Rubbing your reddened forehead, you pasted a little piece of paper on a peasant's door lintel, saying "Watch your head."

In the closets at the Panzhihua City Office of Artifact Management, there are two bright red, bright red quilt covers. Gently whisking off the light dust we see you again, rushing from the far side of the great ocean, laughingly taking your seat at a peasant wedding banquet. That year's bride and groom have long been someone's parents, but every time their eyes light on that coverlet, every time their hands feel the cover, maybe they think of you. And you, in far off Seattle, USA, do you also have a flash of memory? You can't forget far-off Panzhihua, the people of far-off Panzhihua; three years after your initial visit, you journeyed again to Panzhihua. Tramping through the mud of the rainy season, carrying half trouser legs of muddy water, you went visiting; you didn't need a guide—the old roads were still the same, the familiar people still the same! Held up by the heavy rains, you walked with Mao Chunnan, your peasant friend from Yishala Village, singing, dancing, talking. Rain? Tears? It was hard to tell black eyes from blue eyes.

When you first met Mao Chunnan, he told you in plain words: he had participated in Resist America, Aid Korea. You plainly replied: "I was still little then, and never fought against Chinese people. But my father took part in the 'Second War,' so we're allies."

Two pairs of hands, one yellow and one white, shaking with a tight grip. Mao Chunnan had found a foreign soul-mate, and took out hidden genealogies, contracts, even proclamations from the Qianlong period for you to see.

You uphold the pure and simple virtue and humanity of the ordinary Chinese; you're not like most Americans who let old folks live alone, but you brought your old mother to live close by, seeing her morning and evening. You said, Mother is very aged, the next time I come to Panzhihua, will be after I have accompanied her to the end. Confucius of China said, "Don't travel far while your parents are alive; if you travel there has to be someone who stays close."

Coincidentally, on the thirtieth of the old year, when you received New Year's money from the father of Professor Deng of the Panzhihua City Artifact Office, you ceremoniously knelt down and properly knocked your head three times. What stopped you in your tracks, what moved your feelings and brought forth your tears, was it your old mother, wishing in America for her son's return, or was it the white-haired old Chinese man in front of your eyes?

You said: Panzhihua is beautiful, beautiful, like my old home, Seattle; I love Panzhihua.

The natives here say: Panzhihua also loves you.

Today, as the Panzhihua flowers are about to burst forth, as the phoenix trees are greening, when will you come again? Come to dance the peasants' round dances, come to eat the boiled meat of the Yi, come to play "blow the feather" or tug-o-war, to go together visiting over mountains and ridges, come to swing your long legs, to hold forth in your Beijing accent!

You said, you have already chosen a new research topic. Well, then, it can't be very long until we, along with the blue sky and bright sun of Panzhihua, call out in welcome, "Hello, Harrell! Stevan Harrell, Hello!"

At the time the article appeared, Zhou Jifen had never met me; the stories she used to write her account came from Lao Deng. The essay won second prize for the best descriptive essay published in the *Sichuan Ribao* in 1992. I have hazel eyes; the man in Yishala was named Mao Chunlan, but he wasn't the one who showed me the proclamation; and anyway, it was from the Shunzhi period, a hundred years before Qianlong. Ren Hai was the one who kept bumping his head (I was tall enough to have learned to duck long before; he was just tall enough to bang into those short doorways) (see fig. 5.6). I compared Panzhihua to Los Angeles, and it was Lao Deng's father-in-law that I laughingly knocked my head to on New Year's: The old man thought it was a good joke, too.

The article made me wonder how much I get wrong when I tell stories or write ethnographic articles. But Zhou Jifen (whom I later met and liked) did get one thing right—after my mother died in January 1991, I went back to China in September of the same year to investigate the possibilities for a new project, this time in collaboration mainly with the Sichuan Nationalities Research Institute, but unequivocally on the topic of ethnic identity and relations. And I would do most of the research in Liangshan Prefecture, though there would be some to do in Panzhihua as well.

On that brief visit, I spent about ten days in Chengdu and then headed south, this time to visit Xichang with Zhou Xiyin, director of the Sichuan Nationalities Research Institute. Director Zhou was thin, tired, and in poor health, but he gamely accompanied me, partly because we were planning to apply jointly for a big research project to cover aspects of ethnic relations in Liangshan and two other areas in Sichuan. In Xichang, I was introduced to Qubi Shimei, head of the prefectural institute, and one of the young researchers there, Gaga Erri (Gaga Lyssyr). We discussed plans for the general project, and also for my part in it, which would involve fieldwork the following year in Yanyuan County, as well as in Panzhihua.

Gaga and I had a good time that afternoon visiting the Museum of Yi Slave Society and then climbing a mountain, and I hoped he would accompany me to Yanyuan the next day. But in the morning, he came to wish me well and to tell me that another fellow, a native of Yanyuan, would be going with me and Director Zhou instead. Ma Erzi (Mgebbu Lunzy) was a quiet, dark-skinned fellow who seemed cautiously interested in what I was doing. The trip to Yanyuan takes five hours via what I had christened in my mind the Dear Sweet Jesus Road, madly careering past wobbling trucks, around outside curves on the sides of cliffs, bouncing on rutted tracks, or maybe just tracklike ruts, stopping for many minutes because of traffic or landslides or someone blocking the road—who knows? Up one mountain range, down to the hot valley of the Yalong River, and then along the Yousuo River up to a 3000–meter pass leading into the plain that houses the city of Yanyuan.

Cadres from all over Liangshan were holding a conference on poverty and development in Yanyuan at the time; this meant that rooms were scarce at the county guest house, but somehow Director Zhou finagled us some. We found a little restaurant for lunch (Director Zhou was afraid it wasn't too clean), and afterward Zhou finally excused himself for the afternoon (looking quite pale) while Ma Lunzy and I took the jeep to his hometown of Baiwu, where we might be able to do research the following year. A young woman with a baby wanted a ride partway out there, and as we rode I tried out my Nuosu language on her. There was no response at first, but Ma knew what I was up to, and repeated my question to her, after which she recognized what I was doing, and I was then able to ask her simple questions about her family and her baby boy. After she got out of the car, Ma told the driver that I was quite unusual—that they should give me a Yi name right then. "We'll call him Meigui Muga." "Meigui" is the local Han dialect pronunciation of "America," also borrowed into Nuosu usage, and "Muga," (pronounced

7.1 *The first picture of Ma Lunzy (back left) and Stevan Harrell (back right) together,
Baiwu, 1991.*

"m-ga") is a common Nuosu name. I was unambiguously Meigui Muga
until late 1994, and people in Yanyuan still know me by that name.

The reception in light drizzle at Baiwu, a little one-street town about
an hour from Yanyuan City, was remarkable. Ma Lunzy knew everybody, of course, but as we stepped out of the jeep, I was the main attraction. Dirty, smiling children swarmed around me and the young fellow
that Ma had instructed to walk me around town until he could find some
cadres (fig. 7.1). When the cadres arrived, having been prompted as to
what I was about, they said, "Well, if you're interested in *minzu*, and
you can only stay one afternoon, then we'll just visit one household of
each *minzu*." And we did—Naxi, Zang, Menggu, Han, and Yi,[2] I madly
asking whatever questions came into my mind and scribbling them as

---

2. This is the way the inhabitants of Baiwu are classified in the official *minzu* des-
ignations. In terms of more local ethnic identity, those classified as Yi are Nuosu, those
classified as Zang are Prmi, and those classified as Menggu (Mongolian) are Na or Naze.
For a further explanation of this tangle, see Harrell, *Ways of Being Ethnic in Southwest
China.*

fast as I could in a pocket notebook. We would, of course, stay while they slaughtered a sheep and we could eat and drink together. I begged off on account of sick, worrying Director Zhou, but it wasn't easy; I had to promise to help consume plenty of sheep in Baiwu a year and a half hence, and I kept that promise.

We got back just in time for the opening banquet of the poverty and development conference at the Yanyuan guest house, and I toasted every cadre who approached me out of curiosity or politeness or both—"*Zzymo ggehni*," (roughly, "Best wishes")—without waiting to be advised of the particular cadre's ethnicity. The next morning, we hurtled all the way back to Xichang, had a noontime banquet with the prefectural research institute, and then met Driver Dai from Panzhihua, who drove me the six further hours to Panzhihua, giving Dai and me time to discuss Chinese and world affairs, and for this loyal Communist to ask me how many people were really killed in Beijing on June 4, 1989. Then, after Lao Deng's usual whirlwind rounds of visits to city officials, we paid a visit to Yishala (the rainy visit described in Zhou Jifen's article). The next day we headed for Miyi County, where we spent an informative afternoon in a Hui village, and the following day we visited another possible field site—the remote township of Malong, where, along with the more accessible Puwei, there are at least four "branches" of the Yi *minzu*—in addition to Nuosu, here called Liangshan Yi, there are Yala, Tazhi, and Abu. This was an even shorter visit than the one to Baiwu— we did visit a Yala family briefly—but there, clearly, was the other field site for 1993.

My proposal to the Committee on Scholarly Communication was considerably more sophisticated this time; I would make two visits to Liangshan and Panzhihua in 1993 and 1994, to study ethnic relations in a variety of local settings.

My tentative plan would be to spend Jan.–March 1993 and Jan.–March 1994 in a series of field sites in this area . . . In each field site, I plan to conduct the following kinds of research:

1. Interviews of each household in a small community, or a randomly selected sample of households in a larger community. In addition to cen-

sus data on household members and their ages, kin relations, educational and work histories, etc., I would also interview about ethnic group membership, ancestry and history of migration, languages spoken and the context in which they are used, holidays and their celebrations, patterns of intermarriage, and perceptions of the nature of their own and other ethnic groups.

2. Detailed investigations of kin networks in each ethnic group in each community.

3. Interviews with cadres and other key leaders about the history of the community and its internal and external ethnic relations.

4. Participation in holidays, weddings, funerals, and whatever other occasions arise, to observe the conscious assertion and, if possible, effectiveness of ethnic claims.

5. Collection of whatever local documents are available that provide historical and economic background to the local area, as well as possible information about ethnic identity and relations.

For the first period of field study, I had tentatively selected three research sites. I would spend half or more of my research time (six weeks or so) in Yuanbao [Baiwu] District, Yanyuan County, Liangshan Prefecture. On a brief visit to Yuanbao, I found out that the district is composed primarily of Yi, who are very forward in asserting their ethnic identity, but also contains Han, Zang (Prmi), Naxi, Meng (Mosuo), and Nu people.

After Yuanbao, I planned to spend one and one half to two weeks each at two sites in Miyi County, Panzhihua City: the townships of Malong and Puwei, both of which I have visited. Malong is primarily Yi (Nuosu), but contains Yala, a group that does not admit to its Yi designation, as well as Han and Bai. Puwei is primarily Han, but has at least three and perhaps four ethnically distinct groups that are classified as Yi, as well as some Lisu and Hui.

For the second three months of research, in 1994, there were two possibilities. One was to concentrate on the ethnic identity and relations of Lisu communities in Yanbian, Miyi, and perhaps Dechang counties. The other was to concentrate on the Yi side of Yi-Tibetan or other Yi-Zang relations in Muli or Jiulong counties. The exact plans would, of course, be greatly influenced by the results of the first research term.

I received the funding, along with an admonition that I needed to stay longer in China to do all the research procedures mentioned in the proposal. I also received promises of cooperation from the various research institutes, based on the implicit assumption of a quid pro quo trip to the United States for the four senior leaders of the institutes and an application for a large joint grant to carry out a three-year project.

8

FIRST CONTACT, 1991

MA LUNZY

From the time the Liangshan Nationalities Research Institute was established at the end of 1990, several leaders responsible for its establishment had repeatedly asked me to come "promote the usefulness" of their research. Not wanting them to lose face, in the fall of 1991 I reluctantly left the familiar Museum of Yi Slave Society and walked in the gate of the research institute. What to research? How to research it? I hadn't been there long when I went with several colleagues who had come to the institute a few months earlier, and, with an insufficiently serious attitude, attended a conference on Southwest ethnology that the institute was hosting. The evening after the conference was over, institute director Qubi Shimei asked me to go to his office, where, with an officious air, he outlined Stevan Harrell's biography and emphasized the importance of his upcoming trip. The main point was that he wanted me to accompany this famous professor.

The next morning Qubi Shimei and a driver took me to the Qionghai Hotel, where we were introduced to Zhou Xiyin, director of the provincial Nationalities Research Institute, and to Stevan Harrell. When I had gotten out of the car, without Qubi's telling me, I had guessed that the tall fellow standing next to Zhou Xiyin was the professor I was supposed to accompany. During the brief introductions, we both measured each other with our eyes. I joked in Nuosu to Qubi, "There could be a lot of mineral resources in that high mountain; but there isn't much vegetation growing on top, and I don't know if it will be able to stand the searing sun of Yanyuan." Qubi answered in the same vein, "Smart people use their brains too much and it hurts their hair, just as if there are too many loggers on a mountain, the trees will diminish. The reason the two of us have old-growth forests is because we don't exercise our brains enough." I said, "Smart or not, I have no choice but to accept your arrangement and lead his horse on the road." In Liangshan society before the Democratic Reforms, leading a horse for one's lord was called *muke si*, and meant "to serve someone."

After a few polite words, we took off for Yanyuan. In truth, I didn't understand the purpose of Harrell's trip until we were on the road. On the way, Harrell and Zhou Xiyin kept bringing up several scholarly and professional affairs, and at one point took out a map to see where we were. I half closed my sleepy eyes and thought about what I had read concerning the United States—Alexis de Tocqueville's *Democracy in America*, John Hope Franklin's *From Slavery to Freedom: A History of Negro Americans*, and Wang Jianhua's translation of *Selected Inaugural Addresses of American Presidents Through History*, along with some stories I had heard on Voice of America about the great tide of research on China.

At 12:30 we arrived at the Yanyuan Government Hotel, and the receptionist there told us that because they were hosting a prefecture-wide meeting on poverty alleviation, there were no rooms. Director Zhou seemed agitated, and proposed that we immediately find the county leaders to settle the situation. I thought that there was no question that we could find a place to stay, and that looking up the leaders during the noon rest period was not only a bad idea, but also a waste of our time. So I informed Director Zhou that we had time to get to Baiwu and back, and suggested that we find a little something to eat on the way, and then hurry on to Baiwu. We ate at a small restaurant, and Director Zhou vacillated between coming with us and staying behind, and finally decided that he would stay and connect with the leaders. He incessantly patted me on the shoulder and told me to be sure to take good care of the professor. I was a bit puzzled: Why was Director Zhou, whose health was not good, worrying about somebody much healthier than he was— was it out of politeness, or was it because he was required to welcome a professor whose level of knowledge was higher than his own, which made him feel small and inferior? On the dusty road, I got the feeling that this professor, who was looked upon by Qubi and Director Zhou as a "Giant Panda," was much more amiable than they were.

As we were driving on the road to Baiwu, we ran into a lot of Nuosu people looking for rides, and they all looked familiar, but I couldn't remember any of their names. I knew their hardships, so we picked up as many as would fit in the jeep, and the car was crammed full. Harrell not only didn't complain but cheerfully turned around to a young woman with a baby and emitted a few words of Nuosu. Hearing a professor from across the Pacific who had made the effort to spit out a few words of our language was naturally quite touching. His fearsomeness seemed to diminish before my eyes, as did the distance between us. I waited until the mother and child got out of the car along the way, watching their hardship , and then gave Harrell a Nuosu name, Meigui Muga. Muga was originally a birth-order name, meaning "second son," but it has a common meaning of praise. On important occasions, Yi people use "Mother's Muga" to formally announce someone's clan name and personal name. My giving him this name should indicate my initial impression of him. In Yanyuan it practically replaced Harrell's English name to the point that later on, a lot of Nuosu people only know Meigui Muga and had never heard of Stevan Harrell or Hao Rui (his Han name).

When we got to Baiwu, which, of course, is my world, I told friends in the town about the reason for Harrell's trip, and confidently turned over my "horse leading" work to them. A township vice-head and cousin of mine, Li Zhiyuan, and others took Harrell to people's houses to interview them, and introduced the basic situation of Baiwu to him. I sat leisurely in a township leader's apartment and gossiped with familiar people. At 5:00 they came back to the township government headquarters, and Harrell was very satisfied; this was what I had expected.

Director Zhou, who had remained behind, had already contacted the leaders and had telephoned to tell us to hurry back to town for the evening banquet. I thought that our driver must be exhausted, and, after apologizing to him, we quickly returned to the county seat. At 6:00 we got to the hotel and saw Director Zhou with a smile on his face: he had arranged living quarters for all of us, and urged us to go to the restaurant to partake of the banquet with leaders and friends who were attending the poverty alleviation meeting. The "horse leader" felt happy that both the professor and the director were satisfied.

During dinner, Harrell became the focus of attention, and several prefectural leaders separately toasted him, so that each of the county leaders had to do the same as their superiors and toast him too. From start to finish, Harrell came forward to clink glasses with each person who toasted him, and repeated the phrase *zzymuo ggehni*, or "good wishes." Most of the leaders at the meeting were Nuosu acquaintances of mine, and, like me, when they first heard him speak Nuosu, they thought it was quaint and touching, and every one delightedly praised him—*Aguo! Ssahxo!* ("Able! Smart!") When the banquet was just about over, I separately said a few words to County Party Secretary Yang Zipo, a former teacher of mine who had taught with me in Yanyuan, and also (according to Nuosu genealogical calculation) a member of my uncles' generation. I said to him, "Your domain is still a closed area at present, and foreigners who want to come here have to go through a lot of paperwork; Harrell did not have time to do all the bureaucratic procedures. If by some chance the public security personnel should come over and ask, I yield to you." He looked at me and laughed, and didn't say a thing. When I left the restaurant, I began to be afraid that security would bother Harrell and Director Zhou directly, and purposely said to the person responsible for security at the meeting (sent from the public security bureau), "Please take good care of Secretary Yang's foreign guest." Sure enough, this had its effect—that evening, not a few public security personnel questioned Yang Zipo about the matter. Only when they knew that Harrell was Yang's guest did they quit inquiring.

The next morning when we saw each other, Yang immediately asked, "What kind of special agent did you bring to Yanyuan, anyway? Last night public security people interrogated me several times." Laughingly, I answered, "Have our Yanyuan police eaten too much salt [a product of Yanyuan] and not been able to sleep? If he is a special agent, how come he's not operating in Beijing, Chengdu, or Xichang? Would he be coming to a poverty-stricken place like Yanyuan? Next time they want to have a look at an American devil, send them straight to me to buy tickets. If they treat me as a traitor one more time, I'll get my relatives and friends together to show them a little justice." After this little exchange of wit, he went upstairs with me, as if nothing had happened, to say good-bye to Harrell. I want back to Xichang with Harrell and the rest of them. Until I wrote this, I never told this story to Harrell or to Zhou Xiyin.

9

ALMOST REAL FIELDWORK, 1993

STEVAN HARRELL

In January 1993 I flew from Hong Kong to Chengdu once again, and was met by Director Zhou. From my past two experiences, I had expected to spend at least a week or two in the dismal provincial capital, getting permissions and seeing the people I had to see, so I was delighted when Zhou told me we would be going to Xichang in two days, and to Yanyuan not long after that. Sure enough, on the morning of January 9, having taken the overnight train to Xichang, Zhou and I, along with Gaga Erri, Ma Lunzy, and several of the latter's relatives, piled into an ancient Land Cruiser for the trip up and down and up the mountains. After one night in the county guest house, meals with a few officials, and a shopping trip to buy vegetables—unavailable in the countryside—we were on our way to Baiwu to begin fieldwork. We rented some rooms in a little local hotel, hired a young village woman to cook for us after an attempt or two at preparing our own meals, and we were ready to collect data.

Gaga didn't last very long. Although he was a fine writer and archival researcher in two languages, I think he felt somewhat superfluous in this field location, and after a few days even stopped coming along when Ma and I went to interview someone. So after about a week, he decided to go home to his native Ganluo for the Han New Year, and left the local guy and the professor on their own.

Altogether, the two of us spent three weeks in Baiwu, and another two in and about other parts of Yanyuan and neighboring Ninglang. This period was extraordinarily productive. We interviewed every family in the two villages attached to Baiwu Town—the Nuosu Hongxing and the ethnically mixed Lianhe. We also censused all the families in Yangjuan, a village about a forty-minute walk away, where Ma (whom I learned to call by his Nuosu birth-order name, Vurryr, pronounced "vu-jr") had grown up and where his father, formerly the young scion of a slave-owning family but now an ordinary peasant, and several of his eight siblings still lived. We traveled to a Prmi village called Changma, and interviewed there. We went to two Han, one Prmi, and three Nuosu weddings, plus a Nuosu funeral. We observed local elections and interviewed at the local primary and secondary schools. We copied agricultural and population statistics, and interviewed local cadres about various aspects of their work. We went with Han families to sweep the tombs a few days after the New Year, something that Vurryr had never done before. We recorded basic vocabularies in as many languages as local people could remember, and recorded a Prmi genealogy that Vurryr said would have been impossible for him, a local Nuosu, to record alone. We participated in the celebration of the electrification of the town (but not yet the attached villages, let alone the outlying ones), and we even received a visit from County Party Secretary Yang Zipo (Atu Nzypo), who had brought Wu Ga (Luovu Vugashynyumo), a Nuosu graduate student from the University of Michigan, to visit the tall, bald American, who Wu Ga had rightly guessed was me.

After a week in Baiwu, I had a free afternoon, and climbed one of the hills next to the town, where I could see the checkerboard pattern of the walls around the newly planted apple orchards, punctuated by the institutional one- and two-story buildings of the township government, the schools, and the various offices. A week in a place like that lulled one into the misleading feeling of being in a traditional society, a little community, with customs undisturbed by forty years of revolution. I wrote:

This is no place for bandits, or for lovers
Where would either one find shelter here?
Not in the bubble hills, among the spindly pines
Not beneath bare apple branches, on the winter plain
Not even tucked in corners of the mud-wall grid.
Surely the wind would give them up, or the slanting sun.
    No, this place is not for outlaws
    To flee the socialist order
    Or the stricter net of custom
    It's far too cold outside.
Only the floor-hearth warms
With glowing logs
With songs in many tongues
With shallow bowls of strong drink
With the comforting, smothering knowledge
That you, too, have a place inside.

Now, this was a community that had been through the Democratic Reforms, the Great Leap Forward, the Cultural Revolution, and the recent market reforms of China's economy. Still, it gave a visiting researcher a feeling of being somehow traditional, old-fashioned, unchanged, exotic. I was running into the paradoxes of ethnic revival in the 1990s.

Data of all sorts continued to pile up, and we could perhaps have stayed in Baiwu for five or six weeks or more if we had made a special plea. But I ran into the methodological expectations of Chinese ethnology, and the ethnic viewpoint of my friend Vurryr. My journal for January 29 reads:

I'm also beginning to think I'll be pretty satisfied with a little over three weeks' fieldwork in this one place. I'd be dishonest if I didn't admit to personal comfort and freedom from cold as one motive, but that's not all of it. . . .

The more of it is that there is a limit to what I can find out with my level of linguistic ability, unless I stay really long. I guess the difference is between the kind of fast-paced *diaocha*[1] fieldwork we've been doing, based mostly on

---

1. Usually translated as "investigation."

interviews, with observation of rituals, such as funerals, weddings, New Years and civic ceremonies; and the slower, ultimately rewarding but not for the man who misses his home and family (let alone the busy administrator) mode of true participant observation. What I'm saying is that staying two months, I'd run out of obvious, intensive-mode things to ask, and it would be six months or more of hanging out and really learning the language before I could begin to reap those deeper, more elusive rewards. . . .

The other factor is the presence of Ma Lunzy, along with a potential trip to Lugu Hu with the local Black Yi scholar Hu Jin'ao, and the documents that have all been promised me—this means there is a lot of material. It also means, paradoxically, that it's more difficult to develop the fieldworker-directly-integrated-into-the-community persona, without staying for a long time.

So is this a justification or a rationalization? It's an admission of my own limitations more than anything else. I have seen way more of real life in China than I have seen in all my previous visits (by an order of magnitude, at least) and I should graciously accept these limitations and move on to the next things, which are first looking at connections to some other places we've been, as well as collecting documentation, and then moving on to the warmer shores of Panzhihua.

In other words, I was being even more strongly implicated in local ethnological practice than before. Though the conception of the project was mine, as was the theoretical rationale, the practical details were Vurryr's, and I was not set up to contradict either him or the traditions he had been educated in. And even if I could have, I think it would have been wrong to do so, in a sense. Whatever ethnography I ended up writing would of necessity derive its authority from a conjunction of cosmopolitan ethnographic practice of "real" fieldwork, Chinese ethnological practice of *diaocha*, and local discourses. The short-term, extremely intensive *diaocha* is one of the contributions of Chinese practice. I could, at least, *diaocha* in a lot of different places, while real anthropological fieldwork would only afford time for one site.

At the same time, I was inhibited in another way by my dependency on Vurryr, which was partly the result of my own linguistic incompetence, and partly the result of the institutional structures in which I was working. On January 22, I had written in my journal:

Having Ma Lunzy here is an incredible help, revelation, and comfort; and at the same time an unsurpassable block to my field work, especially at my level of Nuosu *ddoma* [language]. Here is the way it works:

With any Nuosu people, he's an immediate entry. He sometimes, at the weddings, sent me off to interview certain households by myself, while he played chess, and I've had several independent conversations with people here in the *danwei*. But mostly, he's there.

This means that we haven't yet gotten much that would speak from a viewpoint opposed to his, either ethnically or in class terms. I think the ethnic barrier is more translucent. For example, the old Bazong[2] families, Naxi and Zang, have given us some things contradictory to what [Ma] has said about prerevolutionary Yi-Buddhist relations, though the issue is hardly earthshaking now. And it's clear that he doesn't much care for the local Han, though he has plenty of Han friends, and we are invited to the Xu family for tonight.

But the class barrier is going to be tougher. [Ma's] father was officially a slave lord, and he has an interest in a certain version of slave-lord relations, which is that yes, slavery was wrong and it's good that we abolished it, and now the evidence is that we get along well with our former slaves—he planted some trees as part of the collective period, which are now [very] profitable for one of the ex-slave families, and he has taught and encouraged many of their people as lower- and middle-school students, and he has no objection to marriage between slave and *quho* [commoner], and the old versions of Liangshan society derived from a mechanical application of Morganian theory[3] are silly and in need of revision, etc., etc., and I believe all of it, to a point. When an ex-slave graduates from middle school, that's a fact, as it is a fact when one marries a White Yi, which has also happened. And he freely admits that some of the older guys in his clan are not so open-minded, espe-

---

2. "Bazong" was the Chinese title of the Prmi local agents of the King of Muli, a monkruler of a domain that included most of today's Muli County, plus parts of north-central Yanyuan, including Baiwu. The Bazong's descendants, classified as Naxi and Zang ("Tibetan") *minzu*, still live in Baiwu Town.

3. The theory, derived from the writings of U.S. ethnologist Lewis Henry Morgan (1818–1881), postulated that all societies progress through a uniform series of stages and transformations, from savagery to barbarism to civilization. Marx and Engels used Morgan's writings to formulate a comprehensive model of society's progress toward eventual communism.

cially on the issue of intermarriage. Still, there is another side to the story, and it's one I'm going to find probably impossible or nearly impossible to get, given the nature of the relationship.

I especially regret not pushing the language harder, though there's no time or systematic way to do it now to get it to anywhere near the level it needs to be at before I can get much independent information, except perhaps from some of the younger guys who can hold reasonable conversations in more-or-less accented Putonghua [standard Chinese].

I was beginning to learn how to look at the world through the eyes of a formerly slave-owning Nuosu, a commoner. I could get glimpses of how things might look to an aristocrat, a slave, or a Prmi, but just glimpses. To get more would require fieldwork, and by this time I was firmly committed to *diaocha*.

So we left Baiwu on February 1, and returned to Yanyuan County Town, where I received my first mail from home in over three weeks, but still no bath—the bathhouse was closed down for several weeks because of the New Year holiday. But we did interview a large number of *nuoho* (aristocratic) families in two suburban settlements, and ate several fine animals. On February 5, Vurryr and I, along with the local Nuosu scholar Hu Jin'ao (Luoho Tuha) and his wife and son, embarked with a cadre jeep caravan to visit the fabled "Country of Women" at Lugu Lake, and incidentally to negotiate a timber agreement between Yanyuan, Muli, and Ninglang counties.

This junket, which I have analyzed in detail elsewhere (Harrell 1996) was probably the first time I ever merely acted as a participant in any PRC context. It was certainly the first group activity in which I had been assigned a protocol rank somewhere near the bottom; on that trip, I didn't sit anywhere close to the head table at any of the banquets. County Party Secretary Yang Zipo had invited me along because I was the first foreigner to spend more than a day or two in Yanyuan since Joseph Rock, and because it added to his prestige and panache to have a captive *lao wai* (foreigner) to show off to his friends and bureaucratic associates. For example, when we arrived at one hotel, he motioned to me to come to the guest room to sit and talk with some local notables. Vurryr and I were headed off somewhere (anywhere to be out of reach of the cadres), so I tried to decline, but Secretary Yang shot back, "You're in China; you obey my orders."

Still, show-horse duty typically took up no more than an hour or two a day for the six days of the trip, and the rest of the time Vurryr and I, along with Hu Jin'ao and Mr. Hu's nine-year-old son, were left to our own devices. My devices included a little random ethnography, such as an unscheduled visit to the local Hui restaurant, which led to an afternoon at a local Hui scholar's house and a nighttime visit to a Na village with Vurryr and Mr. Hu. I also got my first bath in a month at a local hot spring. But I was mainly concerned with the picture of reform China painted in the civic rituals of Secretary Yang and his bureaucratic colleagues. The picture of China they painted, partly for me but mostly for each other and for the local citizens, was the China of the *tongyide duominzu guojia* (united country of diverse nationalities), where members of diverse ethnic groups lived side by side in harmony; at the same time each group developed its own unique languages, customs, culture, and ceremonies. Everywhere we went, we were greeted by maidens in the local native dress, serving ethnic specialties and singing ethnic songs, even rowing us across Lugu Lake in their ethnic canoe (fig. 9.1). We joined in the circle dances, where members of every *minzu* all dance the same steps to the same tune, but each in their own differently colorful outfits. Han army veterans, Yi scholars, and even a Na incarnate lama took part in these nightly "unity-in-diversity" rituals.

This China was also the less explicitly ethnic one, where discourses of development and cooperation had replaced Cultural Revolution themes of class struggle and local autarky. The timber treaty that the three counties were signing, the ostensible reason for the whole trip, exemplified the common use of resources to build the socialist market economy and raise the standard of living in this rather remote area. The multicolored lights in the ballroom of the Ninglang County Guest House were as much a part of the message of this trip as the colorful balconies of the Na and Prmi houses around Lugu Lake.

At the end of the trip, Vurryr and I parted ways for a while. I hitched a ride with some cadres from Muli Tibetan Autonomous County (Muli Zangzu Zizhi Xian) to their home county to visit for a few days and explore possibilities for fieldwork there by me or some of my graduate students. At the high mountain pass that separates Yanyuan from Ninglang, the jeep caravan halted, and we had a half-drunken pistol-shooting contest, in which I somehow managed to hit two beer bottles. Then Secretary Yang, who would be returning to Yanyuan City, bade me a fond farewell, saying, "This is not a separation, just a parting of our roads." Then there was a several-hours-long, half-drunken ride to Muli, the last part of which turned out to be the real Dear Sweet Jesus Road—800 meters up the side of a cliff above the Yantang River—narrow, slippery with mud in places, and the driver taking swigs in turn as the passengers passed the bottle. I spent the next three days in Muli, where local cadres kindly accompanied me on a visit to the Muli monastery, former seat of the lama king, and to several multiethnic villages (fig. 9.2). In my notes, I called it FBK—Fabled Buddhist Kingdom—and I was able to confirm some things about Prmi culture and the relationship of the Prmi to the Zang *minzu*, but the place still remains shrouded in fable for me, and I have not gone there again.

Yanyuan seemed like home when I finally got back—cold, yes, but safe and comfortable, with good friends and familiar surroundings. Vurryr and I spent one more day there and then finally headed back to

9.1 Rowing across Lugu Lake, 1993. Secretary Yang Zipo is in the stern.

Xichang and the Anning River Valley, where I booked a room in the lakeside Qionghai Hotel, expecting three days of rest, sunshine, and data consolidation before heading to Panzhihua. It rained the whole time.

In Panzhihua, there were more rounds of city officials with Lao Deng, of course, and then it was back to Miyi County, to the field sites we had scoped out in 1991. First was Puwei, only forty-five minutes from the county capital on a newly paved road, a place I had been briefly with Ren Hai and Li Mingxi in 1988. I remember we had gone there after the village family survey project, to see yet another kind of Yi, this time the Red Yi, who had come from Guizhou. I was trying to establish the affinities of their language, and we pulled up to a village somewhere near the main road in a two-jeep caravan with a trail of cadres, since Miyi in 1988 was still officially closed to foreigners. Nobody who came out to greet us remembered anything of the Red Yi language, but one middle-aged man in a dusty, faded turban thought that his octogenarian mother might be able to help. Someone assisted her out into a chair on the concrete porch surrounding the courtyard, and started asking

9.2 Stevan Harrell with monks at Muli monastery, 1993.

her, "Ma, how do you say 'father' in our language?" She couldn't hear, so they yelled, "Ma! How do you—" She still couldn't hear, so they yelled right into her ear, and I was beginning to feel acutely uncomfortable, something like Radcliffe-Brown in his Andaman police station would have felt if he had had a postcolonial conscience.[4] No luck, so we visited an old water-driven rice mill, then had lunch at the house of Ma Wenlong, also a Red Yi and a local entrepreneur and relative of Ma Weixin in the Culture Bureau, and drove back to the city.

This time, in 1993, I was going to get the ethnic relations straight here. The *Miyi Minzu Zhi*, or *Record of the Minzu of Miyi*, said that in addition to the Nuosu from Liangshan, there were four small branches of the Yi in the county: the Yala, Tazhi, Abu, and Niluo. All of them could be found in either Puwei or Malong, so those would be the two places we would visit. Miyi was still not used to foreigners, so when Zhang Yong, a young cadre and researcher at the county cultural bureau, accompanied me to Puwei, Vice-Chairman Yang of the county nationalities commission (*minwei*) also came along. The three of us, plus Driver Dai, took rooms in the now-deserted forestry guest house. The forestry bureau, having cut down all the worthwhile trees in and near Puwei, had moved elsewhere, and there were only a few retirees and dependents left.

At an elevation of only 1,650 meters—900 lower than Baiwu—Puwei was in full springtide in early March. Wheat in the terraces on the long, narrow plain and on the gentler hillsides was in the pool-table green phase, when the sprouts have grown enough to hide the brown earth but have not started to turn the least bit yellow or even lighten, and everywhere there were fruit trees at the peak of their bloom—pink for the peaches, and white for the pears. Except for the first night, when it sprinkled a bit of snow that was gone by morning, I could discard my long underwear—more like Xichang than Yanyuan.

This was a style of fieldwork altogether different from what I had

---

4. The great British functionalist anthropologist A.R. Radcliffe-Brown conducted fieldwork in the Andaman Islands in the early years of the twentieth century. Tribal legend among anthropologists has it that he got information by asking the colonial police to go out and round up some knowledgeable "informants" and bring them in for (scientific) questioning.

done in Yanyuan, or even in the Panzhihua villages in 1988. Zhang Yong, my nominal field assistant, was busy with family affairs and not entirely pleased to be there. Driver Dai, a valued and straightforward confidant after all those curves and hills, told me later on that Zhang had also been displeased because I never paid for cigarettes. I had to confess that he was right. I know Chinese etiquette fairly well, and could once drink with the best of them, though it gets more difficult and distasteful as I get older. But I draw the line at tobacco—too many people I have known have died of it. I hoped to just fudge the issue, but Dai, in his typical manner, wouldn't let me off the hook. Dai himself won't touch either tobacco or alcohol, but he knows courtesy and discourtesy when he sees it. Anyway, the upshot of it was that sometimes I was with Zhang Yong, and sometimes I wasn't; Dai was there with the car sometimes, and not at other times, and I usually had a cadre or a storekeeper or somebody that knew somebody to help me when I went to villages. In eight days by jeep and on foot, I think I superficially straightened out the mysteries of the Yala, Tazhi, Abu, and Niluo.[5]

When I had a free morning between village visits and copying records in the township office in Puwei, I outlined what was, with one more season of fieldwork, to become *Ways of Being Ethnic in Southwest China* (Harrell 2001). It was getting toward the end of this field visit, and I had one more field visit planned for winter 1994. I was horribly homesick by this time, and wanted to cut the next visit as short as possible. I also knew by now that I wanted to write about different modes of ethnic relationships in different localities and among different configurations of *minzu*, and that I could probably concentrate on three basic modes of ethnic identity, as represented by three modes of ethnic communication or representation. The first of these was represented by the Nuosu. I had decided that all of the Nuosu communities I had ever worked in, from Gaoping to Baiwu, were at some middle level of acculturation—living in a mixed environment with local Han and other ethnic groups, but still retaining endogamy and many other clear ethnic markers. I decided that I should explore two other contexts to broaden my knowledge—one, a place like Yuehua, an hour north of

---

5. See chapter 13 of *Ways of Being Ethnic in Southwest China* (Harrell 2001).

Xichang near the Anning River, where Nuosu people have adopted many Han ways in the last two centuries, and the other somewhere in the heart of old Liangshan, where Han influence was at its minimum and the population all Nuosu. So those would be two field sites for 1994. Then, to add to my knowledge of the Prmi, whose identity had a second mode—contingent and shifting—I ought to compare them to the Na, who seemed to have an even more fluid and contextual identity, and who lived in various enclaves around and about Yanyuan and Muli. So I should spend some more time in Yanyuan, but this time at the east and west ends of the county, where the Na lived. Finally, I should go back to Muli. I didn't really have a clear idea why—maybe just because it was so remote—but I would spend two weeks there. The third mode was represented by the Han, but I did not feel I needed any more fieldwork in Han communities.

After nine days in Puwei, Dai took me and Zhang Yong to Malong, a two-and-a-half-hour drive over a road that lacked the dangers of the Muli highway but was even bumpier and dustier. Zhang Yong seemed sick in the back seat, and when we got there, he was coughing up blood. Township Head Yang had remembered me from my brief visit in 1991, and had it all set for me to interview folks in and around town, as well as to spend a night in a pastoral area several hours away (I had told him I wanted to visit a remote area, and he, guileless, had simply arranged for a couple of young cadres to take me to one, no questions asked). So when Zhang Yong guiltily asked me if it was all right if he caught a truck back home to his girlfriend, I quickly agreed. Nothing in it for him here, and nothing in it for me having him here.

I managed to interview quite a few Yala people this time, and record a basic vocabulary of the Yala language as well as a census of fourteen Yala households in town. But the highlight of this visit was the hike to the pastureland. I packed my knapsack with everything imaginable— my overnight kit full of medicines and lotions, a dry shirt, camera and extra film, notebook and journal, flashlight, sweater, and drinking water. My two young companions considered taking their toothbrushes, but then thought better of it. They did carry the two bottles of liquor I had bought as a present for the unknown host. The hike took about three hours—800 meters elevation gain—and I was drenched in sweat by the time we reached the high plateau. When we got to our host family, who were fairly close cousins of my companions, the daughter-in-law and her father-in-law were at first afraid to speak with me, just looking me over with an intense stare. But eventually they sized me up, and we had a great afternoon and evening, I trying to dry the sweat out of my fast-wicking ski underwear by turning one side of me and then the other to the sun while it shone, and to the fire when we went inside. They killed a sheep, and we talked while it boiled in the big wok set on the tripod in the middle of the floor. We ate most of it, Nuosu style, which is to say in big chunks with our hands, while sipping its broth with long-handled wooden spoons, or *itchyr*. They put us to bed in a spare room with no windows or outside doors, and the first thing I knew it was morning, and they were calling us to eat again. This time the occasion was not ceremonial, and the sheep was cooked Han style—stir-fried over rice and eaten with chopsticks. I then took a family photo that I said I would send them as a memento, and we started off down the path. After a few minutes, Gaga, the son who had entertained us the night before, came running after us with a camera in his hand—he thought he'd like a picture of us, too. It's always good to reflect on the subject-object encounter in ethnographic fieldwork.

We returned to town, but by a different route. In a village down the valley, there were reputed to be three families of the Bai *minzu*; I wanted to interview them, and so I did. Their identity cards said Yi, and they came from what I knew to be a Yi (Lipuo) area that is now part of Renhe District in Panzhihua.

And that was the end of my fieldwork in 1993. After the last phase in Puwei and Malong was over, I felt acutely that investigating little vestigial groups that claimed to be *minzu*, however important it was to the structure of my forthcoming book, took on a great artificiality. These people were, for all intents and purposes, ordinary rural southwestern Chinese. They were no doubt the descendants of people who were once culturally and linguistically quite different, and it was possible that they might still consider this important in an emotional sense, or in the practical sense of using it to get affirmative action benefits. But I was in another epistemological bind, though one somewhat different from that I had experienced with Ma Lunzy in Baiwu. Here it was not my collaborator's presence that raised an issue but rather mine, in my announced capacity of studying *minzu*. Were all these facts about customs and languages and ancestors and marriage practices really important to these people, or did they just dredge them up because I came around? Were they important when I was not there? I knew they were important for the Nuosu, whose lives are so different, and even for the Prmi, who bear many outward signs of their ethnicity consciously and proudly. But was being Tazhi or Yala really important to these folks? There would be no way to know without more of the real, participant observation fieldwork that I had sacrificed in the interests of breadth of knowledge, not to speak of personal comfort. So my research had passed from the phase of exploration to the phase of concentration; already my sights were narrowed in anticipation of writing my book. But I still had one more field season to go.

10

IN THE MONTH OF THE SNAKE, 1993

MA LUNZY

I had just about forgotten the trip to Baiwu with Stevan Harrell, when Director Qubi summoned Gaga Erri and me to his office on January 5, 1993, and, just as in 1991, explained the purpose and importance of receiving Harrell again. He told us to arrange things well at home, because we wouldn't be able to return to Xichang for at least a month and a half. He particularly emphasized security and satisfaction in research cooperation. Accompanying Harrell the second time wasn't something I could put off; whether I was happy about it or not, according to organizational principles, I had to obey my superiors.

For a long time I had been perusing articles, data, and reports about the Yi of Liangshan written by outsiders, both Chinese and foreign, who had left behind a large number of influential investigations, explanations, and dialogues about the area. Without exception, I got tangled up in unfortunate descriptions of pre-Democratic Reform society, descriptions that I really couldn't shake, and that sometimes made me angry. Whether the writers had set out from Han areas around Xichang, or from Leshan or Yibin, or had started from Leshan and gone to Xichang, they had all prepared before they entered Yi territory as if they had only one chance in ten of surviving, and it seemed as if in their writings they all foreshadowed their own glory in daring to brave the dangers of dying on their journeys. It was not difficult to see that they were trying to emphasize their own self-sacrificing spirit and using their own behavior on the trip as a device to exaggerate the suspense of the tale. Some people, even though they were accompanied by Nuosu guides and received hospitality from clans and their affines (who often presented them along the way with pig heads, sheep shoulders, or beef shoulders), still wrote about these acts of courtesy as examples of a primitive, raw-meat-eating way of life. Their trips to Liangshan were represented as once-in-a-lifetime struggles in which they had fought their way to Liangshan in order to have the opportunity to see and hear what they termed the "savage."

What makes one think even more deeply is that a later group of moralistic fellows, imbued with modern civilization, arrogantly took upon themselves the responsibilities of civilization and progress, assuming the position of saviors who braved bitterness and difficulties and ignored the native Nuosu culture. Their system of knowing and their moral principles led them to use downright hateful language, and contributed to a deeply etched shameful impression of this ethnic group. Superficially, these prejudices were simply a personal or scholarly matter, but for a long time they were the theoretical basis for those who directed the reform of Liangshan Yi society, and thus turned into a pretext for political repression. This had manacled the Nuosu people. I thought about the professor that I was supposed to accompany—what attitude did he have? Would he, in his articles, intentionally or unintentionally harm the subjects of his research and carve a hero's image for himself? If so, what would I be, as a collaborator in name but a translator in fact? Of course, I wasn't hoping that he would make the Nuosu into a symbol of human civilization or a people to be looked up to and admired. This would also be a disgrace to scholarship.

From another angle, from the time my generation had entered school clear through to the reform and opening up,[1] in textbooks and in public opinion, we looked upon the United States as an enemy country, and upon Americans as a people who would stop at no evil. When I

---

1. The name for the policy of dismantling aspects of state socialism, which began in late 1978 and has now lasted longer than state socialism itself.

was little, I had, under a teacher's direction, made pointy paper noses to play the roles of figures fearful and hateful to Chinese people, such as Lyndon Johnson and Richard Nixon. At this particular time, the anti-American feeling in China was not small. How should I respond to this *ggashu qobo*, this "friend on the road" who came from America? The villagers that we wanted to interview would be even more likely to feel this way; during the period of collective agriculture they had sat for long hours in collective meeting places by the light of coal-oil lamps, discussing American imperialism, cutting off capitalist tails, and other political campaigns. In their minds, America was nothing better than a robber. Would we be able to melt the ice crystals of longtime anti-American propaganda into a colorless, tasteless, clear water that would lubricate mutual friendship? Although Americans were our enemies, we also remembered a Nuosu saying: *Sucy fuddu yy; fupur jjijji la, sumu jjiddu yy, jjibur qoji la.* "If crude people deal with their affines, the affines will become their enemies; if civilized people deal with their enemies, the enemies will become friends."

On January 9, 1993, I crowded into a Toyota SUV rented from the prefectural People's Congress, with Harrell, Gaga Erri, my wife, and my four-year-old son, and took off for Yanyuan. The place next to the driver was the roomiest, and ought to have gone to the renter, but Harrell gave up his place to the mother and child. After bumping along the road for several hours, Director Zhou saw that Harrell's body, tall as a cow and big as a horse, was squirming back and forth in the crowded space, and out of concern quietly told me to put my wife and son in the back. When I immediately asked the driver to stop, and presented this idea to Harrell as my own, he not only didn't agree, but angrily got out of the car and said loudly, "This is too unfair. You all go ahead; I'll walk." I felt somewhat taken aback; on the one hand, I shouldn't have arranged things according to our mountain people's custom and squeezed everyone into one car; on the other hand, I thought that no matter who they were, visitors ought to act according to local customs. I was secretly happy about Harrell's behaving in accord with Nuosu feelings, so I chased him and offered a solution. I invited him to take a picture with us as a memento (fig. 10.1); this calmed him down. To this day, when I look at this picture in my album, it transports me to the memory of that time

of interwoven feelings of surprise and happiness. You could say that at the time this picture was taken, I first made up my mind that I would do what I could to help Harrell with his fieldwork.

That evening I took my wife and son to my father's house. The next morning I contacted the township leaders and friends there, and settled Harrell in one room and Gaga and me in another room of a local guest house. When I told Harrell that I had heard on the street about there being a funeral the following morning for an old granny who had died at a place called Lamatang, about four kilometers from Baiwu, he asked me to prepare the way because he really wanted to observe the funeral. Gaga and I knew that anyone who went to participate in a funeral, whether an acquaintance or a stranger, would be given a big chunk of meat and a buckwheat cake. But we didn't know Harrell's eating habits, and we were afraid he wouldn't be able to eat the food and would go hungry. Gaga and I talked it over, and I went to an acquaintance to borrow a wok, some firewood, matches, and potatoes, and at 4:30 in the morning the two of us got up and boiled the potatoes. At 6:00, with sleepy eyes, each of us peeled a boiled potato; we had to force ourselves to eat, and we felt that maybe this hard labor had been for naught. Impatiently, I comforted Gaga in Nuosu: "Don't blame the two of us. Eating potatoes boiled under the stars is like eating stolen food; nobody likes it." Gaga turned his back to Harrell and secretly laughed without stopping.

When we got to Lamatang, Harrell observed the funeral scene; he saw the relatives weeping for the deceased, and heard the rifle shots echoing in the mountain valleys. He was particularly energized. He would take up his notebook and pen and write without stopping for awhile, then take up his camera and incessantly snap pictures. Direct relatives were circling around the corpse, Harrell was circling around the relatives, and a herd of curious children were circling around Harrell. Not until the corpse was placed on top of the pyre on the cremation ground did Harrell follow the crowds and come back to where the beef was being divided. When the division came, he took a piece and began to gnaw at it like everybody else. I had no way of knowing whether he noticed my and Gaga's manner, but I quietly observed his every move as closely as I could.

When we had eaten a little beef, the funeral was finished by firing rifles in the air. I said good-bye to friends, and we headed back to Baiwu. On the way back, I told Harrell about all sorts of pertinent customs, such as the duties that should be performed by affines, agnates, parents and children, brothers and sisters, husbands and wives, neighbors, lords, and vassals. He listened intently and questioned diligently and strangely. I asked Gaga if such Nuosu funeral customs were influenced by the attitudes described by Zeng Zi in the *Analects*: "Pursuing distant origins to the greatest possible extent, the virtue of the people becomes ever thicker." Why do we bankrupt ourselves for the sake of a dead person? Amid incessant discussions, before we realized it, we were back at our quarters. After having a bite to eat and taking a little rest, we began again with our "scattershot" field interviews.

I have taken part in many different kinds of field investigations—organized by popular, collective, or official organizations, or just my own private fieldwork—and no matter what methods one uses, if the interviewer and the interviewee have not established good relations, then some interview subjects will refuse to participate, while others will irresponsibly answer with nonsense. Speaking frankly, I don't blame them—ever since Liberation, all kinds of political, economic, and scholarly work teams have incessantly run around in Nuosu villages, and every villager has been part of some kind of investigation. The attitude of villagers toward researchers has been, "When you come it's a bother for me; when you don't come, I'm happy." Since the 1950s training in polit-

ical struggle has made every Nuosu person capable of unthinkingly cursing ten thousand evils of the old society and fluently spouting off the
experiences of transformation undergone in the new society. And the
poor, frustrated people around us were still incapable of moving away
from this mode of description. Someone who did not have longtime
experience of society in this area would not easily understand this. In
Baiwu, every time I took Harrell to someone's home to interview people,
whether they be Han, Prmi, or Nuosu, they would ask me in Nuosu,
Geahmu pugo li dda; shurmugomu pu mi? (Should we tell him the truth
or weave him a tale?) I told them sincerely and seriously, "Harrell is
my friend; please tell the truth; otherwise he's wasting his time here."
In order to help rid them of their feelings of strangeness and suspicion
toward Harrell, whenever a lot of people where together in one place,
I would use jokes to introduce him.

When we hadn't been in Baiwu for very long, we attended the wedding of the son of my grandfather's dry son Shu Shengyin,[2] and we
went to attend. I formally introduced Harrell by the name Meigui Muga.
That evening there were line dances. According to Ozzu customs, the
women are permitted to get together and tackle and carry off any male
who is there. When Muga and I were participating in the dance, one of
the Ozzu women asked me, "Can we play a joke on this Muga friend
of yours?" Without thinking I responded, "Who knows with you?" When
several tens of us had danced line dances for over an hour, so that we
felt a little bit tired and were getting ready to go back to our hotel, we
heard the screams of a herd of women, and a group of more than ten
of them suddenly surrounded Muga and tackled him to the ground,
then randomly took up his four limbs and lifted him into the air and
swung him around. When Gaga went to "rescue" him, they put Muga
down and tackled Gaga in the same manner. This is a kind of fun that
people often have at weddings in that area, commonly called "picking
up the dead bitch." Until it happened, I hadn't thought that the ques-

---

2. The Shu family were of Ozzu ethnicity, classified as Naxi in the 1950s. Ma's grandfather and father swore ritual brotherhood with many Ozzu and Han neighbors, taking
on their children as "dry relatives." See the account of this practice in chapter 8 of *Ways
of Being Ethnic in Southwest China* (Harrell 2001).

tion that the Ozzu women had asked me was part of a "plot," but luckily neither Muga nor Gaga was hurt or had his glasses or camera knocked off and broken; I would have regretted it without end. I carefully observed my two companions, and they didn't take offense at the custom of "picking up the dead bitch," nor did they think it was a crude custom just because they had gotten a little mud on themselves. On the contrary, they enjoyed the playfulness and directness of the Ozzu. Afterwards, people judged Muga and Gaga as open-minded, with personalities like minority people.

After a week or so of concentrated interviewing in Baiwu, Meigui Muga became a hot topic. If he went strolling on the street, there were always a knot of Nuosu children milling around him, and sometimes they would blurt out "Laowai!" (Foreigner!) or "Hello!" When friends and relatives that I hadn't seen for a long time found out I was in Baiwu with a foreigner, some of them would come around to see the action, and others would invite us to eat. My seventy-five-year-old aunt specifically sent someone to tell me, "Don't hang around with this foreigner." Americans and Han used to be enemies; I should be extra careful, in case the Hans' policy changed. When I took Harrell specifically to see her in 1994, she was extraordinarily polite to him, calling him "My Muga" and insisting that she kill a sheep for us, only relenting after my repeated pressure to just kill a chicken and serve some preserved pork. When Harrell and I walked on the street, people who hadn't seen him before asked, Ni Muga ngenge? (Is this your Muga?), and when I appeared somewhere else by myself, they all asked Ni Muga kabbo o? (Where did your Muga go?). Wherever we went to interview, people often asked, "How far away is America?" "How come he's bald?" "What does his wife do?" "Does he have children?" "How much money does he make every month?" and so on. When we went to interview at somebody's house, often Harrell would be asking about their basic situation, and they would be asking me about his; from my standpoint this was an unavoidable piece of boredom. After a while, when Harrell had learned to speak considerable Nuosu, he could answer these questions himself, and this gradually reduced my burden.

At the beginning of our research in Baiwu, Gaga and I were rather nervous. In the first place, we were afraid that this foreigner's lifestyle and sanitary expectations wouldn't adjust and that he would get sick. In the second place, we were afraid that his research results wouldn't be at a high level or would be less than genuine, and that he wouldn't be able to accomplish his original goals. Every evening, behind his back, we would evaluate the day's results (depending entirely on his tone of voice). If at mealtimes he ate a little more or if during interviews he wrote a little more, then we felt our plan was working. In truth, we had accompanied a lot of professors. What had made them happiest during their work in Liangshan had been the hospitality and directness of the Nuosu; and the hardest thing for them to take was being urged to drink. I know that gentlemen addicts among the Nuosu often used the excuse of "Yi customs" to pour full glasses of white liquor to entertain guests. And the guests, not knowing that clinking glasses and drinking madly is a "custom" that has been cultivated only recently by gentlemen addicts of all ethnicities in Liangshan, but wanting to respect the native customs, drank down glass upon glass of the fiery liquor for one or two days, and afterward were rendered weak or limp and unsure of spirit, impeding their work and wasting their time. In Baiwu, though I was powerless to criticize the custom of singing drinking songs (*yinry liyi*) that had become so popular among officials there, I still had to allow Muga to complete his research responsibilities in a sober or at least only half-drunken condition. When people toasted him, I always told them, in Nuosu, that Muga couldn't drink much. Frankly speaking, in addition to protecting Harrell's ability to carry out his responsibilities, this excuse also had a lot to do with my own preferences. Since I was young, I haven't drunk much, haven't smoked, and have even been disgusted by drinking and smoking. In this, Muga and I worked together. We became offensive and defensive allies, protecting each other, avoiding spending our time in Nuosu areas perpetually drunk as skunks.

There was another custom that was a continual bother to us during our research in Nuosu areas. If we had good relations with affines or if their social position was high, whenever we visited them they would insist on sacrificing an animal to entertain us. A lot of outside guests don't understand this; they think that they and the host aren't very well acquainted, why should the host be so overly polite the first time they meet? This is a misunderstanding on the part of the guests; the hosts are actually using the name of the guest as a way to be able entertain their old friends. This kind of hospitality does not require immediate return, but one does have to interact in a polite way, and if you have an opportunity to meet later in your own home area, you need to entertain them in some way, or else you're being discourteous. When I took Muga to interview in households, every family wanted to kill an animal to entertain us, and according to manners one should not refuse. As a Nuosu, when one goes away and comes home, people should ask *Sso wewe?* (Were there animals killed to entertain you?), and if none were sacrificed, it meant that you didn't have any face. Temporarily leaving aside the question of the goodness or badness of this kind of custom, it has planted its roots deeply in the consciousness of every Nuosu person. Even cadres and intellectuals who have lived for several decades in distant places such as Chengdu or Beijing cannot separate themselves from this custom, and when honored guests arrive, they pay no attention to fine restaurants that may be close by; only if one scours the city for a live pig or sheep to kill does it count as *ssoji*, or entertaining guests. Whenever this kind of entertainment takes place, according to Nuosu customs, the host and guests need to sit and converse, and the guests need to see the live, scurrying stock transformed into fresh meat under the hands of the host and to eat *shefu sheji*, cooked meat that has a ceremonial nature. If one proceeds this way, it takes a minimum of two hours. I thought that if I arranged to take Muga every day to eat *sheji* twice a day, then the majority of his time would be wasted. Because of this, except for weddings or funerals (cattle, sheep, pigs, and chickens killed for weddings or funerals would not be slaughtered specifically for us, and when Muga went to such events, he would have a lot of people to interview, no matter how long he stayed), I asked relatives and friends not to kill pigs, sheep, or cattle, but asked them to cook some preserved pork or kill a chicken or two; preserved pork cooked together with a free-run chicken is quite aromatic and appetizing. Both Muga's and my appetite could be counted as considerable, and when our hosts saw that we both enjoyed the food, they were very happy. The two of us not only ate well, but also saved money and did not add to our account of *ssoji*. We also had the feeling of closeness embodied in *zhe nyi vabu hlo* (only for members of your own clan do you kill a rooster). What a happy solution!

As the days went by one by one, and as the number of households interviewed increased, Muga came to know more and more people, and our research results were better than we expected. Even though I had been born and raised in Baiwu, and name just about everyone in Hongxing and Lianhe,[3] still about their genealogies, the migration of peoples, and the glories and events of their past I actually knew very little. In the past I had often come and gone along with my father, and was on brotherly terms with the Shu family, but until this point I didn't know that they weren't Zangzu but rather Naxizu, and I also learned for the first time that some of the Han uncles with whom my father had the closest relations (he called them "brothers"), had actually experienced the bitterness of having been captured into slavery by lawless Nuosu. One could quote the poet Su Shi, "I'm not familiar with the true face of Mount Lu; only because I have lived in the mountain myself." The history of the superficially tranquil peoples of Baiwu was filled with interaction and conflicts, struggles and reconciliations. This period of research tied together some historical circumstances that I had known about, and later on I used them to write two articles: "Nuosu and Neighboring Ethnic Groups: Ethnic Groups and Ethnic Relations through the Eyes and Ears of Three Generations of the Mgebbu Clan" (Mgebbu 2003), and "Researches into the Changes and Accommodating Behavior between the Yi and Han in Liangshan," which I have presented at Chinese and international conferences.

In the process of this field research, as Muga and I walked on the barren yellow earth and into the winter wind that stirred the red dust, I often recalled two pictures of the life and society of my youth. I was a descendant of a somewhat famous local slave lord, and in my youth, Grandfather was forever taken to be struggled against. Father was also a wealthy person, and a target of reform, so that I became someone saddled with the double hats of the slaveholder and wealthy classes, and so whether at school or on the way to school, I was often subjected to insults. Actually, from the time I was born, my grandfather and parents had become poor peasants, and I wore only tattered clothes, was mostly barefoot in

---

3. Hongxing is a Nuosu village attached to the north end of Baiwu town; Lianhe is a Prmi and Han village attached to the south end.

all seasons, and was hungry throughout most of my elementary and junior high school years. Every summer before the new harvest was in, our family members gathered wild herbs and buckwheat leaves to relieve our hunger. Because we ate these things for every meal in the summertime, every year we all got a kind of sickness called *mgavu*, so that when we encountered sun and wind in the daytime our faces hurt as if we had a high fever, and our arms and legs got numb. This is a kind of life that today's children and anthropologists could never experience.

Even though the incessant class struggle campaigns made everybody afraid, still the natural environment that we lived in made people happy. At that time, we all lived in a land of big trees, in lush forests with their luxuriant leaves reaching to the sky, where on the way to school we would often encounter flocks of pheasants, foxes fighting, white pheasants calling at the sun, and even wild animals mixing with the domestic herds. Decades of unceasing government logging, growth of the local population, expansion of agricultural areas, wood lost to domestic construction and firewood burning, not only have caused the obliteration of the old trees reaching to the heavens and the green grass growing verdantly, but have left the larks with no place to roost. Looking at this landscape, I often wonder, whom should we blame for the infantile political class struggle and the mistaken forest clearing? Who should be held responsible for the sufferings of the aboriginal peoples and the damage to the material environment?

When Harrell was in Baiwu, he wanted to interview at two or three houses each day. I was aware of the primitive nature of the sanitation and the Nuosu lifestyle, and that Harrell suffered every time he went into a house. Nuosu have a saying, *Iddi si co ta bbo* (I shouldn't show my bad side to others). Every time I went into a house with Harrell, I thought, "When he sees our low-ceilinged, dirty, messy, poor bad side, what will he think of me and my compatriots?" Was it sympathy? Pity? Condescension? Contempt? What use was his research for the Nuosu or the ordinary people in the area? Was I, as a "horse leader," *Iddi sijjo hna ti dahly* (one who set our own bad points out for other people to see)? This is a question that has for a long time permeated the thoughts of us locally born and raised translators. A lot of people like me who had been half-guides and half-translators had told me that they have run into some arrogant outsiders who, with contemptuous expressions on their faces, have pointed out and laughed at the poverty and backwardness of ordinary Nuosu people, causing them to be hurt and angry.

Before accompanying Harrell, I had run into this once. I had taken a group of high-level intellectuals from big cities in China to the Nuosu core area to interview people in their homes, and one day at noon an enthusiastic farm family had slaughtered a small pig at their own expense to entertain these guests. Among them was a scholar who sat there mumbling in his grimy little dialect, squinting his beady little eyes behind his thick glasses, looking at me contemptuously, and asking repeatedly, "Is this okay to eat?" I felt incredibly insulted, but suppressed a belly full of anger, and said to him half-jokingly: "This herd of mountain savages that are sitting here only need to be rinsed off with a bucket of water, and neither their build nor their appearance would be any worse than yours. Who knows, if they could read a couple of books, their knowledge would probably exceed yours. They've been eating this stuff all their lives; it's hard to understand why you can't eat a single meal." He kept working his mouth into an unappetized expression, but forced himself to pick up the first piece of meat, and in the end, he ate more than anybody. This kind of scene can really make one furious. Of course, the majority of people are not like this at all—no matter whose house you take them to they take the approach "When in Rome . . . " and present a friendly and sympathetic manner, or at least the outward impression of it. If we accompany outside friends to poor Nuosu areas to conduct research and cause outsiders to develop sincere friendships with and sympathy for the local Nuosu, then we urban Nuosu will feel pained and embarrassed about the horrible life conditions of today's village Nuosu and will worry about our own helplessness. When I was accompanying Harrell during his research in Baiwu, every time we went into the dirty and empty houses of my elders and neighbors, I developed a taste in my mouth that I couldn't describe.

One day in Baiwu, Secretary Yang Zipo brought Wu Ga, who was studying for a Ph.D. in Michigan, to see Harrell, and with him were the head of the organization department, the head of the language committee, and the head of the economic restructuring committee. The local canteen, which ordinarily offered nothing but pickled vegetable soup and potatoes, had already piled the tables high with fresh chicken and mutton. The usually casual local officials were sharply dressed, and they had straightened out the meeting room very neatly. When they heard the sound of the car engine, they all said "They're coming; get ready." When the line of three little cars carrying more than ten people rolled so elegantly into the four-sided courtyard of the township government, even people who couldn't be called unfamiliar with the world, including Harrell, were quite excited. This was not just because the bureaucratic system had trained people to jump and spin whenever they saw bureaucratic superiors, but rather because Secretary Yang Zipo was known to be close to the people and because Wu Ga was looked upon as an object of pride among Nuosu women for her pursuit of a Ph.D. On that occasion, there was nobody who threw his weight around because of his high position or talked like a big shot, there was no attempt to seat people by their rank, and there were no formal and pretentious reports, but everybody acted as if they were among ordinary Yi people— there was talk, laughter, and repartee. Years later, there are still a lot of people who mention that day to me as *ggesa jjy ggesa*—a really good time.

After enjoying the Nuosu-style hospitality, I suggested to Yang Zipo that we take Harrell to Lugu Lake for a short-term research trip, and asked if he could help us with transportation. He said that they were about ready to hold a joint meeting at Zuosuo[4] between two provinces and three counties (Yunnan and Sichuan provinces; Ninglang, Yanyuan, and Muli counties) about timber sales, and invited the two of us to go along. It was really a case of "Asking not being as good as just running into"; I asked Hu Jin'ao to go along, and he agreed (fig. 10.2).

Harrell and I stayed in Baiwu for another week, and returned to Yanyuan Town on the first of February, where Hu Jin'ao arranged for Harrell to do some research with *nuoho* (aristocratic) families that had just moved to Yanyuan. Later, on the basis of this research, I wrote an article entitled "Developing the Market Economy is the Key to Poverty Alleviation Among the Yi," and in it I brought up the idea that emigration is the only way to alleviate poverty in poor Nuosu areas. Dur-

---

4. A town on the Sichuan shore of Lugu Lake, which sits atop the Sichuan-Yunnan boundary.

10.2 *Hu Jin'ao and son, Lugu Lake, 1993.*

ing our research, I had now and then taken up with Harrell some of the research that had already been done on social organization among the Nuosu. I had mentioned that there were divergent viewpoints on questions of the stratification system. I brought up the viewpoints that the *nuoho* were not nobility, that the *quho* (commoners) did not belong in the category of "slaves," that the *mgajie* (unfree peasants) were not slaves, and that the *gaxy* (house slaves) were not slaves for life. I was hoping that Harrell would take up an interest in these questions. But, unfortunately, when people looking for medicinal plants enter the mountains, they only see medicinal plants, and when hunters enter the mountains, all they see is game. Harrell listened, but except for his interest in ethnic relations, he didn't express an opinion about Nuosu social organization and history.

On February 5, Harrell, Hu Jin'ao, and I went along to Zuosuo with officials and timber entrepreneurs in a car that had been provided for us by Secretary Yang. We went into a logging yard in a sparsely populated area, where the mountainsides were covered with nothing but stumps, and the logs were piled up like mountains beside the roads. We pulled up beside a pile of ramshackle sheds to rest for a few minutes, and the businessmen brought out a few bottles of famous-brand beer that were difficult to get in Xichang. It was really a case of if a poor person goes to a crowded market nobody pays attention but if a rich person goes to the deep mountains there are distant relatives around. It was probably about three o'clock when we came to the border between Yanyuan and Ninglang, where the welcoming committee had been waiting for a long time at the pass for the important guests to arrive. They took up rifles, pistols, and assault rifles and started firing into the air to welcome the representatives from Yanyuan and Muli, and the Yanyuan and Muli people took out their pistols from their waist holsters and fired into the air, all to express mutual respect. At first Harrell didn't know what was going on, and I joked, "Maybe the Iraqis learned that an American has entered their territory, and they're firing to resist," and everybody laughed. In fact, I was feeling strangely uneasy. The self-proclaimed servants of the people, the basic-level Communist Party leaders, the descendants of a generation of liberated slaves, in the end still insisted on such luxurious ceremonial. From the mountaintop, where the leaders of the two provinces and three counties greeted each other in such a "humble" manner, in all four directions one could see poor people everywhere; it was a stark contrast in lifestyles.

After a flurry of busy introductions, handshakes, and toasting (fig. 10.3), we were led by the welcoming convoy of Ninglang to make a grand entrance into the county guest house. We received the highest standard of hospitality in the hotel: there were famous dishes and famous liquor on the tables, not to speak of famous cigarettes; the best-known personages and singers of the county all mounted the stage to entertain; and every person was given a carton of Hongbaota cigarettes,[5] which were accessible only to cadres and entrepreneurs at that time. The leaders of Yanyuan and Muli were all acquaintances of mine, and between us there were no superiors or inferiors. Even though I have never held any sort of official position, and although I left Yanyuan rather early, because my clan had a rather high position in Nuosu history and because I was seen as someone with a high standard of both Yi and Han languages, I formed good relations with my peers, and they all looked upon me as an intellectual with a high social reputation. This produced an invisible net of connections, and whoever I asked to help would generally recognize his debt to me. But, perhaps because of my personality or my likes and dislikes, when people are happily extending their political, social, and economic networks all over heaven and earth, I do what I can to avoid and hide these kinds of relationships.

---

5. A high-end brand from Yunnan.

10.3 *Official greeters at the pass between Yanyuan and Ninglang, 1993. The woman on the left wears a Na or Mosuo dress; the others wear Nuosu dresses.*

When Harrell arrived, I certainly did not go out of my way to go and look for help, and whatever I could handle by myself I handled myself, though I was not too polite, of course, to take advantage of opportunities when they presented themselves. Our trip to Luguhu happened in just this way. It goes without saying that food, drinks, rooms, and travel were all paid for, and every evening we were able to see and join popular performance activities in tourist villages, as well as jump into the hot spring pool and soak for free. Despite all this, any time I could hide from the administrative officials, I hid, and I did not like having to appear on their account. We ran into some unfortunate incidents on the trip: the driver and several fellow travelers with high positions screamed at the driver of a coal truck for not moving his truck while his workers were in the middle of unloading coal; a driver made Harrell mad because he wouldn't let him get his bag out of the car; and when we were visiting the Yongning monastery, as Harrell was hurriedly interviewing adult and teenage monks, a bureau head urged me in Nuosu two or three times to hurry up and get moving. Still, I felt enormous gratitude to Secretary Yang Zipo for offering the two of us this opportunity.

After five days of bumping in the car and interviewing in all directions, we returned again to Ninglang in the convoy, and I handed Harrell over to my compatriot, Dong Yunfa, who was serving as magistrate of Muli County. Hu Jin'ao and I stayed behind in Ninglang to conduct research on the history of Nyizu Anyo, a famous woman of the *nuoho* caste in Ninglang before Liberation, and on several *nuoho*, *quho*, and *mgajie* who had been unsatisfied at the time of the Democratic Reforms and had taken to the hills to become guerillas. Three days later Harrell and I met as arranged in Yanyuan, and two days after that we returned to Xichang. When I had seen Harrell off, my "horse-leading" was done, my translating was done, and my cooperation was done, chalked up as one more experience.

During this time, I had gotten to know Harrell a bit better. He was very dedicated to his fieldwork, had a strong adaptive ability and diplomatic skills that allowed him to form relationships with strangers quickly. If he had lived in the Chinese social system, he would have had good interpersonal relationships all around. He could adapt much better than I ever could to the realities of society.

Over a month of busily sharing joys and sorrows caused a dramatic change in our relationship. At the beginning I had really not been glad to be with Harrell, and I didn't want to accept his overtures of friendship or look at his shiny bald head or his browless eyes. I had suspected that he had leprosy, a disease that traditional Nuosu people feared more than death. Dealing with him was something I was forced to do; I had to obey the arrangements of my leaders. When we were first in contact, I "respected him and kept him at a distance";[6] when we ate together I quietly made sure not to come close to things he had touched. I don't know what happened, but in about three to five days, I adjusted to his looks. I can't say if I got used to him just because I knew there was no way out. But in the following days, we formed friendly relations, and his appearance not only didn't scare me anymore, but became a nice symbol of him, and I would take advantage of times when he wasn't paying attention to touch his head jokingly and felt happy about it.

The rough living conditions of my home in Baiwu were fundamentally unsuitable to receiving people from outside. Harrell aside, even I who had grown up there felt it was somewhat of a hardship when I went home. And on top of this, we lived in Baiwu at the time the Nuosu call

---

6. When Confucius was asked about whether one should sacrifice to gods and spirits, he replied *"Ji guishen er yuanzhi"* (sacrifice to the gods and spirits and keep them at a distance).

the snake month, when the heavens are frigid and the earth is frozen hard, when eggs freeze from the frost. There was no way I could help my friend overcome a lot of these difficulties, no way in these conditions to reduce his sadness at having left home. All I could do was take a basin of burning charcoal to him in his room in the evening, or a thermos of hot water, or, at most, when I guessed that he was homesick, to send him a little thread of a smile; or, when local people didn't understand or didn't accept his fieldwork, to take the part of a host and explain to them or maybe even criticize them. With regard to his research, I felt that he had not only added a thick stack of field data to his notebooks but had also added a new layer of Nuosu-American relations to the history of Baiwu. In the midst of the hostility between the Chinese and American governments, giving the local people a chance for reciprocal knowledge on a civil level and creating a friendly atmosphere on both sides was a harvest that neither side had expected.

11

FIELDWORK WITH MUGA, 1994

BAMO AYI

T he time had come to say good-bye. The next day, Harrell and I would each go our separate ways, he to Yanyuan and I to Meigu, to carry out our own fieldwork. For twenty days, I had accompanied him to Manshuiwan and Mishi, going into villages and hamlets, climbing mountains and crossing ridges, interviewing and researching. Now, as we were going our own ways, the feeling was not one of a great burden being lifted or of getting away from a bother, nor was it one of finishing the job without pain or joy. When we shook hands firmly at the Liangshan Hotel where he was staying, there was a tacit expression of mutual good wishes.

It was probably near the beginning of 1994 that I unexpectedly received a letter from Professor Stevan Harrell of the University of Washington. Up to that time, I had never met Professor Harrell, and had never heard of him. In the letter, he introduced his own research on the Yi, and said that he was in the process of applying for funds to hold an international conference on the Yi in Seattle in 1995. If the application proved successful, he would invite me to participate. From that time, we exchanged letters. Probably around the time that the 1994 summer vacation started, I found out that Harrell was planning to go to Liangshan to do research in the fall, and I wrote him a letter saying that when I finished my investigations in Lijiang at the beginning of October, I would return to Liangshan, and hoped that we would have an opportunity to meet then. On the fourth of October, when the China-Japan Southwest Folklore Investigation Team finished its work in Lijiang, my sister Qubumo and I returned from Kunming to Xichang. In addition to visiting my parents, I intended to continue doing field-work on *bimo*.

When I got back to Xichang, I heard that Harrell had already arrived, and my sister and I immediately invited Harrell and Ma Lunzy from the Liangshan Prefectural Nationalities Research Institute to have din-ner together at a Yi restaurant across the street from the Liangshan Hotel; we would wait for them at the hotel gate. As we were waiting, a black sedan pulled in through the gate, and behind Ma Lunzy there emerged a foreigner, tall and shiningly bald. Without Ma Lunzy's introduction, I knew it was Professor Harrell. He introduced himself, saying that he had a Yi name, Meigui Muga. We had dinner against the background of light Nuosu music in a little room decorated with pictures illustrat-ing Nuosu themes. During the conversation, I heard that Harrell was looking for a place to do fieldwork in the Anning Valley on the topic of ethnic relations. I proposed that he go to Manshuiwan, a Yi village com-pletely surrounded by Han, and recommended myself as a good guide. My father was from Yuexi, but as a boy had spent time in his mother's native village of Manshuiwan, and he had a lot of feeling for the place. From the time I was little, every year or two our whole family would go to Manshuiwan with Father. Though I had always thought that our rel-atives there were too Hanified, and we couldn't get used to their con-tempt for the Nuosu living in the mountains, I knew that it would be an ideal place to research ethnic relations. In addition, there were a lot of useful resources there, including free room and board and conven-ience of interviewing. I thought that Harrell and Ma Lunzy were prob-ably frustrated, because Harrell wanted to go to Meigu, but Zhaojue County, which was on the way to Meigu, was quarantined by a cholera epidemic; Harrell also wanted to go to Yanyuan, but Ma Lunzy was busy at the moment and couldn't go with him. Inserting myself at just the right moment, I felt like I was "taking up a position in the middle of a crisis." I also felt that I owed a debt of gratitude but had no way to repay it. Besides, it was tempting to me to see how an American professor did fieldwork. Time was precious; Harrell and I conferred and decided to leave for Manshuiwan the next afternoon. After a pleasant dinner, my sister and I invited Harrell and Ma Lunzy to go back to our house and talk. When Father heard that I wanted to take Harrell to Manshuiwan, a place dear to his heart, he expressed enthusiastic support and agreed to take us there himself.

Arriving at Manshuiwan, forty-eight kilometers from Xichang, we quietly entered the village without sword or spear. Walking into what had formerly been my grandmother's courtyard, we could see that the splendor and market-like bustle of previous years had faded with time, and with no hope of returning. The rich rice-and-fish village in the Anning Valley had long been unable to hold the descendants of the Jienuo clan, whose first ancestor had originally come from Puxiong to escape the death penalty and to find a place to settle down in the valley of rich soil and clear water. Now descendants of the Jienuo were leaving the valley one after another, entering the even more splendid outside world and following an urban lifestyle completely different from the ancestral one of going out to the fields with the dawn and returning at dusk. The old swing next to Grandma's front gate, which had carried me back and forth as a child, was nowhere to be found; the tall, wide stable to the left inside the gate, which had been full of cattle and horses, was now completely empty; and the old toilet with the shit pit in the middle had gotten a hole in the roof from years of disrepair. Even though I felt a little sad, I enthusiastically took Harrell in one door and out the next to show him everything. The watchtower between the west wing and the main room of the house, which had been used as a lookout and defense against approaching enemies, was the only building in the courtyard that had any Nuosu flavor. The room in the west wing next to the watchtower had been my Grandma's bedroom. One could still make out the couplet "Raise my head and look at the bright moon / lower my head and think of my old home." The main parlor, with the table against the back wall as a Han-style altar for worshipping the gods of heaven, earth, and country, as well as ancestors, is something one won't find in villages in concentrated Yi areas (figs. 11.1 and 11.4).

The inhabitants of this four-sided courtyard house, which was built

11.1 *The courtyard of an old Chinese-style house in Manshuiwan, 1994.*

by my grandma's grandfather, the Qing dynasty military *xiucai*[1] Wang Wenming of the Jienuo clan, were two poor septuagenarians. One was my father's third maternal uncle, and I called him Third Granduncle. He was the husband from whom my aunt had separated but not divorced many years before. In my memory, he wasn't the boss there but rather a kind of spirit who was always in the house and could never lift his head or stand straight. The other inhabitant was Father's fifth maternal uncle's wife, Fifth Grandaunt. Her maternal family was of the Aju, another big Nuosu clan in this village. Here, as in Nuosu mountain villages, they practiced the system of ultimogeniture, so that the compound originally belonged completely to Fifth Granduncle. But because Fifth Granduncle left when he was young to take an outside job a hundred kilometers away in Yanyuan, he asked his third brother to help him take care of the house, with the condition that he would give two rooms in the west wing to his third brother, who had lost his property and his wife to his opium habit. When Fifth Granduncle and Fifth Grandaunt

---

1. Colloquial name for the lowest civil or military degree in the Qing examination system, formally called *shengyuan*.

retired, they returned from Yanyuan to attend to their ancestral property and spend a peaceful retirement.

Fifth Grandaunt prepared rooms for us, Harrell in a guest room in the east wing, and I keeping Fifth Grandaunt company in a bedroom right off the main parlor. At first Fifth Grandaunt was telling Harrell and me at great length everything that was wrong with Third Granduncle, and after a while, when I took Harrell to pay his respects to Third Granduncle, he didn't shy a bit from the foreigner, but told us about Fifth Grandaunt's shortcomings. In the short time we lived in that courtyard, Harrell and I both got a sense of the enmity between the two from listening to their mutual recriminations and complaints. This made me feel a little uncomfortable. Ordinarily one doesn't hang one's dirty laundry in public, but there was no way around it, the "American Devil" Harrell was going in and out of this four-sided courtyard, and what could escape his sharp eyes? What wouldn't appear in that field notebook of his, where there was nothing he didn't write down? If I had wanted to hide anything, I wouldn't have been able to, so all I could do was console myself that this was also a part of life, and that is was a rare opportunity for an American anthropologist to see the trivialities and petty squabbles of a Chinese village, particularly a Yi village.

We had no contact with township officials, and thereby possibly saved ourselves both banquets and formal procedures, and so quickly moved into research mode. I had always assumed that there were just two clans in Manshuiwan, which intermarried with each other: the Jienuo, whose Han surname was Wang, and the Aju, whose Han surname was Li. This time I finally got it straight that the village above the highway, which was mostly populated by the Han Wu clan, also belonged to Manshuiwan. In the village, in addition to the sixty households of the three big surnames—Wang, Li, and Wu—there were also seven households of later-arriving people who relied on their kinship relations to these three surnames. We did a census, recording the names, ages, levels of education, language abilities, marital status, and kin relations of each household. Harrell and I went to every household from the lower to the upper village; we had but to see that someone was home, and we went there. Without any prior arrangements having been made, we were welcomed by smiling hosts. Harrell thought that this was because I was along, since almost everyone knew me, and called me by my childhood name, "Ngan Lan," a name that was already strange to me, and which, when Harrell heard that I still had a Han name, he probably thought quite curious. But I think that even if I hadn't been along, the sight of a tall, big-nosed foreigner knocking at their doors would have been enough to make the villagers curious and to stop what they were doing long enough to figure out what the foreigner was up to. What kind of questions would the foreigner want to ask them? Most of the Wus in the upper village didn't know me, and I didn't know them, but there, too, our investigations didn't run into any coolness or refusals. As I look at it, this was not because of me, but because of Harrell's tall frame, long face, and foreign status, and also, of course, because of the villagers' own friendliness. Because everything was clustered closely together, we could interview in the Han language, and the people were not like those Nuosu up in the mountains who placed great importance on slaughtering animals to entertain guests, we saved time, and our research proceeded quickly. In less than a week, we had been everywhere in the upper and lower villages, had visited every household, and had collected complete data on every household and inhabitant of the village.

In addition to the household census, we concentrated on interviewing old people and cultured people in the village, attempting to straighten out their genealogies, understand the origins and migration histories of the village clans, and comb through the village history. The person we ought to credit with giving us the most help with this was my maternal granduncle Wang Chenghan. Granduncle Chenghan had formerly been an associate translations editor in the Liangshan prefectural translations office, a man of letters known throughout the prefecture, and, from the early 1950s onward, a specialist in oral and written translation between Nuosu and Chinese. He was at that time basking in retirement in his native village, enjoying the bucolic life. The two things of which he was the proudest were, first, that when a delegation of high-level ethnic personages had traveled to Zhongnanhai in Beijing in 1956 to see Chairman Mao, he had been the translator in attendance; and, second, that his grandfather, Wang Wenhan, had won the titles of *xiu-*

cai and *juren*[2] in the Qing dynasty and, at the beginning of the Republic, had been the head of the educational bureau of Mianning County, where Manshuiwan is located. Granduncle Chenghan invited Harrell and me to his home. Granduncle's compound had been built at the same time as Fifth Grandaunt's house (where we were living), and was an equally exquisite typical Han-style four-sided courtyard, with its open space in the middle paved in the same intricate patterns made from different-colored pebbles. What was different about Granduncle's house was that the flower ledges displayed carefully pruned expensive plants, the corridors were hung with squawking caged birds, the desk in the study in the west wing held brushes and writing ink, and the bookcases were full of books, so that it had a bit of the flavor of a rural gentry Chinese courtyard of old.[3]

After lunch, Granduncle told the story of his clan —the convoluted and glorious history of the dominant Jienuo clan in the village. The first ancestor of the Jienuo, Jienuo Mosi, was originally a member of the aristocratic ("Black Yi") Ahxo clan living around Puxiong. In a dispute over rights to fish on a particular stretch of river, he had unintentionally killed a classificatory younger brother of his own clan, and was *luoyicy*, expelled from the clan. Accompanied by his wife and children, Mosi brought his slaves and drove his cattle and sheep across mountains and rivers, and came to live at a place called Magongjia. Mosi had two sons. The first was called Sala, who gave himself to a Han landlord as a "dry son" and later became his son-in-law, changing his name to the Han surname Wang; his descendants became Han people. The second son was called Sada, and the Jienuo of Manshuiwan are his descendants.

Because there was long-term friction and conflict in the area of Manshuiwan in the Anning Valley between the Nuosu and the Han military colonists sent there by the authorities, commercial activity was difficult to undertake, and social conditions were chaotic and unpeace-

---

2. The second Qing examination degree, which usually qualified the holder to take up at least a minor official position.

3. Translator's note: I visited Manshuiwan in August, 2005, and found that Wang Chenghan had died. His house was unoccupied, but we found someone with a key. It seemed smaller without living people or plants in it, but it was still in good condition. We hope that someone will restore it as a historical landmark.

ful. Granduncle told us that the Nuosu name for Manshuiwan was Mosifa, meaning "a place where there had been the confusion of battle." The local government assigned the Jienuo, who had good relations with the Han and also commanded respect from the Nuosu, the responsibility of adjudicating disputes between Yi and Han, as well as promoting commerce, and granted the Jienuo a large expanse of land, including Manshuiwan.

Granduncle used his practiced narrative skills, honed in his translation work on government documents, to sum up the role of the Jienuo in the Anning watershed. He said that the Jienuo had made great contributions to the solidarity between Yi and Han, to social stability, and to economic development and flourishing in the Anning Valley for a long time. The history of the Jienuo was extraordinarily interesting; their relations with the Han were far from new. But what made me feel a little unsettled was that beforehand I myself had "proudly" told Harrell about the origins of the Jienuo in the Ahxo clan of Nuosu aristocrats, but had not brought up such things as one of my Jienuo ancestors' marrying into a Han household as a son-in-law, then changing his name and becoming a Han; or of my ancestors' close relations with Han officials; or of their service as a mediator between Yi and Han. I hadn't been deliberately hiding these things or lying about them. I had repeatedly been told about the Jienuo origins in a high aristocratic Nuosu bloodline, and of their move from Puxiong to Manshuiwan; what they neglected or forgot to tell me was about their ancestors' rise to fame and the inseparable relations between their eminence and their connection to the Han. Admittedly, I, who was one-fourth Jienuo, had intentionally or unintentionally "flaunted" to outsiders (including Harrell) the high-ranking Yi origins of the Jienuo. If I hadn't gone there to do research with Steve, I fear I would never have known of those details or stories that people other than Granduncle Chenghan had no desire to bring up or to go into.

What the people being interviewed found curious about Harrell was that a foreigner could speak such fluent Chinese. But to Harrell, what was interesting about the people he was interviewing was not that they could speak the Han language but rather that they still preserved the knowledge of their own language—Nuosu Ddoma. Harrell discovered that the Yi villagers of Manshuiwan could to a person all speak completely accent-free Chinese to us, and then turn around and speak with each other in Yi. Harrell felt that this linguistic switching phenomenon was quite extraordinary. The Han in the village spoke Chinese; the people outside the village spoke Chinese; when villagers went to school they learned the Han written language; even the couplets pasted on Yi doorways were written in Han—so the most important thing was that the villagers were all able to command the Han language, and that the language they used in reading and writing was Han and not Yi. In a word, as a communication tool, the villagers of Manshuiwan did not need Nuosu. But then why was the Nuosu language still in daily use in Manshuiwan, still flourishing there?

Harrell wouldn't let this question go. He wanted explanations. He didn't get answers from every interviewee, but a maternal great-granduncle of mine, the village head Wang Kaifu, had thought a little about this question himself. Harrell worked out a conclusion: He thought that this was an expression of feelings of ethnic identity, which resulted in people's intentional retention of their own language. That is, the Yi villagers of Manshuiwan, who as far as I was concerned were already so Hanified as to practically have become Han, held on tightly to the only conspicuous ethnic marker that could differentiate them from the Han—that is, their Yi language—precisely in order to prove that they were Nuosu people. Harrell thought that for the Yi villagers of Manshuiwan, whose clothing, houses, and lifestyles were already practically indistinguishable from those of the Han, the Yi language had become a symbol of their ethnicity, an important part of their feelings of ethnic identity. To me, the fact that my relatives in Manshuiwan spoke Yi was nothing new or curious. But why had this linguistic isolate not been obliterated? I had never conscientiously thought about this or researched it. Could the continuation of the Nuosu language be attributed completely to ethnic identity? Was the need for ethnic identity sufficient to preserve a language? To prove that you were a Yi, was it enough to simply hold tightly on to your own language and not let go? I thought that Harrell's explanation was fresh and new, but to this day, I still carry a question mark in my mind.

While the Yi villagers of Manshuiwan preserved their ethnic identity and their ethnic language, they paid a lot of attention to their successes and failures in the Han world and the areas outside the village. Historically, the Jienuo had built a village school, which had also admitted children from the Aju and the Han Wu lineage. They had hired a Han teacher to teach the Four Books and the Five Classics, so that their young people enthusiastically took part in the examination system. Even people like my grandmother were sent to school for Han-language education. Nowadays, all the Yi children in the village go to school. And a large proportion of the Jienuo and a fair number of the Aju have tested into vocational middle schools, higher-level vocational schools, and even universities, and after graduation have stayed to work in the cities. The Han Wu lineage, on the other hand, has suffered greatly in comparison, and has been very unsuccessful at education. I remember interviewing the family of Wu Fangyou, and being shocked that his seventy-three-year-old wife didn't remember her own name; she only knew that she was Mrs. Wu, née Lei. Frankly speaking, this period of fieldwork changed my view of my relatives in Manshuiwan.

Just as Harrell had expressed, the Yi villagers of Manshuiwan did retain their feelings of Yi identity. In addition to their memories of their Yi origins, in addition to their retention of their Yi language, they did not intermarry with Han—at least not with Han from their and the neighboring villages. In the sphere of Manshuiwan, at least, the line between Yi and Han was clearly drawn. Even though there were a few sons and daughters who had married Han in the cities where they had gone to work, because they didn't participate in Manshuiwan's activities, they did not harm the structure of the village. And when Yi villagers took Han wives from outside, once the Han girls had entered the village, they were absorbed into the Yi clans, and became part of the Yi, and did not influence the structure of Yi-Han relations in the village. Think about it: If a little Yi island like Manshuiwan were to open the flood gates of Yi-Han intermarriage in a great Han sea, what would ensue? The example of Sala was a warning. Not intermarrying with Han was a firmly held belief of the Manshuiwan villagers. The Jienuo in the village, in addition to intermarrying with the local Aju, also intermarried with lowland Yi from several villages scattered about the Anning River floodplain, such as Yuehua, Xinhua, Mianshan, Shijia, Yangjia, and Luo-jia, or even with the Bamo clan, who live interspersed with Han in distant Yuexi County. But the Manshuiwan villagers did not intermarry with Yi from the mountains. Both Jienuo and Aju villagers recited a wide variety of reasons for this, such as the inconvenience of transport in the mountains, the poor sanitary conditions, the difficulty of making a living, and the remnants of the former caste system. This is all to say that the identity constructs of the Manshuiwan villagers are layered. They identify with the Yi, but they also feel that they are different from the wild, backward Yi in the mountains; they are plains Yi, advanced and civilized Yi.

At the time of Fifth Granduncle's death, I had been unable to come back to participate in the funeral events, so I took advantage of the convenience of being there for research in order to "go to the grave." Nuosu ordinarily practice cremation, and don't build graves. Even prefectural and county-level cadres and professionals are cremated on wood pyres when they die. But in Manshuiwan, they bury their dead according to the Han custom, so they also visit the graves. This was my first chance to do so. Fifth Grandaunt's legs were in poor shape, and she limpingly and haltingly led Harrell and me up a short stretch of mountain trail to the front of the graves. She pointed out the nearby graves, and, not lacking in pride, said that Fifth Granduncle's grave was the nicest and most imposing. Following her instructions, I poured some liquor into the glasses we had brought along for this purpose, and knelt down in front of the new grave. Fifth Grandaunt faced the grave and said, in Yi, "Muga [Fifth Granduncle's name was also Muga], your granddaughter Ngan Lan is here to see you; she has brought you some liquor, and you should protect her so that she will be peaceful. . . . " After she finished, she told me to knock my head on the ground three times. On the way up to the graves, I had felt a sense of sadness; my honest, sincere fifth granduncle was already an ancestor. But when Fifth Grandaunt told me to kneel, and then to knock my head, I felt silly and unnatural, it was almost funny. This is the only time in my life I have ever knelt and knocked my head in front of a grave. There was no reason for Harrell to offer liquor or knock his head, so he took pictures of me doing so (fig. 11.2). On the way back, I said to him, "Yi in the mountains have never knelt or knocked their heads, whether it's to spirits, ancestors,

11.2 *Ayi kneeling at the grave of her fifth granduncle, Manshuiwan, 1994.*

ghosts, or living people." I used the grave visit to explain to Harrell the Hanification of the villagers of Manshuiwan.

In the middle of our research, Harrell and I returned once to Xichang, in order to take part in my little sister Vusamo's engagement party. When the ceremony was over, we returned to Manshuiwan to do more research. This time, whenever we went out the door, we ran into my uncle Wang Zhengxing, and every time he would bashfully issue an invitation to go to his house to eat. Even though Harrell and I had already surveyed his household, it was difficult to refuse his enthusiasm, so we eventually decided to accept the invitation. It wasn't until we got there that we discovered that this banquet wasn't without a purpose. The host family wanted this foreigner from across the ocean to be a dry father to their grandson. When the mother, still in her month-long postpartum confinement, and with her head wrapped in a cloth, unexpectedly stated this wish, I froze up. But Harrell calmly consented. The host family explained that the child cried at night and didn't sleep, and, according to local custom, taking dry relatives could cure night crying. Harrell said that he was a little old to be a dry father, but about the age to be a dry grandfather, and took the twenty-one-day-old infant from his mother's arms. According to custom, Harrell choose a name for the baby, and it was a foreign name, "Henry"—Hengrui in Han characters (fig. 11.3). Harrell explained that phonetically Hengrui was a lot like his own Han name,

11.3 Stevan Harrell holding "dry grandson" Wang Hao (Henry), Manshuiwan, 1994. Photo by Bamo Ayi.

Hao Rui, and that semantically, "Heng" meant "smoothly" and "efficaciously," and Rui meant "happiness" and "good fortune." I suspected that Harrell knew something about these characters because of his own name. He had not chosen the foreign-sounding "Hengrui" for himself, but rather the authentically Chinese-sounding "Hao Rui." Alerted by his being taken as a dry parent, we quickly discovered that, although there was not one example of these villagers' breaking the prohibition on intervillage Yi-Han marriage, the reciprocal interethnic recognition of dry relatives was a common phenomenon. Wang Chengliang, another granduncle of mine, explained to us the process of recognizing dry relatives, as well the purpose of the practice, which was to assure the trouble-free growth of the child. Without doubt, this was another example of the ethnic relations that we were searching for.

During the fieldwork in Manshuiwan, besides helping Harrell with his research, I also helped Fifth Grandaunt prepare the two daily meals. Fifth Grandaunt had spent her working life as a cook in a work-unit dining hall, and had quite a good hand in the kitchen. I was the so-called helper cook, but actually I was limited to helping her pick vegetables, wash woks and pots, and add wood to the cooking fire (fig. 11.4). Fifth Grandaunt was really good at combining vegetables and meat, with vegetables picked straight from the garden—very fresh—and meat bought in the local town market. I told Harrell that I had never been as comfortable with the food in the field as I was this time, and he agreed that

11.4 *Bamo Ayi, Fifth Grandaunt Li Wanxiu, and Stevan Harrell, Manshuiwan, 1994.*

of all his trips to Yi villages, the food there was the steadiest and most enjoyable. I remember seeing his face light up every time he saw the fresh vegetables on the table. As for me, I like meat, and what I can't forget to this day is Fifth Grandaunt's deep-fried salt pork. She made it by taking good lean meat, rubbing it with salt and Sichuanese flower pepper, and hanging it up by a wood fire to smoke for three days. The flavor was indescribable. Still, every time the three of us noisily dug in to her fragrant dishes in the corridor outside the main reception room, the sight of Third Granduncle lonesomely holding his rice bowl in the doorway of the wing disturbed me. Later on, in America, I spent time with Christians, who were always talking about tolerance and forbearance. Thinking back on my days with Harrell in Manshuiwan, and the consternation brought to me by the inability of those two people to coexist, wasn't the cause the lack of tolerance and forbearance between people?

Our fieldwork in Manshuiwan was over quickly. Before we left, Harrell asked my fifth grandaunt to buy a gift for his little dry grandson to complete his ritual obligations. When we heard that little Henry's night crying had stopped because he had been given a dry grandfather, Harrell said happily that he was of some use as a dry grandfather; it hadn't been in vain. Later on, when Harrell had returned to Xichang from his work in Yanyuan and was preparing to return to America, he left 200 yuan for me, asking me to buy two suits of clothing to give to little Henry at the Han New Year, and I did as he asked. The enmity between Fifth Grandaunt and Third Granduncle hadn't changed at all. After returning from my fieldwork in Meigu, I went back to Xichang and rewrote the genealogy that Harrell and I had worked out for the Jienuo clan, making it into a complete genealogical chart, from Sada to little Henry. I made two or three copies and gave them to my relatives in Manshuiwan. This was a kind of payback to them for the bother we had caused, and was also my contribution as a granddaughter of the Jienuo to my grandmother's clan. Every time I gave a copy of the genealogy to my relatives in Xichang, I always had to joke, "You Wangs ought to slaughter a cow to thank us."

On the twenty-second of October, after we had returned to Xichang and straightened up our affairs, the prefectural Nationalities Research Institute sent a car to take Harrell to Mishi in Xide, accompanied by Nuobu Huojy of that institute and by me. Mishi is quite a famous place among Nuosu, for one reason, because in the late 1950s and early 1960s it was where the thunderous "bandit" Loho Muga started his rebellion, and for another, because the local dialect was chosen as the phonetic standard for the written Nuosu language. Going to Mishi to do fieldwork, I felt pretty relaxed, on the one hand, because Nuobu Huojy was along—he was from Xide and had lots of friends and relatives in Xide and Mishi, so I didn't need to worry myself about finding places to research or setting up people to interview. But on the other hand, I felt

a little worried and curious. I was worried because Mishi was very different from Manshuiwan, and I didn't know if Harrell could hike the mountain trails or eat the chunky meat. There was also the language. Mishi
is a concentrated Nuosu area, and the people there wouldn't be like the
Yi in Manshuiwan; most of them would not be able to understand the
Han language. Even though Ma Lunzy had told me that Harrell could
get along in everyday spoken Nuosu, and Harrell himself would sometimes come out with a few sentences in that language—as well as insert
a few sentences of Nuosu writing in a letter, or a greeting of *zzymuo
ggehni* or "best wishes" at the end—I was worried. I was also curious
about why Harrell, who was doing fieldwork on ethnic relations, wanted
to go to a place where there were no ethnic relations. Because Mishi is
a wholly Yi area, I was afraid that he would only find household relations, clan relations, caste relations, but no ethnic relations; What would
he have to work on? That's what I was thinking at the time.

After a sumptuous noon banquet given by the Xide county government in the county seat, we arrived at Mishi, twenty-seven kilometers
from the city. Every Party or government leader of Mishi who was in
town came out to see us, and gave us an introduction to the place and
helped us gather research materials. We quickly gained an understanding
of the basics of Mishi township, and on the second day, we began visiting villages. Our first station was Matolo Village, about a two hours'
walk from the township headquarters. The muddy mountain trail led
straight into the village. These villages here were not like Manshuiwan,
which had a road, a creek, and concrete courtyards; instead, the houses
were arranged in no particular order, following the topography of the
land. When we walked into the house of the village head, Alu Osse, I,
walking in front, mischievously perked up my ears, expecting to hear
behind me the "Peng!" of a head banging into a door frame. But when
I turned around to look, Harrell was already standing behind me. His
six-foot frame had not bashed into the lintel. Nuosu houses are not very
high-ceilinged, so that the door frame is ordinarily only about 1.65 meters
high, and a majority of grown Nuosu men have to duck their heads to
enter. Outsiders are not used to ducking, and frequently bang their heads.

The host family welcomed Harrell, me, Huojy, and the township
cadres that were escorting us to sit in the upper seats by the hearth. Vil-

lagers are accustomed to putting mats on the ground to sit on, but will always have ready two or three little wooden stools for guests from outside, particularly for cadres "coming down" to the village. The host handed two short little stools, casually knocked together out of boards, over to Harrell and me. Harrell is tall and long-legged, and looked a little awkward sitting there on the stool, and I said to him in an exaggerated manner, "Careful, don't tip over the stool." As Huojy and the township cadres introduced themselves to the hosts, people from the village kept crowding into the house. It was the perfect season for doing fieldwork, since there was not too much farmwork to do. Besides, Yi people have a tradition of enthusiastic hospitality, so that the guests of a single house were the guests of the whole population. In addition, today's guest was a long-faced foreigner who was neither Yi nor Han. Later on, we recorded that there was a villager whose name was Yare ("foreigner"), but I dare guarantee that the majority of the villagers had never seen a foreigner. Because Xide was not officially open to foreign visitors, it was rare for them to come here. People twirled in their hands the white liquor we had brought, took up the candy and cigarettes we had brought, and carried a look of curiosity in their eyes. Harrell had probably never seen so many people in one room—on the floor, on the beds and benches, even on the ladders—it was full of men and women, old and young. Harrell, sitting on the upper side of the hearth, curiously craned his neck back and forth, counting how many people were in the little room after all. He told me the result; I don't remember exactly, but I think it was close to thirty. It looked like research would be easy there; we could do the entire household survey of the village right there in that room. It was quite a contrast with the calm research done in Manshuiwan, were we needed to visit every household. This was one difference between Yi in purely Yi areas and Yi in mixed areas.

The research began. Without waiting for me to speak, Harrell, speaking Yi, began to ask the first interviewee, Azo Mujy, the father of the village head, "What's your surname?" He didn't immediately reply, but turned to face the people chattering away at the lower side of the hearth, and announced, "Hey, this American understands Nuosu language." At this, the room quieted down considerably, probably because people wanted to hear the American speak Yi. I was not surprised at this; the previous day, Meigui Muga had already shown off his Yi-speaking ability to the cadres. But still, as the questioning continued, I was happily surprised to see that Harrell could not only use Yi to ask about the main topics of his research—such as names, ages, horoscopic animals, family membership, marital status, kinship relations, and so on—but could also use Yi writing to record the answers. When people then found out that this foreigner could write the script of the Yi, they began to turn to each other and whisper, *Meigui co cyma Nuosu bburma syr* (This American can write Nuosu characters). The curious ones even stood up and leaned over Harrell's notebook to observe.

As the questioning continued, the frantic sounds of a pig scream-ing came in from outside, and the people sitting below the hearth stood up and vacated the area while a forty-*jin* pig was hauled in. Harrell looked at me anxiously, and I politely told the hosts not to slaughter the pig. But it was useless. The smell of pig hair being singed in the fire suffused the room, a smell to which I was well accustomed, and which I rather liked. But I thought that Harrell would certainly not be used to it. Huojy had long ago gone out to look for relatives, and was nowhere to be seen. We proceeded to interview; when the representative of one family had finished answering, we went on to the next one. But one thing was rather hard to take—the smoke. We were sitting at the upper side of the fire, and the smoke kept blowing upward. I felt my eyes stinging to the point that I was about to cry, but Harrell didn't seem to be affected by the smoke, and kept up his detailed questioning, writing the results with flying fingers.

About an hour later, chunk meat, rice, and broth appeared. I guess that Harrell was hungry, because he not only didn't wince at the meat in the wooden dish with the remains of singed black hair on it but eagerly ate one chunk after another. When Nuosu kill a pig or a sheep, a cour-teous guest will eat two or three—or, at the most, four—chunks, and then lay down the *itchyr* or wooden spoon and pass the food back to the hosts. Being a guest often means not getting one's fill, unless an ox has been killed, in which case it's fine to stuff yourself. Even though it's said that slaughtering meat is for the guests, everyone should have a portion of the sacrificial meat. In the villages, it is still the custom for the guests to eat first, but those who are guests should eat a bit and then let other people eat, particularly the children whose mouths are watering and whose eyes are about to fly into the meat dish. I remember that afterwards, behind Harrell's back, I said to Ma Lunzy, "This *bbozze* [buddy] of yours can really eat chunky meat. When I'm a guest with him at somebody's house, it gets to the point that I'm embarrassed on his behalf." Ma Lunzy was of a like opinion: "This Meigui Muga doesn't know politeness." It was only later, when I went to America, that I learned that this was the way of Americans; once they are invited to eat; they eat until they're full. Nevertheless, what the villagers of Matolo expressed about Harrell's "wolf tongue and tiger mouth" was pleasure and enjoyment; they didn't use the standards of Yi manners, or *bbuyy*, to evaluate this American, because in addition to discovering that he could speak and write Nuosu, they had made another discovery: that he could eat chunky meat with their *itchyr* spoon. In the past, when I had gone to villages to interview, everyone's attention had been concentrated on me, the daughter of Bamo Lurhxa's household, the city girl from Beijing, who understood the knowledge of the *bimo*. This had made me feel important, and at the same time was very tiring. Coming here, Meigui Muga was the point man and the focus of everyone's attention, and I was satisfied.

Our research in Matolo was like that in Manshuiwan, primarily recording the family members, ages, kinship relations, educational levels, Han language ability, history of migration, caste position, and so on, of every household in the village. Because we asked just about the same questions of each household, and drew the same kinds of genealogical charts, the research almost became dry and boring. Even though the questioning had to be carried out in Yi, Harrell's Yi-language ability was sufficient, and he only needed help when he discovered an interesting question that he wanted to understand in more depth. Because of this, there wasn't much need of actual translating, other than establishing relations with village leaders and discussing the arrangements for interviewing. After the first two trips to the villages, Huojy said to me, "This Meigui Muga's questions back and forth are still all the same, and are not interesting." He was not very active about the remaining research, maybe because he discovered that once we got to a village, he was not needed for the interviewing; that he himself was not of much use; that if a question did come up, I would be around; and that the relations with the villages were handled by the cadres who accompanied us from the township. Besides, he was an elephant-chess fanatic, and there were good chess players at the Mishi township government, so he continually stayed at the government and played chess, and didn't go with us on every subsequent trip to a village.

Even though the Yi in the villages didn't have phones or telegraphs, news didn't necessarily spread slowly among them. Visiting relatives, going to market, herding animals, and gathering firewood were all opportunities for spreading the latest news. Altogether we went to five or six settlements. Every time we came to a new village, people had heard about Meigui Muga and Bamo Lurhxa's daughter and their "census" (they still had clear memories of the census a few years before), and that Meigui Muga could speak and write Nuosu. I remember that later on, when we went to interview in Jiemo village, as soon as we walked into the village, people yelled "Meigui Muga is here!" Before we set out for every village, we prepared a big plastic jug of clear liquor and a few packs of cigarettes. Every time we interviewed in the village, there was the same loud confusion, with people all crowded together, drinking and smoking, waiting in turn for our "interrogation." Every time we went to a new research site, the villagers would want to kill a sheep or a pig for us. After a few villages' worth of research, we could begin to discover the webs of kinship within and between villages; identify the patterns of marriage relationships between clans; see the interaction, the migration, and the reasons for it; and figure out the different castes. Paying close attention, we could even discover which people had "Han roots," and which of them were true Yi.

Two incidents impressed me deeply. One occurred when we were interviewing in Jiemo. During a break, Harrell said to me quietly, "The people in this village definitely have Han roots." I asked him how he knew, and he said that even though the villagers in Jiemo were better off than those in other villages, he could see in their dispositions and in their eyes a kind of modesty that was unlike the fortitude of the real Yi people in Matolo. The people in Jiemo spoke Yi, wore Yi clothing, and lived in Yi houses; I hadn't thought that, among all these Yi, one would be able to distinguish Yi with Han roots from true Yi. Afterwards, when we returned to the township headquarters to confirm this with township Secretary Yang Ziha, sure enough, most of the people in that village were descended from several generations of Han-root slaves, and at the time of the Democratic Reforms were classified as liberated slaves; the village had previously been known as Liberation Village. Because nobody wanted anyone to be reminded of their Han origins, they had later changed the name of the village. This gave me a new knowledge of this Meigui Muga: he really did already have a relatively deep understanding of Yi people, and was quite sensitive to the fine points of ethnic relations.

The second incident that made an impression on me was discovering the rate of illiteracy among villagers. Before we had gone to the villages, the township cadres' introductions and the statistical materials that we examined in their offices had reflected a high rate of illiteracy in the area. According to what we recorded in our household interviews, the people in Mishi were very enthusiastic about learning to read and write Yi, and several villagers had at their own initiative started Yi script classes, so that a large number of Yi men and quite a few Yi women could read and write the language. But the standard for the official statistics was whether or not they could read and write Chinese. Harrell pointed out that using this standard to measure illiteracy was wrong. If Han writing was writing, wasn't Yi writing also writing? Harrell's observation touched a nerve. Why until now had all of us thought that measuring literacy or illiteracy by the standard of Han writing was a completely natural thing? And why for so many years had Yi people thought exactly the same way? Was it that Harrell was the only one who really respected Yi language and writing, who knew what it was to treat different cultures equally?

Lacquerware from Mishi is famous, and Harrell and I were both interested in it. On the twenty-sixth of October, we crossed a local river and climbed a trail for about two hours to visit the cliff-side lacquer village of Apu. In Apu we not only watched and photographed the entire traditional process of making and painting lacquer vessels (fig. 11.5), but also bought a large number of different kinds of lacquer eating utensils. Harrell also bought a set of lacquer-making tools for his university museum. It was in Apu that I felt for the first time that I hadn't

11.5 *An artisan from the Jjivo clan painting a lacquer bowl, Apu Village, Xide, 1994.*

come to Mishi for nothing. Despite the fact that I have always been proud of Yi lacquerware, to the point of taking large amounts of it to Beijing and displaying it in my house, as well as taking it to America, France, Germany, and Japan as gifts for friends, I had not known how traditional Yi lacquerware was produced. When I saw that Apu villagers could turn out a wooden blank on a local foot-pedaled pit lathe in ten minutes, and, without making any preliminary sketch, could paint the beautiful and intricate designs right on the wood, I felt a gasping admiration and pride in their knowledge and skill. Today the production of lacquerware has already entered the factory; it won't be long before nobody knows anymore how these ethnic markers for the Yi were traditionally produced, and I will be able to tell them what I saw, be able to show them my pictures. I am joyous to have seen the traditional Yi art of making lacquer vessels with my own eyes.

When we left Apu, after about three and a half more hours of climbing, we came to the roadless headquarters of Yilu Township. Before we left, the township cadres had told me to warn Harrell that Yilu was very high up, and that we would have to hike for five or six hours. Harrell had answered that he hiked in America, too. I had feared that this American fellow, used to riding in cars, would suffer having to climb around. But on mountain trails, long-legged, long-strided Harrell left me far behind.

After Yilu Township had killed a sheep to entertain us, they organized a line-dancing party for us. Harrell, a head or two taller than anyone else, stood like a crane among chickens, holding hands with people in a circle and imitating their steps: one foot forward, one back, left-left-right-right. Because he had to look at other people's steps to be able to do the dance, he was often half a beat behind, and sometimes he got his hands and feet all tangled, putting his left foot where his right was supposed to go. In the dance line, I secretly laughed at him, not at his wrong steps but rather at his earnestness. The line dance is second nature to me, and after dancing awhile, I came to the front of the line and became the leader.

The Yilu people's dress caught both Harrell's and my attention. The dress of the young people in the dance line, of the township cadres, and of the people from households near the township headquarters were mostly Han-style shirts and pants, and even many young ladies wore only a hand-embroidered head cloth for decoration. Yilu was a high-mountain Yi area, where even the shadow of a Han person was hard to find. Many of the villagers, I fear, would have had a hard time speaking even in simple Chinese about eating and sleeping, but Han-style clothing had become a local fashion. I was very disturbed by this, and also felt embarrassed that Hanification had come to a place where there were no Han people. But Harrell allowed that it was probably because there were no Han in the vicinity that the people here wore Han clothes. He thought they wore Han clothing because in an area like this no one needed a marker to distinguish ethnic groups.

School education was also a part of our research. On the morning after we had arrived in Yilu Township, we went to see the township elementary school. The old and dilapidated desks and tables in the teachers' quarters and the classrooms formed a heaven-and-earth contrast to the elementary school in Mishi. We talked to a few of the children playing in the schoolyard, and as soon as we heard that they were too poor to buy textbooks, that only the teachers had copies, Harrell told them, "You will have textbooks next term." From the numbers of students that the teachers had told him, and the numbers of classes and texts for each student, he figured out a rough estimate, and said that he'd like to contribute 1000 yuan, and asked the school to take on the responsibility of buying the following term's texts for the students. Later, when he returned to Xichang and exchanged the needed money into *renminbi*, he sent the money as promised. I was quite moved, even though I never told him this.

11.6 Boys in the village school at Matolo, Mishi, 1994

11.7 Lacquered sheep-horn cups made by Jjivo Vuqie and given to Stevan Harrell by Mishi Township Party secretary Yang Ziha in 1994.

In the village school of Matolo (fig. 11.6), and in the elementary and middle schools of Mishi Township, we separately listened in on classroom education in Han language, Yi language, mathematics, and English. When Father was the vice-prefect in charge of education, he had taken me with him many times to visit schools. I remember one time when we went to see an elementary school at Sikai in Zhaojue County, looking at those dirty little creatures, repulsive and lovable at the same time, I was really moved, and thought that going to a small town or village school to be a principal or teacher might be a more worthwhile pursuit. But on those few visits, the most we ever did was stand outside a classroom for a little while and listen to the teacher's voice and the voices of the children reciting; mostly we looked at the teachers' quarters and sat and discussed things with the administrators and teachers. This time, under Harrell's influence, I actually went into the classrooms, in order to understand village Yi education, and recognized some of the problems of Yi language and Han language education. Later on, Harrell and I wrote and published an article together on Yi language education (Harrell and Bamo 1998). This was inseparable from what we learned on this research trip and from the discussions that we had between us.

In Mishi, we lived in converted sickrooms in the township clinic. One day, a young female doctor from the clinic invited us to dinner. Her surname was Hxielie; the Hxielie and Bamo clans have a common genealogical origin, which is to say, we belong to a larger, exogamous clan unit. When she heard Meigui Muga introduce his own English surname as Harrell, she immediately said, "This is Hxielie, too; we are all one family, and after this, you are Hsielie Muga, not Meigui Muga." I thought my relative was just speaking casually, but Harrell seemed very interested in this new Yi surname. He immediately said to me, "After this, we can call each other 'brother' and 'sister.'" He was *hmazy*, or "brother," and I was *hnimo*, or "sister." I didn't say anything one way or the other, because I didn't want to spoil his nice idea, but privately I thought it was just wishful thinking. Yi people emphasize genealogical origins and pay a lot of attention to roots, or "bones," and no clan has the custom of adopting sons or taking in people from other clans. In the past, Han captives could go several generations without people forgetting their Han origins. After Harrell returned to America, he wrote several letters addressing me as *hnimo*, but in my letters back I couldn't bring myself to address him as "brother." I mentioned my feelings about this to my sister, and she agreed that giving Harrell a Yi surname would be difficult to get people to accept. But her reason was that everyone liked to call Harrell "Meigui Muga," and that this name expressed a Yi identity with him on the part of villagers or others who knew him. If he added a Hxielie surname, it wouldn't be good: not only the Hxielie but other clans wouldn't allow it, and at the very least Ma Lunzy wouldn't be happy; Harrell belonged to everybody. Meigui Muga was more natural; it didn't attach him to any particular clan, and also expressed Yi people's general acceptance of and identity with him.

Overall, the work in Mishi went very smoothly, but because we were eating meat and drinking liquor all day long, my toothache really began to bother me. It wasn't just a teasing annoyance, but a pain to the point of wanting to hang myself, as I said to Huojy, using a Yi expression. At the beginning, pain pills could control it for two or three hours, but later on, not even the painkilling shots that I got from the clinic could rescue me. The township clinic didn't have a dentist or any medication especially for toothaches. My Hxielie relatives had me use a Yi folk remedy, and gave me several *huajiao* peppercorns to put between my teeth, but it still hurt as much as ever. Not caring how ridiculous I might look, I spent the whole day with the heel of my hand pressed against the part of my jaw where the toothache was, and that way it was a little easier to endure. In addition, Harrell started to have intestinal pains and diarrhea. On the way to visit Jiemo village, I was pressing on my face and he was holding his stomach, and Harrell joked that we looked like a pair of male and female ghosts on the mountain path. At that point, even the most delicious pork or lamb didn't whet our appetites, and we could only eat a little bit to express our appreciation of our hosts' hospitality. When we got back from Jiemo, Harrell seemed down, and as he sat on the bed in his room, working over his notes, I went over to see him. With a sad face, he told me that he was homesick, thinking about eating foods from home, thinking of speaking his own language, thinking of his daughters. Looking at him and hearing him talk, I got very sad, but I could think of no way to comfort him.

I had always felt that the household census we were doing reflected very little in the way of ethnic relations, but Harrell said that there were things: commercial goods from Han areas, the villagers' ability to speak Han, the teaching of Han language in the schools, Han-style clothing, the suspicion of government cadres, the Han wife of a peasant entrepreneur, and so on. As he wrote later on, for the Nuosu, the Hans are a kind of haunting presence in their absence, even here in a concentrated Nuosu place where there weren't any Han.

But whether or not Harrell had reaped any results from his research on ethnic relations, or how much he had reaped, on the material side, he was returning home with a full load. In addition to the lacquer utensils and the tools he had bought in Apu, he had also purchased a beautiful Xide-style vest from one of the doctors at the clinic. But what made me most envious, even jealous, was the gift that township Party Secretary Yang Ziha gave him: a pair of beautifully formed, exquisitely lacquered sheep-horn drinking cups by the hand of famous Apu artist Jjivo Vuqie. Secretary Yang was probably afraid of neglecting me, so he told me and Huojy in Nuosu, "This Meigui Muga that you brought along is really like us Nuosu people. We like him a lot, and want to give him these sheep-horn cups as a memento" (fig. 11.7). On the thirty-first of October, the township held an evening going-away party for us in the courtyard of the township building. Harrell, Huojy, and I all made speeches expressing our enthusiastic thanks. At the dinner preceding the party, in order to express our sadness at leaving, Harrell and I had both drunk a few extra cups, and the drunken feeling spread out to the evening party, expressed in dance and song. I competed to lead every one of the line dances until the end, and Meigui Muga voluntarily asked to sing songs, ranging from American, Italian, and Irish folk songs to Yi drinking songs. The trip to Mishi came to its end amidst the sounds of dancing and singing. When we were leaving Mishi, Harrell told me, "It's not that I couldn't stand to live here longer; it's that we really shouldn't stay. If we stayed on, the ecology here would be ruined; the pigs and sheep would all be slaughtered."

12

GETTING FURTHER IMPLICATED, 1994

STEVAN HARRELL

My next field season did not begin in January 1994, as I had hoped. The Sichuan Nationalities Research Institute was refusing to sponsor my application for a visa, since they felt I had so far not held up my end of the bargain—there was no large-scale grant, and I had brought none of the leaders to the United States. When I talked to my American China Studies associates about it, they were outraged, though not surprised, at the perfidy of the Chinese, but I had to admit that the folks in Chengdu were right. I had as yet done nothing in return. So, instead of going to Liangshan again, I sat home and wrote proposals for a conference on Yi studies, which would be held in Seattle in early 1995, and to which I would invite at least the two Nuosu of the four leaders to whom I owed trips. I wrote proposals to the National Science Foundation (NSF), the Wenner-Gren Foundation for Anthropological Research, and the Joint Committee on Chinese Studies of the American Council of Learned Societies and the Social Science Research Council. I also asked for some money from the China Studies Program at the University of Washington. I figured that if I got a couple of these grants, I could at least have a small conference, which would allow me to fulfill half of my reciprocal obligations. By May I was notified that all but the National Science Foundation had awarded me money. When

I wrote to Chengdu, they said fine, they'd love to come, and, sure, I could come and do my fieldwork in the fall.

And so I was in Chengdu at the beginning of October 1994, and again the formalities went fast, so I quickly proceeded to Xichang, the increasing casualness of the interaction indicated by the fact that the institute sent only a junior researcher[1] along with me this time.

Vurryr and some other friends met me at the train, and I asked what plans had been made for this year's fieldwork. None. I had been in touch with the Liangshan institute about my plans for several months, and had also been in communication with Bamo Ayi, a young Nuosu scholar who taught at the Central University for Nationalities in Beijing and also had a research organization of her own in Xichang, and whom I had invited to the conference planned for the following spring. But Director Qubi was out of town, and nobody know where Bamo Ayi was. We could not go to Yanyuan, because Vurryr had a writing deadline, and we could not go to the field site in the original Nuosu homeland in Old Liangshan, because the central counties were quarantined on account of a cholera epidemic. It looked like I would be in Xichang for awhile, though I might be able to go with one of the junior researchers to Yue-hua to study the lowland Nuosu who had adopted Han customs and lifestyles. That, at least, did not require a police permit. In the meantime, we went to look up Martin Schoenhals, a young American professor with whom I had corresponded, who was doing a study of the Ethnic Middle School in Xichang City. He was a nice young fellow, I thought, very serious.

The following evening, Vurryr and I were sitting in his apartment, trying to put together some kind of dinner in his wife's absence, when a messenger came to tell him that he had a phone call. It was Bamo Ayi's younger sister, Bamo Qubumo, inviting us to dinner at the Liang-shan Hotel, the classiest place in town. She and her older sister, Ayi, had been in Zhaojue County, where the cholera epidemic was, and had not been able to get out until the county police chief had escorted them back to Xichang in his own car. We turned off the stove, got the driver

---

1. Yuan Xiaowen, a young Tibetan scholar who became the institute's director in 2003.

(since Vurryr had been promoted to associate professor, he had access to the driver without asking the leaders), and headed for the hotel. Standing in the driveway was a young woman with long hair and thick glasses, smiling and waving to us to park the car; she introduced another, thinner, woman as her sister, and directed us across the street to a restaurant run by a "brother" of theirs. Later on, I learned what a "brother" was: any male of your own clan, with clans extending clear across Liangshan. I guessed these must be the Bamo sisters, and the one with the thick glasses must be Ayi.

At dinner, we talked about anthropology, fieldwork, ethnicity theory, mutual friends, next year's conference (I didn't have enough money yet for Vurryr, since he was junior at his institute), and my frustrations. When I mentioned that I was stuck in town without police permits to go into closed counties, and without the possibility of going to Yanyuan (because of Vurryr's schedule) or Old Liangshan (because of the epidemic), Ayi said, "Well, why don't I go with you to Manshuiwan, where my father grew up? It's just like Yuehua; we can stay with one of my relatives, and—we'll go tomorrow afternoon." She had to be back in four days for her youngest sister's engagement party—to the second son of Secretary Yang Zipo of Yanyuan—but we could come back for a couple of days and then go out again, since it was only about a two-hour ride.

After dinner, the sisters invited Vurryr and me to their house, in the City Party Committee compound up on the hill. It was a privately owned house, and the nicest place I had ever seen in China. In their new, upstairs rooms, there were fake-leather overstuffed chairs on a polished tile floor, an oil portrait of a Nuosu maiden on the wall, and a pillar finished in silver-colored Nuosu designs. The adjoining bedroom had a similar pillar, finished in gold. Before long, Ayi and Qubumo's father, former vice-prefect of Liangshan, Bamo Lurhxa, joined us and broke out the liquor, and not long after that Ayi had sweet-talked her father into escorting us out to the village in his Land Cruiser the next afternoon.

My journal for October 8 reads:

So what's happening is that, willy-nilly and seemingly through neither wish nor fault of my own, I'm getting hyper-connected with the Yi elite. And they just confirm, over and over, my impressions from last year of how chauvinist they are. In the Hong Kong-luxury styled apartment, what kind of cups and bowls do they serve Yanyuan apples and *baijiu* [liquor] in?

It took less than two hours to get to the village at Manshuiwan the next afternoon, and we were soon settled in a classic if decrepit Chinese-style four-sided courtyard house, complete with an open courtyard in the middle, where the full moon could shine in, and a four-story tower formerly used for defense against hostile Han from the surrounding villages. The house belonged half to Mr. Bamo's mother's third brother, a widower who lived in two rooms on one side, and half to the widow of his mother's fifth brother, who had three rooms plus a kitchen on the other side and also made use of the common room in the middle. Within an hour of our arrival, each had come to tell me (and Ayi, who had heard it all before) that the other was a no-good, lying slime. We interviewed some people after dinner, and then I was put to bed in one of the rooms along the courtyard, while Ayi slept with the old lady in another room off the common room. My next journal entry is dated October 12, 4:30 a.m.

OK, fine, so I can't sleep and have to keep getting up (actually, only twice so far) to pee in the stupid chamber pot, and the bed smells like the must of a cool graveyard, and I'm getting old and I think I might be hungry and I know I'm thirsty even though I've been peeing, and the toilet is the pigpen and they like to eat salty, salty ham with a faintly rancid taste and there've got to be rats around because the old lady was baking rat poison and pretty soon the cocks will start crowing and the old lady hates her brother-in-law and vice-versa and they have both told us so and Ayi keeps reminding me that this is really nice compared with what it will be when we go to a real Yi place and all this makes me a WIMP WIMP WIMP and that in itself is enough of a worry to keep me from sleeping which means that all tomorrow I'll be sort of out of it and unable to function in this language which is hard enough for me to start with and tires the brain cells in its own right even if you had a good sleep the night before.

We did manage somehow. After all of my pretenses at being an anthropologist in Mainland China, here I was living in a village for the first time. Ayi helped her aunt cook while I wrote field notes, and we went out interviewing together; she, being younger, healthier, and probably more conscientious than I, was always urging me for just one more interview or visit, and I was always shamed into it. Since everybody knew her (they used Han names here, so they remembered her from her childhood as Ngan Lan), there was little suspicion, and we collected enormous amounts of data in a very short time. We worked with another great-uncle of Ayi's, Wang Chenghan, who was a professional interpreter for Nuosu politicians and a local scholar, and we managed to draw a complete genealogy of the Wang (Jienuo) clan, something he had been trying to do but had never gotten around to finishing. We almost finished the genealogy of the Li (Aju) clan, but had to leave a couple of gaps. We got quite complete census information, and a lot of people's opinions about the relationships between lowland Nuosu (themselves), highland Nuosu (whom they ordinarily didn't marry), and Han (whom they sometimes did marry). I became godfather to a colicky baby, since the custom is to ask someone of another *minzu*, and I named him Henry because his Nuosu name meant "rich" and "powerful," and his Han name began with an "H," and because Henry was my maternal grandfather's name (see fig. 11.3). I bought him a little suit of clothes, and left some money with Ayi to buy him a New Year's gift.

We did return to Xichang in the middle of the Manshuiwan project, and Vurryr and I went as guests to Bamo Vusamo's engagement party (fig. 12.1), where we saw Secretary Yang and more of the ethnic cadre and intellectual elite. After we came back, Vurryr and I paid a very interesting, one-day visit to a local Hui township, accompanied by Wang Wenzhi, a Na cadre in the *minwei* who was a great joker—except when I suggested that the Na were a matrilineal society, an offhand remark that sent her into a rage and led her to ask me if I wrote that, why didn't I write that the Han had whorehouses? She also admonished me to make sure to write the truth—that the Na were Mongols, not some other *zu*.

Ayi and I were soon off again to our next field site, this time the promised village in a purely Nuosu area, Mishi Township in Xide County, northeast of Xichang. We went with Nuobu Huojy (Huojy is Nuosu for Hongjun, or Red Army), another researcher from Lunzy's institute, a native of Xide County and who would be able to smooth our way using his personal connections.

12.1 At the engagement party for Ayi's youngest sister, Bamo Vusamo, at
the Bamo family compound in Xichang, 1994. Left to right: Stevan Harrell,
Bamo Qubumo, Bamo Ayi, and Bamo Vusamo. Photo by Bamo Erfu.

Mishi required yet another style of field research. For our ten-day
stay, we were almost completely in the hands of officials—although it
wasn't unpleasant, because of the extraordinary cooperativeness and
friendliness of many local cadres, particularly township Party Secretary
(boss) Yang Ziha. We were deposited by car in the concrete courtyard
of the township government on October 22, and sat around the township office the entire sunny afternoon, interviewing cadres and copying statistics of various sorts. We had no idea where we would eat or
sleep, but by dinnertime there we were offered the meat of an enormous sow, Nuosu style; we would eat from her carcass, Han style, at
breakfast the rest of the week. Other than that, we systematically
depleted the livestock supply of the township. We partook of:

October 22: The original pig from the township government
October 23: A pig in Matolo Village
October 24: A sheep in Matolo Village
October 25: A sheep in the afternoon at the town elementary school
           A sheep in the evening at the town middle school
October 26: Two chickens at noon in Apu Village
           A sheep in the evening at Yilu Township

October 27: Two chickens at a relative of Huojy's who was a doctor in the
local hospital
A sheep slaughtered by the township government to feast
visiting police come to investigate a murder
October 29: A pig in Jiemo Village
October 30: A pig in Lieto Village

Meat was overshadowed, however, by drink. On every village visit, we
would pack a ten-gallon plastic gasoline jug filled with corn liquor or
buckwheat liquor, and offer it to the locals while we sat in their courtyards or on the floors of their houses by the fire and did censuses and
interviewed them about local history and conditions. We, of course, could
not offer liquor and not partake ourselves, so our condition at the end
of each day ranged from mildly tipsy to totally blotto, particularly Ayi,
whose family was famous all over Liangshan, and I, who was a foreigner
who spoke a little Nuosu. It got worse toward the end, partly because
drinking has a cumulative effect, and partly because we were getting
sick. Ayi had developed a bad toothache, and was plodding along the
steep muddy trails with the heel of her left hand held against her jaw,
and my digestive system was beginning to lose the battle to the twin
demons of liquor and fat meat. I remember thinking as I downed a
farewell toast in Matolo, "Nothing like a good shot of rotgut to get you
going down a slippery trail."

The one night when there was no animal to eat, one of Huojy's relatives, a medical worker in the local clinic, invited us to eat potatoes
with hot peppers, and, of course, to drink liquor along with it. The doctor was really intrigued with a foreigner who could speak rudimentary
Nuosu, and pushed me to the limit of my language ability, which I greatly
appreciated. She also asked me what my surname was in my own
language, not in Han but in the language I spoke at home. This was a
question I almost never got asked in China. I said "Harrell," and she
immediately shot back "Hxielie" (she was also Hxielie). And so I was
no longer Meigui Muga, but Hxielie Muga, placing me in the Nuosu
kinship and caste system. I was immediately a brother to Ayi, because
the Hxielie and Bamo clans are linked (they do not intermarry), and,
of course, that made me a *quho*, or commoner, because Hxielie is a com-

moner clan. They told me I should be glad of this, because the aristocratic Nuoho oppressed the people (in Han, *yapuo renmin*), appropriating official discourse, as people so often did, to make local jokes. Later on, at Secretary Yang's house in Yanyuan, when I called Vice-Prefect Bamo *pavu*, or uncle, he doubled over with laughter, and had to tell the story to everyone present. Secretary Yang said "Yes, that's much better. We have to switch. Hxielie Muga." When I visited China in 1999, everybody seemed to have heard of me as Hxielie Muga, especially in Meigu. But neither Ayi nor Ma Lunzy ever liked it, and in Yanyuan, at least, Meigui Muga seems to be permanent.

In addition to complete census surveys of four villages, our trip to Mishi also included an overnight trip to the neighboring roadless township of Yilu, mainly for the purpose of visiting the hillside village of Apu, where, according to local researchers, the Jjivo clan invented the manufacture of the red, yellow, and black painted wood dishes that now grace the tables of every elite Nuosu family in Liangshan, as well as the floors of most of the peasants. Most of the dishes sold in stores are made in factories at Xide and Zhaojue, but in Apu, they are turned on a pit lathe and painted by hand. We documented the whole process, and I bought a burlap sack full of dishes, which a young local man carried down the mountain to Mishi Town (see back cover).

The other thing that began in Mishi was a focus on local schooling. Vurryr and I had drafted an article on local education the year before (see Harrell and Ma 1999), and I had become increasingly interested in schools as sites of nationalist discourse and local ethnic mixing. So in Mishi I began visiting schools, interviewing teachers and administrators, collecting statistics, and auditing classes wherever I went. In Mishi I spent time at the township elementary and middle schools, as well as the village schools in Matolo and Apu.

On October 31, the night before we were scheduled to leave Mishi, Ayi and I were walking along the road with township Secretary Yang Ziha, who pointed to the last leaves clinging to the poplar branches in the wind, and said, "Why don't you stay until these leaves are all fallen, and then go?" He held a song-and-dance party in the courtyard that night (where I made an awkward little speech in Nuosu), and then we all got drunk one more time in the office (where I made a complex and probably overstated "thank you" speech in Chinese). Mishi fieldwork had been just the opposite of fieldwork in Manshuiwan. We had been in Manshuiwan on kinship connections, and had had little to do with cadres. We had lived in a peasant house, had helped cook peasant food (or Ayi had—her great-aunt had made it clear to me that males were not welcome in the kitchen), and had been given a village-centered view of things. In Mishi, we had been there officially, had had everything to do with cadres, had never lifted a finger to cook or wash, and had gotten an official view of the villages, looking from the outside in.

The morning after the party in the courtyard, we took a car back to Xide Town, stayed the evening, and then proceeded back to Xichang. A call home brought not only welcome news of the family, but the report that the NSF had also approved my application for the Yi culture conference—four for four, and the best news was that I could now include Vurryr. The next evening, we attended a dinner for a crew from Central TV in Beijing, who were making a documentary called *The Three Daughters of the Bamo Clan*. After dinner, I said good-bye to Ayi, and two days later was on my way to Yanyuan with Vurryr, this time to study the ethnic relations of the Na.

After a rather wild party at Secretary Yang's house in Yanyuan (one more celebration of the engagement of his son to Ayi's little sister), we were on our way to Guabie, the seat of a Na *tusi* or local ruler of the nineteenth and early twentieth centuries. We had to take a two-hour car ride from the county seat to the road's end at Guanding, and from there take a four-hour walk or horseback ride to the district seat of Guabie, one of two districts (or *qu*, a unit made up of several townships, or *xiang*) in all of Liangshan to lack a motor road in 1994. (A road was completed in 1996, and there are now daily buses, but by all reports it's still a harrowing journey). The most interesting thing in 1994 is that not only was I allowed to go to Guabie and spend time (which would have been unthinkable in 1988) but local officials, up to and including County Secretary Yang, were completely nonchalant about it. They said, "Well, have a good time, and be careful not to get hurt." They didn't send any agents to make sure I couldn't see radars, and they certainly didn't come out to check on me themselves. I was, according to the locals, the first foreigner ever to visit

Guabie—even Joseph Rock had never made it—and as we walked along the trails, Nuosu women would notice me and shout, *Abbe, cy ka da la su nge?* (roughly, "Wow, where did he come from?") I would answer, *Nga Meigui da la su nge* (I came from America), and they would be even more startled, and then we would each go on our ways.

Guabie, the most inaccessible place I had ever spent any time in, was also one of the most pleasant. Located in the deep valley of the Xiao Jin River, its climate is more like that of Xichang than that of the high plateau of Yanyuan City and Baiwu, and there are fresh vegetables all year round, along with sweet, juicy lumpy tangerines and frequently succulent large carp from the river. There were no vehicles there, not even animal-drawn carts; the trails were too narrow to make them worthwhile. Everything was transported by horse- mule-, or human back, and one awoke in the morning to the sound not of engines but of bells. There was only a small amount of concrete, since it, too, would have had to be packed down from Yanyuan; even institutional buildings were made of mud or wood. The keeper of the inn where we stayed was very solicitous of our needs, and not a bad cook, either.

There are Na, Nuosu, and Han people in Guabie, but we mostly worked with Na, who in that part of the country identify themselves as Mongols. We recorded the chants of their priests, or *ndaba*; we censused families in two villages; and we spent a lot of time at the elementary and middle schools, observing classes and getting to know the local teachers, two of whom told us that they had been really scared when we had first arrived and started asking questions, since schools are always under pressure to make their graduation rates look good, and they had assumed that we were one of those investigation teams which would file reports on them. One evening, the teachers asked Vurryr and me to give a pep talk to the middle-school students about education and social mobility and America and anything else we wanted to talk about, and they packed the small classroom. The students were very attentive. At the end, we asked for questions, and they were all silent. One of the teachers suggested that the students might want to write the questions down and submit them, and the torn bits of paper poured in. Most of the questions were about astronauts, space travel, and the possibility of alien visitors to Earth—this from children many of whom had never seen an automobile, and some of whom had to walk two days to get to school.

I wondered at the teachers' social structure. There were twelve teachers at the middle school, nine male and three female, and the male and female teachers seemed to have nothing to do with each other. An impressive (and beautiful) young Chinese teacher, herself a Tibetan from Kangding, seemed shunned by her male colleagues, and spent her free time with Ms. Yang, the head of the local women's federation and a Prmi from Yanyuan, while the male teachers hung out with each other. We socialized with both; Ms. Yang was our guide whenever we wanted to find particular families inside or outside the village, and her two-year-old son, who was always along, finally learned to tolerate me and sometimes let me carry him to give his mother a break.

In the middle of our visit to Guabie, we hiked a steep and sometimes cliff-side trail a further four hours to Dapo, for a celebration of their ten years as a Mengzu (Mongol?) township. On the way back, I told Vurryr the story of Shelley Rosaldo, the talented young American anthropologist who had died falling off a trail in the Philippines; but I kept my footing until we were about 200 meters from Guabie, when, on a broad but slippery road, I slipped and crashed into a bank between terraces, bending my glasses frame, knocking out the lens, cutting my eye, and getting mud all over everything. The next day, the village mute, who had seen me fall, did a hilarious pantomime of it; Vurryr was worried about me, but I was fine. I thought back to the evening in Mishi when Nuobu Huojy had told my fortune and had said that I would have a good time in Yanyuan, but that I ought to look out for my health.

After we hiked back up the hill to the road's end, we proceeded to Baiwu, where we spent two days, including a visit to the middle school to investigate teenagers who had enrolled in a newly begun Nuosu first-grade class, and an afternoon at the home of Vurryr's father's eldest sister, in her seventies. She had warned Vurryr the year before that he shouldn't hang out with foreigners, that the Han would tell him that it was all right, and then attack him when he didn't expect it. But when I showed up, she was delighted, and kept patting me on the arm, saying, *Nga Muga, nga Muga* (My Muga, My Muga).

To pursue the other side of the Na question from Guabie, we needed to go back to Zuosuo, near Lugu Lake on the other side of the county, where we had circle-danced around a big bonfire with Secretary Yang the year before. By public transportation, it would take us three days each way, however, and there were only six days before I was due back in Xichang to travel to Panzhihua. So a nephew of Vurryr's found us a relative who drove his own car for a living, and he agreed to take us there for $300, three crisp Ben Franklin greenbacks. I had the money, so why not? The car was not much—we had to get out and crank or push it now and then, there was no rearview mirror, the seats in the back were not fully upholstered any more, and the steering wheel was so loose that Lalyr had to turn it a full rotation just to go around a mild curve in the road. But Lalyr himself was wonderful—steady and uncomplaining—and he accompanied Vurryr and me to every village and every house at which we interviewed, just for something to do.

What we did, mostly, was visit four villages in two townships (Luguhu, formerly Zuosuo; and Gaizu) to have quick looks at the household structure (one of the Na households, a true matrilineal one, had over twenty members, and several numbered in the teens), language knowledge, and the general situation of ethnic mixing, as well as to interview some priests. It turned out that the Prmi and Na around Zuosuo belong to the Bön sect, which means that when they circumambulate the lake (or anything else) as an act of merit making, they go in the opposite direction from the "orthodox" Gelugpa Buddhists who live at Yongning and Qiansuo. On the last afternoon, we found out that a famous Buddhist priest whom we had been interviewing was the father of one of Vurryr's old high-school teaching colleagues and basketball teammates, so we stayed for dinner at the teacher's house (fig. 12.2), and he rode with us back to Yanyuan in the morning. Vurryr had a network of colleagues, teachers, students, and teammates all over Liangshan that seemed every bit as wide as the kin network he was connected to as a member of the Shama Qubi, probably Liangshan's largest clan.

I had not intended to do any fieldwork in Panzhihua this time at all, but my mind had been changed by the old professors at the provincial institute in Chengdu, who told me they had established a field project in Futian Township—just west of Zhuangshang, where we had surveyed the Shuitian people in 1988, and inhabited partially by the same Shuitian. Futian has been touted as a model for minority development. So I spent six days there with Lao Yan, Lao Deng's hardworking and long-suffering assistant director.

We lived in a little hotel in a brand new town at Futian, built right along the main highway that goes from Panzhihua up to Lijiang in Yunnan. The town had only been started a few months earlier, and featured retail stores, hotels, and restaurants catering to travelers and investors. The air was filled with coal dust and truck exhaust from morning to night, but once again the fish from the Jinsha River (upstream from the power plant) was delicious. From there we made forays into several villages and several ethnic groups—Shuitian, Tai, and Han—together with the township government driver, Little Wang (fig. 12.3).

After we left, in the garden of a hillside hotel above the city, I had an interview, a kind of roundtable talk show with some local leaders, in which I dutifully praised Panzhihua's development, but also lashed out at the leaders for not controlling the ever-worsening pollution from the mines, smelters, and now the myriad trucks. The young cadre from the TV station who interviewed me asked me if, when I returned the next year, they could tape me doing my work with the local people in a Yi village. I had a day left of my trip, so I said, "Why wait 'till next year? I don't even know if I'm coming next year; why not do it tomorrow?" So on my last day in Panzhihua, I was in yet one more 4x4, headed back to Gaoping, where I had seen my first Nuosu village six years earlier. They taped me coming out of the hotel, getting into the car, riding in the car, and throughout our visit to the village. They taped me as we hunted down my old friend Nyite, now the proud father of two school-age children, with a new house, a television, and a photography hobby. They even taped me on the way back, standing in front of a pollution source, to accompany my comments on pollution.

When I returned briefly in 1996, I saw the raw tape, some of which was quite good, but nothing had been done with it. The next time I saw her, I kidded Ayi that she got to be on national TV, and I got to be on Panzhihua TV, which showed our respective ranks. I had seen the program about her and her sisters in Chengdu the night before I flew home from Chengdu, and had thought that it was very conventional and superficial. In Beijing in 1996 the national TV network came to interview

12.2 At the house of Yang Erche's father, Lugu Lake, 1994. Left to right:
a local cadre, Stevan Harrell, Erche's father, Ma Lunzy, and Yang Erche.

12.3 Stevan Harrell taking notes at an interview, Futian, 1994.

me; I was speaking Yi of course, but I don't think that that show got broadcast either. I finally made it, however, when Nuosu TV host, actress, singer, and producer (not to say glamour queen) Shama Ago came to Seattle to make a program about the Mountain Patterns exhibit, and the tape was shown three times on national TV.

I remember that on one of my last days in Futian, as I was walking along one more village path, looking for one more family, ready to ask about one more set of ethnic customs or ethnic relations, I began singing softly to myself (or maybe just in my head), "How many roads must a man walk down / Before they call him a man?" How many more muddy trails, how many more little wooden stools, how many more middle-aged people in faded black turbans, how many more meals around low square tables or out of red, yellow, and black dishes on the dirt floor? Did any of this even count as fieldwork? Does working with cadres disqualify you as an anthropologist? What about moving around, instead of staying in one village for a year like one is supposed to? What about knowing only one and a half of the six or seven relevant languages in the area? Or going home after only three months, instead of spending a whole academic year in China? What about having research collaborators, like Vurryr and Ayi, instead of going it alone like Malinowski supposedly did,[2] or even as I do in Taiwan?

Do I have any ethnographic authority? Where does it come from; what mode is it? Do I gain any ethnographic knowledge if I stay such a short time and only speak one and a half languages? I know I have had the emotional encounter, and have survived it, though, I sometimes think, not without scars. And have I acted ethically? Should I have intruded on these people's lives, for purposes that some of them understand and that some do not? Have I hurt anybody, even unintentionally? What do I owe them in return? Telling the world about the Yi? Saying nice things about them? Keeping up obligations of godfatherhood, or making sure they get a copy of their genealogy when I work

---

2. Having recently read Michael W. Young's biography *Malinowshi: The Odyssey of an Anthropologist*, about how the famous Polish-English pioneer spent a lot of time with traders, missionaries, and novels while he was doing his famous fieldwork in the Trobriands, I now feel much better, at least on this account.

it out? What do I owe the cadres and scholars who have collaborated with me? Glory? Coauthorship? Trips to the United States? Graduate schools for their daughters? Respect for their scholarly viewpoints and approaches, which are so different from mine? Telling the truth, that we are Mongols and not some other *zu*? What about the poor young secretary in the Futian government, who let me copy the impressive village-by-village record of economic development in the 1980s, but was later criticized by his superiors for showing unpublished materials to a foreigner? What could I do for him? I only know that when Bryan Tilt, a graduate student of mine, went to do fieldwork on pollution in Futian in 2002–3, he brought back warm greetings from that fellow.

13

THE LAST TIME I LED THE HORSE, 1994

MA LUNZY

I n October of 1994, Harrell came to Xichang again, and we all went to the station to meet him. The two of us were delighted to see each other, and shook both hands tightly. I took him to a hotel to get settled, and told him about the arrangements. Because I had work responsibilities—one of them editing *Liangshan Minzu Yanjiu* (Liangshan Ethnic Studies) and another editing the *Liangshan Minzu Zhi*, (Record of Minzu in Liangshan)—I wouldn't be able to get away to do fieldwork with him. He was very disappointed, and I did all I could to find someone among the younger personnel of the Institute to accompany him, but he always gave the impression that he was dissatisfied with my choice. We were beginning to feel hopeless.

The two of us were at my house, just getting ready to put some beef into the pot, when we got a phone call from the Bamo sisters—Ayi and Qubumo—asking me to bring Harrell with me to a little restaurant across from the Liangshan Hotel. The two of us put down our cooking utensils and rushed over. Ayi and Qubumo were both members of the Yi elite, so naturally I wanted to "hide by the hearthstones and chew the meat" (*galu nboda shefu xie*), a Nuosu proverb meaning "to take a little advantage of guests or famous people." This was the first time the Bamo sisters and Muga had ever met, and the subject of their conversation was serious and purposeful; they talked about various famous people's viewpoints, the differences between Eastern and Western culture, and things like that, giving the occasion the flavor of a little "cultural dinner." Naturally, occasional witticisms emerged from the mouth of someone like me, who was incapable of putting on the airs of high culture, and it stopped everybody with delight. There wasn't a lot of direct interaction between Ayi and Qubumo and me. I had read with admiration many of their articles, and I particularly liked Qubumo's fluid and sensitive writing style. They brought up a few articles of mine, and in fact mentioned some fine points in my articles that I myself had forgotten; one could say that they were not ashamed to inquire of someone of lesser knowledge. During the meal, Harrell brought up the matter of his not being able to go to Zhaojue to do research (there was a cholera epidemic there), and Ayi suggested that he start out in Manshuiwan and Xide and that she would like to go along. Harrell was very happy, and I was relieved.

The Manshuiwan research was a success; afterwards, when I received an article written by Harrell and translated by Ayi, "One Way of Being Ethnic in Southwest China: The Yi of Manshuiwan in the Middle of a Han area," I felt I had eaten their dust and would never be able to catch up. Even though the writing and analysis had been done by Harrell, still, between the lines one could see the help and cooperation that Ayi and her relatives had afforded him. When Harrell came back to Xichang, he told me that this trip had been very successful, that Ayi had really put her energy into it, that she was an untiring worker—the only problem was that he didn't have as much energy as she did, and felt ashamed.

After a day of rest in Xichang, Nuobu Huojy of our institute accompanied Harrell and Ayi to Mishi in Xide to conduct research. Even though I had gone over the matter of trying to control the slaughter of animals for entertaining with Huojy, when he took charge, he didn't listen to my suggestions, and treated Harrell and Ayi just as a Nuosu person would; he used the web of kin connections woven by himself and Ayi and, intentionally or unintentionally, quietly motivated the people in Mishi to kill animals for hospitality. For a Nuosu person, this is proper behavior; people call it *ssoshe jishe*, "looking for relatives to slaughter animals for hospitality." I knew that Huojy's quiet taking charge of these matters had taken control of the two of them. When Huojy came back to the institute, the first thing he said to me was, *Cy nyima nga shussoby atimu la o* (I got them hospitality too heavy for them to carry). When Ayi and Harrell came back to Xichang, they corroborated his story, rattling off a long list of the animals killed for them. They had eaten until one of them had diarrhea and the other had a toothache. Even though Muga had consequently developed an aversion to too many animals and too much liquor, all in all he was very satisfied with the trip. He told me that he had run into outstanding teachers in Mishi, who had used their own meager incomes to help students with their tuition and book expenses, something that he should learn from. I later learned from Huojy that when Harrell had seen the primitive equipment in the school, he had slipped the school a thousand yuan. Muga, who was ordinarily a bit on the stingy side, had just opened his wallet to help out without making any noise; this undoubtedly increased my good feelings toward him a little more.

When I finished editing *Liangshan Minzu Yanjiu*, I took the unfinished rough draft of *Liangshan Minzu Zhi* and, on November 4, rented a car for us to go back to Yanyuan to do research. Even though I was very busy, I was happy to be "leading the horse" for Muga one more time. The horse-leading duty was different this time, perhaps because we understood each other better and were much more familiar with each other by this time. In my mind, Harrell was no longer a proud professor, and I began to look at him simply as a friend who happened to come from the University of Washington. After we got to Yanyuan at 4:00 in the afternoon, we went to pay our respects to Yang Zipo. At 8:00 the next morning, we went to the Yanyuan county government offices to relate to them our plans to go to Guabie for research, and at 9:00 we left Yanyuan City. After bouncing along the horrible road in the car for a couple of hours, we reached the end of the road at Heihailuo at 11:00. There we rented two horses, one to carry our bags and one for me to ride; Harrell, being allergic to horses, walked (fig. 13.1). In this connection, I jokingly asked him whether this was a case of liberation or a case of there are no heroes in the eyes of the servant? He laughed, but gave no answer, and occupied himself with walking his own road.

13.1 *Ma Lunzy on the way to Guabie, 1994.*

The road to Guabie was a twisty trail, like a sheep's intestine, with slippery slopes everywhere, and it was humid. We arrived, sweating, at 4:00 in the afternoon.

At 5:00 we linked up with the local Party Secretary, Ji Guangguo, and told him our purpose in coming; he expressed support. I was surprised to run into my cross-cousin Ashuo Vuda (Jiang Kegao), who was the township head there, and I felt much more secure. After discussing the matter, the two of them decided to appoint vice-secretary Nie Fuzhen (an ethnic Na, a member of the Mongolian *minzu*) and a chair of the women's association named Yang to accompany us on this research. I was relatively familiar with both Na and Prmi, to the point that I understood quite a bit of their daily speech, but because there were conflicts resulting from the identification of ethnic groups within Yanyuan (which could touch in many ways on sensitive issues), and also because someone from a different *minzu* taking part in such scholarly discussions can easily lead to misunderstandings or rise to the level of a dispute of principles, I naturally was not too interested in doing research on this trip. Other than connecting with local people morning and evening to assure that Harrell's research went smoothly, most of the time I stayed in the hotel and edited my *Liangshan Minzu Zhi*. I hadn't expected that in every work unit in Guabie there would be stu-

dents, classmates, or relatives of mine. Because of the support and cooperation of the local government and of acquaintances there, it all went
pretty smoothly, from living arrangements to research.

The climate in Guabie is very good and produced the tangerines that
Harrell loved, and no matter whose house we went to, they would bring
out a plate full of tangerines. And often we would eat fresh fish caught
in the Jin River (the upper reaches of the Yalong River). When we went
back to the hotel to wash or rest, we would listen to proprietor Zou Daokui
talk confidently about how he had established his hotel in Guabie and
his plans for enlarging it in the future. The Na in Guabie could all speak
fluent Nuosu, but their relationships with the Nuosu before the 1950s
were not very good; a few Na had been carried off in chains by the Nuosu
to be slaves, and only at the end of the 1950s had they been released
and able to return home to reunite with their families.

The reasons for the historical hatred between the ethnic groups were
numerous. Even though Guabie has tall mountains and deep rivers,
the climate is still salubrious, and the products are rich; one could say
that it is an otherworldly peach garden plunked down along the Yi-
Tibetan corridor. In the past, the Na had established a relatively strong
political presence there, and had preserved liaison with Housuo in Muli
and with Zuosuo and Yousuo in Yanyuan, forming long-term affinal
relationships. In the beginning, the Na had paid no attention to the surrounding Nuosu, and had used their power as *tusi* to do whatever they
felt like. Later on, when the Nuosu in the core area sought to increase
their territory and began migrating into Yanyuan, a branch of the very
powerful Loho clan migrated to surround the Ji *tusi*. The *tusi* did not
pay much attention to the Loho at first, but in their respective comings
and goings, conflicts gradually developed, which increased daily, to the
point that a life-and-death enmity developed between the two. By the
1920s, the Nuosu, led by the Loho and depending on their own clans
and others, gradually occupied a lot of the Ji *tusi*'s territory, so that by
the 1950s the territory controlled by the Na had been constricted to a
very small area, and their position became more insecure by the day.
As a Nuosu, listening to people who had been chained into slavery by
Nuosu tell their stories, I couldn't help feeling deeply ashamed. After
the 1950s the relationship between Na and Nuosu improved, and some

intermarried. The historical gleam of knives and shine of swords gradually faded over the decades, and became a memory of suffering among the present generation of both ethnic groups.

On November 11, Harrell and I set out from Guabie to participate in the ceremony celebrating the tenth anniversary of the establishment of Dapo Mongolian Township. When we got to the Wodi bridge over the Xiao Jin River, we found a bunch of people of different ethnic groups sitting in a clump chatting, and in the course of the conversation I discovered that there was a woman among them who spoke in the Yynuo dialect of eastern Liangshan. I found that her name was Asi, that her home was in the Lomuhxo Village of Niuniuba Township of Meigu County, and that she had been doing business on the outside when she met Wang Geke, a Na. After being together with him for a long time, she had married him and borne him two sons and a daughter. Marriage to someone of an outside ethnic group had not been tolerated in traditional Nuosu society; before the Democratic Reforms of 1956, marriage with an outsider had been punishable by death. After the Democratic Reforms, the old marriage system had been (officially) abolished, but such long-accumulated cultural customs are difficult to break. The few who do intermarry with other ethnic groups mostly live in the cities or work for government units. Among the Nuosu of Meigu, where Asi came from, marriage with an outsider is still an affair that goes greatly against the grain. That Asi could surmount such a great obstacle and marry someone from another ethnic group from a place far from Meigu was no simple matter. I wrote in my diary, "Asi's courage and resistant attitude make me respect her greatly; breaking through the strict marriage system of the Yi not only requires legal protection but also attack one at a time by people like Asi who are moving toward freedom of marriage. I only hope that in the future, lovers like Asi and Wang Geke in Liangshan will all be able to establish marriage relations."

An iron-chain suspension bridge had been built over the clear waters of the Xiao Jin River, and when the muleteers winding their way on the snaky road met someone riding the other way, whether they knew them or not, they would smile and dismount as a sign of respect, an offering of one's body toward peacemaking. After crossing the iron-chain bridge, a steep, windy mountain path was waiting for us. Halfway there we met up with a group of young Nuosu men who were going to Dapo. They climbed the mountain path with no effort at all, suddenly coming up behind us to ask if we were tired, sometimes chatting and laughing, running ahead, and then having a smoke while looking down at us. I guessed that this irritated Harrell a little; he began to strive for the lead and fear the rear, and when everybody was leisurely taking a rest by the side of the road, he just kept on climbing. On the way back there were similar instances, proving to me that I had guessed right. This round-trip told me that my friend was somewhat competitive. As far as those young Nuosu road companions were concerned, whether we were going fast or slow, I'm sure that none of them were trying to compete.

After several hours of climbing, we finally reached Dapo, and at one glance we could see in the midst of scattered farmhouses and villages on the hillsides a row of neat classrooms and a broad four-sided court-yard across from them: this would be the school and the township office. The township cadres and the teachers and students from the school were standing in long lines, forming a corridor to welcome us. Hearing the teachers and students yelling slogans and clapping was hard for me to take. During the Cultural Revolution, people of my generation had too often been interrupted during classes to form lines and shout slogans of welcome and congratulation to arriving or departing cadres, or take trips of a political nature. I would never have thought that this cultural remnant would have survived in such an out of the way place as Dapo.

In truth, such empty ceremonial could only have survived by being learned from the previous generation. I had encountered groups of high-level leaders on fact-finding visits in just about every county town, with important locals clustered around them, putting on their best faces, and expressing joy in political movements. In the evenings, middle school students would sing and dance for the leaders in outdoor arenas; I have even seen kindergartners singing drinking songs to toast them at 9:00 in the evening. The leaders followed the practice of Chairman Mao by holding babies and exhorting the next generation to "study hard; advance every day." It made me want to puke. As the sounds of Dapo's children's shouting and clapping faded, I thought of a passage from Tao Xingzhi:

What is education? It is teaching people to change. Teaching people to change for the better is good education; teaching people to change for the worse is bad education. Live education teaches people to live; dead education teaches people to die. Not teaching people to change, teaching people not to change is not education.

In an out-of-the-way mountainous place such as Dapo, if teachers unthinkingly taught children to stand out in the scorching sun shouting empty, meaningless slogans to welcome group after group of "leaders," what impression would it leave on the minds of the little ones?

Even though I had run into a couple of Han teachers sent to Dapo from the county seat, as well as some agnates and affines, and even though I could pass the time with them anytime I wanted, still, after a day or two, I felt that a day there seemed like a year. The morning that we were returning to Guabie, I felt as if I would be returning home after a long absence; I got up early and packed my things. Before we left, Harrell asked me to go with him to see the school principal, and in the principal's neat, crowded house, Harrell took out 500 yuan, to help the school conduct some kind of activity for Children's Day on June 1. I knew that giving an elementary school 500 yuan was like using a cup of water to put out a fire in a cartload of wood, but what was interesting was that Harrell didn't give them the money when he came, but when he left. Chances were that he wouldn't have another opportunity to return. Such behavior was in accord with the Nuosu custom of *kadagge* (a thank-you gift), which Harrell didn't understand at the time. I had accompanied a lot of researchers who would show up with all kinds of gifts and invitations, but when their work was done would find it difficult to even take a moment to say good-bye. It was a humble gift expressing deep feeling (fig. 13.2).

When we left the principal's house, the two of us passed on to some of the Han teachers local produce we had been given at the welcoming ceremony, and after saying good-bye to them, we returned to Guabie. On the trail back, Harrell told me of the misfortune of a prominent American anthropologist who had been killed doing fieldwork, and I thought of the unfortunate death of Fei Xiaotong's wife, who died after falling into an animal trap during fieldwork in Guangxi.

13.2 *Group picture with cadres and teachers before our departure, Dapo, 1994. In the top row: school principal (far left), Party Secretary (fifth from right), Ma Lunzy (fourth from right).*

From my point of view, the trail to Guabie wasn't particularly dangerous, but as soon as one stopped being careful, a serious accident could ensue. When we were done climbing the mountain trails and were close to Guabie, something unfortunate happened: crossing over a mud puddle, Harrell jumped onto a round, slippery rock and fell heavily to earth. He had broken one lens of his glasses, and there was blood coming out of the corner of his eye. This scared me to death; I immediately helped him up and brushed the mud off of his face with my hand. When he began to wash himself off with the water from the puddle, I quickly stopped him. At the time, I didn't tell him why: When I was teaching in my old home in Baiwu, I had run into a friend who had washed himself off with pond water after getting a cut on his skin, and had caught tetanus. Even though he had been quickly taken to the hospital, the illness was incurable and within a week he had died. I told Harrell to go to the local hospital to get disinfected, but he said that he had medicine, and when he got back to his room, he put on some medicine to stop the bleeding (which had English instructions that I couldn't understand), and I went back to my room to rest. There was only a wooden partition between our two rooms, and we could hear each other breathing. That night was very hard to get through, as I listened to his movements, and I didn't get to sleep until very late. I didn't quit worrying until I saw no signs of inflammation in the morning.

In Guabie I took hardly any field notes, and, aside from getting a basic understanding of the enrollment and promotion rates of the school, I spent most of my time in my room writing the treatise on ethnic groups. Still, Guabie left a deep impression on me: at all times one could hear the bells of horses arriving from all directions, and one could hear Nuosu, Na, and Han—three languages. Perhaps because everything had to be hauled on horse- and human back, even though every ethnic group wore its own clothes every adult wore a sheepskin or woven wool horse blanket, which was a kind of symbol of the people of Guabie. There the breeze was gentle and the sun was warm, the mountains were high and the waters were deep, and at any time one could eat fresh fruit and game.

When we were through with our fieldwork, it took me two hours to get a phone connection with the county seat; they agreed to send a car free of charge to pick us up at Guanding. In the middle of my early morning dreams, I heard horse bells approaching from far away. Proprietor Zou woke us up, and, after we had a bit to eat, we left Guabie, Harrell walking, and I on a horse.

After stopping to do a little interviewing in Baiwu for a couple of days, we returned to Yanyuan, and the next day went to have a quick look at a Na village in Shuanghe. That wasn't too happy a day, owing to the fierce Mongol sentiment among some of the Na, who didn't appreciate outsiders investigating their history or questioning their ethnic affiliation. The local leaders were quite sensitive to this, and whenever outsiders came to investigate, the duty of accompanying them was given to Na people in the township government. The Na who accompanied us was a young fellow, and he secretively explained the internal policy of what to call the Na and told me what I should be looking out for. I assured him that we would respect the wishes of the local people, and also told him our purpose in coming—that we didn't have much interest in the question of what *minzu* they should be assigned to. Still, when we went to a village, he restricted our freedom; he took us to a few households that had been well trained, and claimed that there was nobody at home elsewhere. At one point, disregarding his obstruction, I knocked on a Na household door, and the person who answered was a former student of mine. She and her parents received us most enthusiastically, and without offending their ideas about *minzu* membership, we learned a lot. She also let me know that Lang Chengzong, well known to me in my childhood as a "Mongol uncle," lived nearby. When Harrell and I were getting ready to go there, the driver pretended that there was something wrong with the car, and it took a lot of persuading to get him to drive over. I knew that there was nothing wrong with the car; the problem was that we hadn't "taken good care" of the driver. I thought of a saying well-known in Yi areas: *Yoshe dudu to, qielur dudu zo* (If you don't offer enough mutton, the mill won't turn very well). On that day's fieldwork we encountered both chill and warmth: The two guides (the driver and the fellow from the township government) received us in a cold manner, while the informants (my student's family and my "uncle") received us with the utmost warmth.

On the eighteenth of November, we rented an inexpensive, old, broken-down car to take us to Zuosuo. The owner of the car was called Mgebbu Lalyr. We were clan-mates, and he called me "uncle," according to the generational order. His father had been a slave lord and had been arrested and reformed through labor in the 1960s; he had nearly lost his ability to work when he was let out. Lalyr, in his fifties, was the eldest child in the family, so responsibility for the family's livelihood fell entirely on his head. Luckily, he had a healthy constitution, and the government took him on as a clarifier in the edible oil industry. He supported his younger brothers and sisters by working hard and saving. During the Cultural Revolution, he had become acquainted with a tractor operator and had signed on as his apprentice, learning to drive. In 1976, when policies improved, he became one of the first generation of Nuosu drivers in Yanyuan. In the 1980s, he learned of the economic advantages of renting out cars and trucks, bought a vehicle, filed paperwork for "retirement due to illness," and began to earn money.

We had had a difficult time finding a driver to take us to Zuosuo;

drivers didn't want to go there, so their rental prices were very high. I went through a lot of acquaintances without being able to come to an agreement. When I asked Harrell if we could take two extra days and go by bus, he refused. It wasn't until 9:00 in the evening that I made contact with Lalyr, who agreed to take us for one-third less than another driver would have asked: two and a half Ben Franklins, which converted to 2000 yuan. At the time, Lalyr didn't know I had talked to other drivers. Later on, when I went to America, he gave me back these same greenbacks at the exchange rate of 1 to 9, so he made a few hundred *kuai*. The car was quite shabby: there was no rearview mirror, the back seats were full of rips and holes, and if you closed the window, the dust blew in all the same. Lalyr was smart. Beforehand he had parked his car at the side of the road, found some passengers, and pretended that they were acquaintances cadging a free ride; actually, he had taken money from them. When we had lunch in Ninglang, he reminded me privately, speaking Yi, that he was losing money on the trip, and asked if I could find some acquaintances that could get us some free gas. He knew that I was acquainted with several officials in Ninglang. It was best to answer him by pretending I hadn't heard. Despite the fact that Lalyr was always trying to pick a little something from Harrell's and my pockets, he and his car were like a pair of loyal friends bound together by money; they reminded me of the relationship between an old ox and a broken-down cart—on the road to income there was never a word of complaint.

After more than ten hours of bumping, we arrived at our lodgings at Zuosuo at around 6:00. By the time we had eaten dinner, the sky was completely dark. We went to a free outdoor movie at a spot not far from the hotel. The audience was unusually lively: almost every man was sucking on a cigarette, so that the lit ends were sparkling in the dark, and almost every woman and child was chewing on melon seeds. The crowd was so bubbly that it was sometimes impossible to hear the movie; people were enjoying the evening, the break from the boredom of their formulaic lives of getting up and working with the sun and retiring when it went down.

The next morning at 8:00 we ate the previous day's leftovers, and at 9:00 we went to the district middle school to investigate the situation there. The principal had not gotten out of bed yet, so the director of studies gave us a simple introduction. We also went to interview teachers and administrators at the elementary school. I hadn't known until I walked in that the principal and the director of studies there were both classmates of mine from normal school seventeen years earlier. I hadn't seen them since graduation, but we still remembered each other very clearly. Seeing their children, I thought of an ancient Han poem: "Long ago, when we parted, you were not yet married; / your sons and daughters suddenly have formed a rank." We got caught up in personal conversation—we couldn't ask enough questions and couldn't stop talking—diluting the research. Only as they were getting ready to lay out lunch for us did I come to, decline with thanks their offer of hospitality, and begin to talk formally again. The two leaders could recite precisely the numbers of male and female students and the numbers of Yi, Han, and Meng students in each class. The cleanliness of the school and the bearing of the teachers and students attested to their professionalism and conscientiousness.

After our visit to the elementary school, we went to visit the son of the last *tusi*—La Pinchu. La and I had worked at the same school in 1978–79, and were very good friends, so when he saw the row of us come into his house, he felt, "Is it not a joy when friends come from afar?"[1] He knew the history, politics, society, culture, language, and religion of Zuosuo like his own hands and fingers, so naturally he used up a lot of Harrell's ink and paper. After six hours of interviewing and talking, we all felt very happy. La's house had a bit of the immensity of that of a *tusi*; the mud-and-wood four-sided courtyard was very broad (fig. 13.3). In back was a community temple, and on the left side, an official elementary school. The main room was large and high-ceilinged; the rafters were hung full of preserved meat, and, in addition, there were four preserved whole pig carcasses on the floor. La's clothes were all sewn with replacement buttons, and he looked nothing like a *tusi*, nor did he look anything like a people's teacher; he looked more like a frugal mountain peasant. In his conversation there were many fond reminiscences of his father, though he seemed to lack a little in self confidence. He attitude toward life was one of falling short of the best

---

1. The second line of the Confucian *Analects*.

13.3 At the home of La Pinchu (center), Zuosuo, 1994. Photo by Ma Lalyr.

but doing better than the worst; you could say he was content with his lot and happy most of the time. He had taught school in Yi areas for most of his life, and could speak fluent Nuosu; in his conversation with us, he often spoke Nuosu; some of his life habits and ways of thinking were very close to those of the Nuosu. He killed a live chicken to *sy nra zzy* (see a bit of blood), according to Yi custom, and then served us a sumptuous meal centering on Naze-style cooking. He asked us several times to stay for a few days. After I told him our schedule, he very regretfully accompanied us to the highway.

After we left La's house, we drove on the highway for fifteen kilometers, then left the car in the care of a road-construction worker and walked for a little over an hour to arrive at Gaizu Township of Zuosuo, where we did a few days of research. Even though we were tired from a day of interviewing and traveling, we needed to make contact with the local authorities, or we would waste the next day doing it. After asking around, we found a deputy township head, a Nuosu of the Mosi clan, and I used a method often used by Nuosu when they are away from home: *Ami xyli nra, tine ji xi jji* (Two Yi, strangers to each other, are still relatives here). We quickly latched on to each other as cross-cousins. Recognizing me as a relative meant that he agreed to help us out; this is called *Nimu ji she zze; shuomu zha lo che* (In Han areas, you depend on commerce to eat; in Yi areas, you depend on your relatives to eat). He figured out a way to get us two rooms, with Harrell sleeping inside the courtyard of the township government and Lalyr and I in a room outside along the road. We had a place to perch; I was very reassured.

The next day we interviewed several households of Meng, Han, and Zang in the villages in the vicinity of Gaizu. There I saw for the first time the undivided matrilineal households of the Na. There were twenty-three people in the household, with four sisters as housewives; they all had children, and the oldest sister was the household manager. It was the first time I heard a sorrowful Han bride, dressed in late-Qing period clothing, singing laments for her natal family; the first time I saw two bridesmaids keeping watch by the bride's side, now crying, now singing, now laughing; the first time I saw the bride's and groom's families grow red in the face and scarlet in the ears with anger over a pair of pants in the dowry. From this angle alone, I can say that I had a big harvest in Gaizu. All of the ethnic groups in Gaizu were rather reticent, and lacked the enthusiasm of most minorities. The relationships between the groups were not very good; they didn't communicate. In other mixed-ethnic areas, every time there is a wedding, people of every ethnic group help each other out in the work of hosting. In Gaizu, each group was only looking out for its own. They didn't speak much about mutual trust or kindness; their hearts seemed narrow. Quite a few households refused to let us interview them. When we went to interview a Han household that was having a wedding, the host family was not very happy about it; they wouldn't let us take pictures, wouldn't let us get close to the bride, and so on. We had to respect their wishes, so we regretfully left the area. This was the first time this had happened to me in over ten years of research in Liangshan.

The twenty-first of November was the most unforgettable day in my research with Harrell in Liangshan. In the morning, we went to interview in Heshang and Sanjia villages, about a two-hour walk from Gaizu. We left the township government and hiked down to cross a river, then went on along a mountain trail toward Sanjia Village. The trail was very steep and slippery; Harrell was very anxious and fatigued. The entire way I quietly stayed near him, ready to give a helping hand if he needed it. Halfway there, Harrell worriedly asked me to stop for a minute. He said that he was in constant danger of falling and dying, so he wanted to make sure to tell me his wife's address in detail, and asked me to get in touch with her through Marty Schoenhals in Xichang if something happened to him. I felt so much sympathy for my friend, and worried about something unforseen happening. I said as many supportive things as I could to try to dissipate the atmosphere of anxiety, and also occasionally told jokes to lighten the mood. At the same time, I laughed inwardly that my friend's dramatic language on this occasion was a little bit childish. If by some remote chance he had actually fallen down and gotten killed, did he think I didn't have the sense to make contact with his family in America? Lalyr told me later on that when he had heard the professor say this, he had quietly wept many tears himself; he felt that if Harrell was that dedicated to his work, it would be worth it to help him out, even if Lalyr didn't get carfare out of it.

When we got to Sanjia Village, everybody was out of breath. I found the group head and explained why we'd come. The residents were mostly Yi. We found out the basic situation of a few of the households. The household heads and their children all looked upon school as something of an add-on; paying money for children to go to school was an unnecessary burden. They figured that even if more of their people went to school, there still wouldn't be a single one who could become an official, so it was better to kill off this kind of thinking and contentedly herd their cattle and sheep and plant their crops. The Nuosu of Sanjia, young and old, male and female, all liked to smoke, and asked me and Lalyr in Yi whether we had any rolled cigarettes. Lalyr took out a pack, but didn't have enough to go around. According to Nuosu customs, they could offer to give us something to eat at noon, but none of the households did. We hungrily pressed on to Heshang Village.

The residents of Heshang were mainly Na and Han, with a few Nuosu. Their climate was slightly better than that of Sanjia; in the fields, dark green wheat sprouts were already growing. When we walked into the school at 3:00, the students had already been let out. All we could see were the shabby classrooms, with desks and benches scattered in all directions. We found out where the teacher lived and went straight on to his house. As we finally opened the teacher's wooden door, amid the threat of innumerable dogs, the person who answered was Wang Dehua, my classmate from Yanyuan normal school, who had been the work monitor for our classroom. He was a local Han and spoke fluent Nuosu. He said, "Welcome, welcome. Come in, come in. We're all old classmates." It was only after I went in that I discovered that the host was another classmate from Yanyuan normal school named Yang; Wang Dehua and Yang had been assigned to the school in Sanjia after graduation. Yang's household had killed their New Year pig that day, and had asked a priest to come read scriptures. This was a case of "Climbing all the mountains and crossing all the rivers, I suspected there was no road/ In the shade of the willow and the brightness of the flowers there was another village": The teachers and the priest that we had wanted to interview were all gathered for the ancestral ritual, and, in addition, we could eat fresh New Year pork; our pens naturally gained energy (fig. 13.4). After chewing the fat for two hours, we needed to return to where we were staying. Wang Dehua asked us many times to stay at his house, but we declined and asked him to show us a somewhat safer trail back to Gaizu. Of course, going downhill was more dangerous than going up, so when we set out, I was very anxious about the possibility of something troublesome. On the edge of the road, I picked out two sturdy wooden sticks, and Harrell and I each took one and proceeded. I went in the front to test the way (fig. 13.5). The trail was still dangerous, but a lot safer than the one that morning. After we finished walking this "skyway," Harrell took up his walking stick and I took a picture of him pointing back toward the way we had come; it looked like a scene of Chairman Mao on the long march, displaying his self-confidence after the march was over (fig. 13.6).

The next day, after a bit of a walk, we returned to the spot where Lalyr's lovable jalopy had been resting for four days. Giving a little money to the fellow who had watched it, we slowly drove back to Zuosuo. We immediately found a student that I had taught when I was a high-school teacher, and asked him to take us to interview a priest. It turned out that the son of this priest had also been a student of mine, by the name of Yang Erche. He was both smart and sincere, and had been well liked

13.4 *Buddhist priest reciting memorial texts, He-shang, 1994.*

by teachers and students alike. We had both been very fond of basketball, and had often been together, and had gotten along very well. Erche and his father opened up the temple for us to take pictures and look things over, and brought out an unusual amount of local products to entertain us. Erche told me that he and his father both participated in the "walking marriage" system,[2] and because of this, he had three homes: his father's, his wife's, and his real house, which was his mother's brothers'. He told us that we absolutely had to go to his real house as guests; friendship and curiosity together made the visit a necessity. On the way there, we ran into students getting out of elementary school; Erche tousled the hair of a young boy and introduced him to me: "Teacher Ma, this is my son; his house is over there." One could say that from this short encounter, we understood the Na family and marriage system in depth.

Erche's mother and her sisters busied themselves for a long time, and brought out many kinds of local products; they killed a chicken and presented us a table richly laden, along with wine that they had fermented themselves, offering us their full hospitality. At the sumptuous banquet, we asked everything we needed to ask and wrote down everything we needed to write; we left nothing out. It wasn't until midnight that

---

2. The Na around Lugu Lake are famous for this extreme matrilineal system, in which people do not marry but remain members of their mothers' households for their entire lives, the men visiting their lovers at night. See Shih 2000; Cai 2001.

13.5 Ma Lunzy (left) with
Driver Mgebbu Lalyr
(center), Heshang Village,
Gaizu, 1994.

13.6 Heroic courage in retro-
spect: clowning after the
scary part of the trail was
over, Gaizu, 1994.

Erche took us back to our hostel. The next morning, before we were even out of bed, Erche came and called us to go drink tea and have breakfast. He caught a live chicken especially for us and told us to roast it on our way back to Yanyuan.

When we left Zuosuo, we took with us a string of memories. As we left the sincere but crafty Lalyr and his old jalopy, we had a feeling of relaxation and release, and at the same time a feeling of not being able to leave them. It was as the Nuosu say: "Ten beautiful maidens want to be beautiful together forever, but they are always divided by their mates; ten brave warriors want to be brave together forever, but they are always divided by their own fights." Harrell and I, in the course of fieldwork, were together through bitter and happy experiences, and had established a real friendship, but when the fieldwork was over, we couldn't avoid each going in our own direction. The lucky thing was that soon afterward he voluntarily arranged to lead the horse for me in Seattle.

14

THE *BIMO* IN THE MODERN WORLD, 1994–95

BAMO AYI

At the beginning of 1994, when I had finished helping Professor Steve Harrell with his research on ethnic identity in Mishi, Steve and I went our separate ways. He went to Yanyuan with Ma Lunzy, and I, after taking care of my toothache in Xichang, wanted to go Zhaojue and Meigu to continue my research on *bimo*. At that time, the cholera epidemic in Zhaojue had reportedly been eliminated. Mother repeatedly opposed my going to Zhaojue, but I stepped onto the Zhaojue road, and Father accompanied me to help arrange my research there (figs. 14.1 and 14.2). While there, I interviewed, among others, Jjike Yuoga Hlumo, reputedly the most famous *bimo* in all of Liangshan, who came to the district headquarters to meet us, and took me along on many of his ritual rounds.

But the most unusual *bimo* I interviewed was Nuobie Yopuo, who lived in Tebulo Township, close to the district headquarters. It was said that Nuobie Yopuo's tongue was half black and half red, and that whomever he cursed with death would die. If he cursed you to die standing up, you would not die lying down, and if he cursed you to die by falling off a cliff, you would not die by drowning; he could even control the date and manner of someone's death. The Nuobie clan had a tradition of cursing people, and it was said that among their ancestors were

14.1 *Bamo Ayi interviewing* bimos *of the Jjike clan, Guli Township, Zhaojue, 1994.*

14.2 *Bamo Ayi with daughters of* bimos *of the Jjike clan, Guli Township, Zhaojue, 1994.*

three with tongues just like Yuopuo's—half black and half red. A *bimo* with a family tradition of cursing people was called *cossy bimo* (*bimo* who curse people) or *bike nuo* (black-mouthed *bimo*). Cursing rituals and the *bimo* who performed them had always been a puzzle to me. Did *cossy bimo* curse people simply to serve their own interests and get ahold of other people's money? Or did it serve a social function?

When my field assistant Lamo and I got to the Nuobie village, Yopuo was out; we waited on the drying ground with the village head and with Nuobie Gohxa Bimo, who had just come back from the fields. There were thirty-two households in the village, all belonging to the Nuobie clan, all descendants of a single ancestor. The lord of Yopuo's family had been a *nuoho* of the Mupo clan; he was very proud that among his retainers he had the famous cursing *bimo* of the Nuobie family.[1] In the several decades since the democratic reforms, the Nuobie clan in the village had produced only seven elementary school students; some had gone on to junior high, but none had graduated. At the time I was there, there were only three children in elementary school, and all of the rest were studying to be *bimo*. None of the villagers had ever held a salaried job outside the village. In 1987 the villagers had started a campaign to teach Yi script in the village, and everyone over the age of thirteen had participated; this, together with the *bimo* studies, meant that a high percentage of the population had good written Yi skills. The village head, Nuobie Ddisse, was an elementary graduate. After the Democratic Reforms, all of his ritual books had been burnt; after that, he had followed the Communist Party and no longer performed rituals. But among the old men in the village, there were only three who did not do rituals; there were over sixty *bimo* in the village.

It was at about the time when smoke began to rise from the gaps between the wooden roof shingles that Yopuo Bimo returned. He didn't show any enthusiasm about our visit, and ushered us into his house without any change in his expression. Our interview started with a series of questions: Was it true that, as long as there was a sponsor, Yopuo

---

1. Despite their high position and the respect with which they have been held in Nuosu society, *bimo* almost always come from *quho*, or commoner clans, and are thus almost always subject to the overlordship of the *nuoho* aristocrats.

Bimo would definitely perform a cursing ritual, no matter who was to be cursed or for what reason? Yopuo laughed and said, "Cursing someone is not a simple decision." One didn't lightly decide to ask a *bimo* to curse someone, because a curse not only had harmful effects on the person cursed but could also harm the sponsor. A sponsor usually came to him only when things had gotten to the point that there was no other way. Yopuo told us a story. The Anre clan, one of the most famous in Yi history, was fighting with the Vasa clan, and the Vasa were defeated; all their men lay dead on the battlefield. The women of the Vasa turned themselves into curse offerings, using their own blood to write the ritual *Vasa Laqie Rre* (Curse Text of the Vasa) to curse the enemies. The result was that everybody on both sides died from the curses, and neither clan had any descendants. If a sponsor doesn't have a valid reason for cursing someone, the curse will not only be ineffective but can also turn back on itself and hurt the *bimo* who supervised the ritual. A *cossy bimo* has to be upright, and can't randomly curse somebody.

Before the Democratic Reforms, cursing rituals were usually prompted by clan feuding—disputes over slaves, homicides, control of territory, stolen brides, unprovoked injuries, or large-scale pillage. Today, the situation has changed, and most curses are performed because of thefts or robberies. Yopuo Bimo gave an example. Property and food was taken from the Tebulo Township government, and the township authorities asked Nuobi Guohxa and Yopuo to curse the culprits. After they did so, the two people assumed to be the robbers died of the spell. Since then, the township hadn't lost anything.

At the conclusion of a ritual, the *bimo* ordinarily can receive as payment only the animals sacrificed at the time, and must wait and see if the purpose of the ritual is accomplished before receiving the final payment, but if the ritual works, the compensation is very high. At the time the invitation is made, the time limit for the curse is set, whether one or two months or, at the most, one or two years. Cursing rituals don't happen very often and are difficult to do, so, unlike *bimo* such as Sadda or Nyieddu, who depend on ritual payments for their living, the Nuobie *bimo* say that ritual payments are like wind and rain from the sky, and can only be used occasionally; their main source of income is farming. Lamo told me that social order was quite good around there; one could leave a herd of sheep up in the mountains for five or six days, and no one would lead them away. Having *bimo* like the Nuobie around was good for social stability.

After spending the night at Yopuo Bimo's house, early the next morning Lamo and I walked down the mountain to catch a bus back to Zhaojue. On the way, I suddenly realized that I had forgotten to look at Yopuo's tongue: Was it really half black and half red? Lamo joked, "If you're really that interested in Yopuo's tongue, then we can go back." Actually, it would have taken only about a half hour to get back to Yopuo's house, but what would we say to him? "Please stick out your tongue so we can investigate for ourselves?" And if we clarified the matter of Yopuo's tongue, what would it explain? Lamo and I kept walking.

After waiting for over an hour, the two of us finally managed to get a lift on a little tractor that was hauling various kinds of tools. As the winter wind unmercifully chilled our bones, and as the plume of gray exhaust spewing out from the back of the tractor gradually dissipated at the roadside, there suddenly arose in me a shameful feeling: Chairman Lamo, almost fifty years old, was not only going up and down mountains with me but was riding on this uncomfortable and dangerous little tractor. But Lamo said that, working in a government office, it was difficult to get out and around, so it was great. The little free ride could only take us to Zhuhe, still twenty kilometers from the county seat. I proposed that we take a bath in the famous hot springs at Zhuhe, and then figure out a way to get back to the county seat. After ten days of being smoked by the wood fires of the hearths, all of the fatigue from hiking and riding completely vanished in the steaming waters of the pool. For only five yuan, I got to spend a beautiful forty minutes in a twenty-square-meter bathing room all by myself; it was heaven.

After that, Lamo and I went to the Daqiao hydropower station in Meigu. We stayed in Lamo's younger sister's house, and interviewed the *bimo* Jjike Azhe, who had been invited there from Ssezhe Lyrgu Village. Jjike Azhe was forty-five years old, not very tall, on the skinny side, and appeared very capable. As soon as we went in, he greeted us in Yi-accented but fluent Chinese. Of the *bimo* I had interviewed, very few were able to converse in Chinese. This time, the first one to express himself was not me or Lamo but Azhe Bimo. He thanked us sisters

14.3 Bamo Ayi and Zhaojue's
most famous bimo, Yuoga
Hlumo, Zhaojue, 1994.

who cared so much about Yi culture from so far away. He said that
through our research, we could correct the erroneous ideas that people
(I don't think he meant villagers in the mountains) had about *bimo*. He
said that the government was currently promoting the Four Moderniza-
tions, with the goal of developing production, strengthening the country,
and enriching the people. The goal of *bimo* was *bushy*, that is, "flourishing development"—the flourishing of livestock, the five grains, the
forests, and the human population for the purpose of people's health
and happiness. The goal of the *bimo* and the goal of the Four Modern-
izations was identical. *Bimo* don't steal, don't rob, don't take drugs, and
don't do bad things, so why didn't the government like them? He couldn't
understand it.

If commoners under the domination of *nzymo* or *nuo* (high-ranking
strata of Nuosu society), didn't like their lord, they could move elsewhere
and rely on a different *nzymo* or *nuo*. Some could even get rid of the
nzymo or *nuo* and become independent commoners. But the Yi couldn't
do without the *bimo*. When somebody dies, you can't do without the
bimo to send the soul off; when somebody is sick, you can't do without
the *bimo* to cure their illness; and, for general prosperity and peace, you
can't do without the *bimo*. It seemed like Azhe's concern was not just
for the clients (*visi*) who invited him to perform rituals or for the influence
of the *bimo* in the mountain villages but also for the image of the *bimo*

in the eyes of the government officials, for the place of the *bimo* in political life. He was concerned not only for the Jjike clan *bimo*, but for all *bimo*. Even though other *bimo* that I had interviewed (particularly the older ones) clearly remembered the oppression and injury that they had faced during the Cultural Revolution, as soon as the government had allowed them to conduct rituals once again, they had became concerned only with their own fame, the glory of their own *bimo* lineage, and they worried only about whether the government might one day prevent them from carrying out their rituals again.

Azhe had studied with teachers everywhere, and had learned rituals from eight different master *bimo;* Yuoga Hlumo (fig. 14.3) was one of them. Azhe felt that his own ritual activities simultaneously incorporated the strengths of many masters; his ritual results were very good, and he was welcomed by clients' families. By his own report, during the busy seasons, he made about 2,000 yuan per month. Azhe's territory included Xide, Mianning, Xichang, Muli, Ninglang, Jinyang, Leibo, Jiulong, Zhongdian, Zhaojue, and Meigu—eleven counties. Clients who hired him to do rituals included not only Yi but also Han Chinese and

14.4 *Bamo Ayi with schoolchildren, Zaluo Village, Meigu, 1994.*

Tibetans. Cadres in offices in Xichang—in particular, the upper-level *tusi* and *nuo* in the People's Consultative Conference—also hired him to do rituals; in addition to doing rituals, he also conducted business on his trips. On the fourth day of our interviews, somebody brought a telegram informing him that there were several households in Muli that wanted Azhe Bimo to conduct a *cobi* ritual to settle the soul of a deceased ancestor in the next world. Azhe figured out some dates, and determined that three days later would be an auspicious day for conducting a *cobi*. From there to Muli was a two-day bus ride. He would have to leave the next day, so we had to terminate our interviews with him early. When we were about to leave, he wrote down his address for me in Chinese: "Azhe in care of Munyo at the Credit Cooperative in Daqiao Township, Meigu County." He said that if there were people who wanted him to conduct rituals or wanted to do business with him, it was all done through his relative, Munyo, or through the fellow who had brought the telegram. If it was an emergency, they contacted him by phone through Munyo.

After lingering a few more days in Zhaojue, I went deep into Meigu again to continue my *bimo* research. Meigu is the core of the Yi district of Liangshan, often called "the origin of the *bimo*." To this day, *bimo* activity there is flourishing, the religious atmosphere is thick, the level of the *bimo* is high, and the ritual texts are numerous and of high quality. According to a recent survey, there were 6850 *bimo* there, constituting 4 percent of the total population of the country, or 8 percent of the males. There were about 200 different rituals performed, large and small, and about 1,150 different ritual texts. I thought that once I got to Meigu, I would be able to do three or four months of *bimo* research (fig. 14.4). But just after the Ddisse Bimo of Lama Village had slaughtered an ox to welcome me, once again giving me the highest honor the Yi could bestow, my relatives sent a car to come get me; there was an emergency at home that I had to help take care of. And because family matters occupied me for a long time, I wasn't able to go back to Meigu. Having broken off that research is still a painful matter for me, but I think that at some time I'll be able to go back there to do more fieldwork.

PART III AMERICA

15

THE FIRST INTERNATIONAL YI CONFERENCE, 1995

MA LUNZY

At the beginning of 1995, I received Stevan Harrell's invitation to attend the International Yi Studies Conference being held at the University of Washington in March, and I was extremely happy about it. Even though I had never asked Muga to his face if I could attend the conference—to the point that I avoided talking about it altogether—partly because I didn't want to pressure him and partly because I didn't want to be seen as exacting a quid pro quo for my "horse leading," nevertheless, to be able to go to America and see it for myself was something I really wanted to do. I was motivated all along by the attitude "Just hearing about it is empty; being able to see for oneself is real." I really wanted to see the paper tiger that we had cursed when we were little Red soldiers, to see the democratic country that was in the thoughts of today's youth. To be able to fulfill this desire through Muga's Yi studies conference was an exciting prospect. I needed to prepare.

Among my old academic paper drafts I found two to submit as papers for the conference. One was richly challenging: "A superficial discussion of the naming system of the Liangshan Yi, along with a discussion of the mistaken concept of the father-son linked name system." The other I had written with Qubi Shimei: "Homicide and homicide cases within the clan in the old society of the Liangshan Yi." Even though the points being made and the evidence presented in the two papers were relatively solid, I still felt that the force of the writing was insufficient, like two loaves of insufficiently baked bread—valuable things and regrettable things were mixed together. I really wanted to make some effort to revise them, but because the time was short and the paperwork required to leave the country was voluminous, I couldn't do anything but put the revisions aside and use the drafts as my ticket to the conference room.

I met the other conference participants from China (Yu Hongmo, Wu Gu, Bamo Ayi, Li Yongxiang, and Qubi Shimei) at the Beijing airport, and we boarded China Eastern Airlines flight 583 via Shanghai and Los Angeles, arriving at the Seattle airport around noon on March 15. Muga and Wu Ga met us at the airport. Muga greeted everyone in Yi, and the participants from Yunnan and Guizhou looked at me incredulously and asked, "He understands Yi?" "When did he learn it?" Thinking about this afterwards, after Qubi Shimei and I returned we wrote a short article published in the *Liangshan Daily News:*

We were fortunate to be able to attend the International Yi Studies Conference held at the University of Washington. When our plane touched down at noon on March 15 at the Seattle International Airport in Washington State, everybody was a bit exhausted from the long trip, mingling with the American crowds walking toward the exit. Then we were met by the chair of the University of Washington Anthropology Department, saying to each one in fluent Yi, "Honored guests, honored guests! Are your families well?"

Hearing this mouthful of standard Yi, we felt very close and very moved; everybody thought that it was no simple feat for him to learn even this little bit of Yi on the other side of the Pacific.

Two days later, he asked all the conference participants to his house to chat, and after everyone had sat down, he cleared his throat, and said simply, in Yi, "Honored friends, you've come here from far away, how can I not be pleased. Let's raise our glasses together, and toast everyone's health and good fortune, and wish that our friendship will be with us forever." Then all the Yi friends seated there stood up, very moved, and without reservation began talking with him in Yi about daily household things.

The next morning scholars from five countries (China, the US, Germany,

France, and Australia) were in a lively discussion of an article on "The double cross-cousin marriage of the Yi of Liangshan" when Stevan Harrell took a piece of chalk and smoothly wrote several pertinent Yi words on the blackboard. At this time, not only scholars who came from other countries, but also the several Yi among us really felt respect in our hearts for his ability to command so much Yi speech and Yi writing. One scholar said to him, "Your Yi speech and writing are really not bad." He joked, quite confidently, "That's because I have a Yi name, Hxielie Muga."

When this article came out in the *Liangshan Daily News*, it caused a reaction. Many senior urban Yi told me, "In America, there are people who can speak and write Yi; we have some children who not only can't speak it but look upon speaking their mother tongue as being beneath their dignity; this is a tragedy." Some Yi in post-revolutionary society were influenced by the policies of the extreme left or the extreme right, and those who were most looking out for their own social advantage would enthusiastically speak Han and tell their children not to speak Yi or to speak it less. Reports like ours couldn't help but incite a reaction in them.

In the late 1980s, when I was a newcomer to Yi studies, I took part in quite a few domestic conferences and meetings. At the larger ones, the chair's platform was usually fully occupied by a bunch of powerful personages. Sometimes even ordinary scholars attending the meeting were not given copies of the conference materials. At the meetings, these leaders lined up to recite the same political economic jargon that appeared in every newspaper and magazine, present their opinions, express their support for scholarly activities, summarize the current situation, foretell the direction that scholarship was to take, and distribute responsibility; we would then sightsee for a day and adjourn the meeting.

In the case of more specialized meetings, the head table would also be full, and after some prominent scholars in the field had finished delivering lengthy reports with shaking heads and bobbing brains, the conference organizers would exaggerate the extent to which the first-rate scholarly findings had achieved this and that kind of breakthrough, and that the achievements were this and that kind of enormous, they would cleverly hand over the responsibility for the conference to some other group, set a date for the next meeting, and then proclaim the conference to be over. The clever, poor *xiucai* would exhaust their mental capabilities, relying on the support of the leaders and their funds; this year they would meet at Mawang Dui, next year at Mogao Jue, the year after next meet at Emei, Huashan or some other mountain, send out soldiers to let Heaven have a look (a Yi proverb, meaning "filling in the ranks with incompetent soldiers"). The units that had a relatively large supply of funds always sent people to big and small meetings; some of them had been to several tens of meetings without having given a single scholarly presentation. We really needed to knock on the door of an American scholarly conference, to see what kind of medicine they had in their gourd.

I wrote in my diary on March 16, 1995:

> There was no chair's table, and no division between leaders and followers; we all sat wherever we wished around a big table. The chair announced the rules of the meeting, the times allowed for presentation, and so on. The twenty-one participants punctually used a minute each to introduce themselves, giving their name, their unit affiliation, their teacher, their specialization, and so on. It was a little bit like a group of Nuosu who were strangers meeting on the road and doing their best to introduce themselves and get to know each other. This beginning gave me the impression that everyone was a host at this conference.

Professor Tong Enzheng's critique of Guizhou Yi historian Yu Hongmo's paper served as the prelude to our exchanges at this conference. In natural and flowing language, Tong Enzheng gave a sincere and biting critique of the theory of the five kinds of social formations prevalent in Mainland China, as well as a critique of Eurocentrism. He advocated a multicentered perspective on historical development, as well as a merging of one's thought into international currents. But his criticism of Mainland Chinese scholarly vocabulary was particularly strong; certainly Western scholarly vocabulary was too democratic. Maybe all of this was obvious, but confirming everything or denying everything was a question that both Chinese and Western scholars ought to pay attention to.

Tong's incisive commentary naturally brought me to thinking about the first national conference on folkloric artifacts held at the Sichuan University Museum in 1987. At that time, folkloric research in Chinese scholarship was at high tide, and a scholarly elite centered around the national museum system had been gathered together under Tong Enzheng's leadership. I was at the Liangshan Museum of Yi Slave Society, which—perhaps because it was the first museum in China devoted to slave society—attracted scholarly attention; otherwise, neither my unit's nor my own position would have qualified me to attend such a meeting. At the meeting, the definition of a "folkloric artifact" had been the hot topic, and when the discussion touched on minority artifacts, many of the scholars had agreed that all minority artifacts should be classified as folkloric. I had had an opposing opinion, and had presented my position, stating that such a conclusion was the functioning of majority ethnocentrism and asking, "Can we say that religious instruments used historically by Yi *bimo* are folkloric artifacts? What about offensive and defensive weapons used in warfare, including armor, guns, and so forth: can we say that they, too are folkloric artifacts?" Professor Shi Shuqing, who was attending the conference, and Professor Tong both agreed strongly with my criticism, and went on to explain it in an acute theoretical manner. From that time forth, I had deep respect for Professor Tong. In his summary presentation on the last day of the 1987 conference, he repeatedly compared cultural research in China and in the West, and mentioned certain nationalistic sentiments. He emphasized that people should not be blinded by the fog of various Western theories, and talked about how one could use a Marxist conception of history to analyze the history of various ethnic groups in China.

The Tong Enzheng of Seattle eight years later had really changed his attitude toward Western scholarship. As I described him in my diary, using Yi: *Hani wo ddur a nyi* (There are no bones in your tongue; you can say whatever you want). It gave me the feeling of being damned if you do and damned if you don't. Later on, when Professor Tong wrote me a letter, his name was fully Westernized as En Zheng Tong. When I went to Han areas, I transformed Shama Lunzy into Ma Erzi; even today I still wonder, if I went to America, would I have to change it into Erzi Ma? Could this be a topic for anthropological research?

In addition to the scholarly theory, some other things made an impres-

sion on people. When the conference chair was announcing the arrangements for presentations and discussants' remarks, Mr. Hsieh Jiann from
Hong Kong raised his hand to warn Mainland China scholars that they
should respect the time allotted for their presentations, and not drag
into the international conference their custom of one person having
the final say. As a result, presenters seldom violated the time specifi-
cations of the conference; but Hsieh Jiann, as the Yi proverb says,
"chewed buckwheat like a sow," meaning that he didn't bring up anything new but rather went over and over things that had been said before,
to the point that the chair had no choice but to firmly cut short his
remarks. Hsieh Jiann had mentioned that when he had crossed Liangshan on a train in the 1980s, he had wanted to investigate reports of
chaotic social situations in Liangshan that he had read in Guomindang
newspapers from the 1940s, but that he hadn't dared even get off the
train. I admired him for speaking so candidly in front of so many Yi
people, but also had a hard time believing that someone who called himself an anthropologist could unthinkingly believe an irresponsible and
uninformed report from half a generation ago.

In sum, the impressions made on me by this meeting were profound.
In the first place, there were so many famous scholars from the East
and from the West joining hands with Yi people, using Eastern and Western theory as well as cultural phenomena from throughout world, to
discuss Yi studies. In addition, the people attending the meeting didn't
feel constrained by each other's academic degrees or by distinctions of
rank, gender, nationality, or career history. Also, the scholarly content
of the meeting was very broad. "Wise people recognize wisdom; com-
passionate people recognize compassion." The scholarly discussions
were very animated and many voices were heard. As Professor Tong
Enzheng stated, when the conference was over, the new Yi studies began.
I thought that this would resound for a long time in Yi studies. Professor Harrell had put a lot of effort into organizing the conference; he
should consider it to be another bright point in his anthropological career.
As a participant, I was also proud.

Just looking at Muga as an ordinary "horse leader," apart from his
roles as a scholar and conference organizer, I couldn't help but be sincerely moved by his consideration. He used his free time during the

conference to arrange for everyone to sightsee around the city, and took us to visit museums, and to taste all the culinary culture, from quick take-out hamburgers to buffet lunches, salmon and crab, a lamb dinner at a Greek restaurant, Korean lunch boxes, Vietnamese noodles, and Chinese food in Chinatown. Even though people were exhausted from jet lag and were still adapting, everyone managed to enter into the excitement of the moment and quickly synchronize their daily schedules with those of the local people. Maybe it was because so many of us were Yi, but when we were walking and chatting on the streets, a lot of people said, "Look at all these foreigners," calling Americans "foreigners" in America. I said to them that here they were the ones who were foreigners, and everybody laughed at the idea.

On the eighteenth of March, Muga took us to a museum at an Indian reservation on the coast. I was quite excited. This name, "Indian," was something we had run into in the works of Marx and Engels, and in the past decade, quite a few scholars had brought it together with the question of the racial affiliations of the Yi. Many textbooks in China had somewhat confusedly made "Indian" into the name of an ethnic group. It wasn't until I went to the conference that I found out this was a mistake. At the museum, I could see the tribulations and bitterness of the Indians in the last 100 years, their development and their fall, and could follow the sound of the rifles of the immigrants. The Indians had lost their homeland, lost their original language, and, in an era of tumultuous development, they had increasingly lost their own culture; even their cultural elites were unable to utter even a few sentences of their own tribal language.

In our conversations with them, it wasn't difficult to discover that their spiritual culture was like a kite whose string had been cut, and was having difficulty finding a place to rest. From this I drew the following warning: The greatness of the Nuosu of Liangshan is due to their stubbornness, and their backwardness is also due to their stubbornness. Maybe our ancestors caused us to lose a lot of our material wealth, but they left us a large amount of spiritual wealth that is more valuable than gold. Maybe in the end the Nuosu will lose their language, their writing, and their ethnic characteristics, but this great transformation will definitely not happen in our lifetime.

That evening when I got back to the hotel, I wrote in my journal:

History and contemporary affairs are playing with people: when Zhyge Alur[1] killed the giant serpent, he was a hero; when Wu Song[2] beat the tiger to death, he was a hero; when their descendants follow their example, they are criminals, because we have to preserve biodiversity. When the European immigrants used knives and clubs to occupy the lands of the American aborigines, they were heroes, when the Descendants of the Dragon assimilated barbarians to Chinese culture, they were heroes; when their descendants carry on this work, they are thugs, because humanity needs cultural diversity. Can we ask when human thinking about heroes and people of great ability will ever be constant?

When we came back from visiting the Indian reservation, Muga invited all of the conference participants to his house to sit and chat; I was of course delighted with the opportunity to meet the "elder sister-in-law" from my longtime fieldwork collaboration (fig. 15.1). When I walked into the house, without any introduction I recognized the Barbara that I had seen for several years in the little book of pictures that Muga often pulled out. She had the same nice smile I had seen in the pictures. In the room full of guests, she called out my name in an extraordinarily clear voice. The Liangshan Yi all called out in Yi, "*Cy ne sy yi ddap?*" (Does she know you?). I joked to them, "*Jjy yyr mgo shyrmgo da sy su*" (We know each other from having had each other's souls and shadows pulled together), referring to a ritual in which a *bimo* pulls someone's soul into a grass effigy in order to curse the person, but here meaning photographs, tape recordings, and the like. They cracked up. Barbara entertained everyone enthusiastically; When we saw that the hostess was so hospitable, we all felt that visiting there was like returning home, and the atmosphere became very happy. It was like "Go out the door and look at the color of the sky; go inside the door and look at the color of her face [the

---

1. The Nuosu cultural hero, born of a male eagle and a female dragon, who performed all sorts of heroic deeds at the beginning of the world.
2. A hero of the Ming Dynasty novel *Shui Hu Zhuan* (Water Margin), by Wu Cheng'en.

15.1 *Gathering at the Harrells' house, Seattle, 1995. Standing at left: Thomas Heberer, Charles McKhann, and Liu Yu. Middle row, left to right: Li Yongxiang, Bamo Ayi, David Bradley (behind Ayi), Wu Ga, Ma Lunzy, Ann Maxwell Hill, Qubi Shimei, Wu Gu, and Lu Hui. Standing at right: Yu Hongmo and Maya Bradley. Seated in front: Barbara Harrell, Stevan Harrell, and Wu Jingzhong.*

hostess]." We all started singing and dancing, with the Harrells leading the songs and dances, and even the taciturn Qubi Shimei said several words of a Meigu *bimo*'s blessing.

On the twentieth of March, Muga arranged for our four elders, Qubi Shimei, Wu Jingzhong, Yu Hongmo, and Wu Gu, to go to some cities on the East Coast, and those of us left behind all slept in. Bamo Ayi and I took some samples of Yi clothing to the Burke Museum to talk about the possibility of an exhibit there, and at 3:00 p.m. we were invited by our Sichuanese compatriot, Peng Wenbin, to go to his house for a marathon evening. We drank beer, talked, and watched four videos, including one in the Yunnanese style of anthropological video from Lijiang. Everybody was curious about some of the content touched on in that video;

there were some scenes that people inside China could not have obtained, which demonstrated that the director had the support of powerful or well-connected people in China.

Wu Ga, Ayi, and I didn't leave Peng Wenbin's house until 2:00 a.m., at which time we had the opportunity to have a good look at Seattle's night scene. Streetlights illuminated all of the main streets, both sides of which were lined with neatly parked cars; all appeared quiet and orderly. At one relatively large intersection, a single small car was coming along the road toward us. When the driver saw the red light, he slowly came to a stop, and didn't start again until the red light had turned green. In China, at an intersection with a signal there would still be cars asserting their right to go through. Wu Ga explained to us that on the whole, American citizens respect laws and regulations, and maintain public order, but that once you break the law, it is merciless. This is the advantage of a society based on law.

On March 21, Muga asked us what our wishes were for the next few days. He asked us to tell him any place that we would like to see; nobody suggested anything. I thought that it would be a big shame to go to America and not look around, so I impolitely asked Muga if he could arrange for us to see an elementary or secondary school, or a basic college class. He agreed, and quickly contacted an elementary school and a middle school, since the university was closed for vacation.

The next day, Harrell took us to an experimental elementary school. A lower-grade class was in the middle of an environmental science lesson. The class was divided into four groups, and acted as if they were four communities. On the tables were pieces of waste paper, empty bottles, and other such trash. The teacher asked the students to talk about what they should do when they ran across such things, then each group designated a representative to report on the group's findings; other members of the group could help answer questions or give the representative reminders. The small group discussions were interesting; some of the students were eating, some lying down on their backs or on their sides, some standing, and some sitting, but they all answered actively; everybody was chattering and yammering about the topic. When the students reported their recommendations for taking care of the trash, one could see the liveliness of their thought pattern: Put the trash into a machine and grind it up, and then use it for something else; send it to the moon; burn it into ashes; bury it deep in a forest to increase soil fertility and nourish the earth; send it to another planet; reprocess it into something that's not harmful.

In another class, the teacher asked each student to take five Post-its and stick them onto five things, without duplicating any, and to indicate what these things had been in the past, what they were in the present, and what they would be in the future. Some of the students stuck the notes on paper, on books, or on pens. Others put them on tables, on their eyeglasses, on their hair, or on their teeth. Some even put them on the teacher's face, nose, or ears. I stared curiously at the notes stuck to the teacher's face and ears, and asked Wu Ga what answers were written there. The answers were: "It used to be skin; now it's skin; in the future it will be dirt." "It used to be a nose; now it's a nose; in the future it will be dead." Many of the answers were related to the children's families' religious backgrounds. This formed the extreme opposite of China's educational style, in which the teachers had a stern manner and an unquestioned high position, and the students acted as little memorization machines, with their heads held straight, never looking to the side, concentrating on the blackboard, reciting stiffly and memorizing precisely, swallowing whole everything the teacher said. No wonder so many people who have lived in America say America is a child's paradise.

After that, we visited a fourth-grade class about the history of the American Civil War. The teacher and the students played the roles of different military men of the time, wearing different uniforms and carrying weapons according to their specialties. They had done some of the needlework with their own hands, and had written battle diaries. The classroom was practically transformed into a stage, and the teacher and students into actors. These studies were extraordinarily lively and involved (fig. 15.2).

In the afternoon, we visited a first-year high-school biology class. Every student was the size of a horse or cow, and dressed very casually. Some of the girls were wearing garlands of flowers on their heads. We were told that the high school had been started by seven teachers who had raised some ideas about educational reform and had been dissatisfied with the lack of response from the government, upon which they had

15.2 *With students in the Alternative Elementary II program at Decatur Elementary School, Seattle, 1995. Top left: Wu Ga, Bamo Ayi, Liu Yu, and Stevan Harrell. Second from right, Ma Lunzy. Photo by Li Yongxiang.*

banded together and started a private school. The education given there was considered quite good, and the school had become rather fashionable locally, so that it had taken on the character of an elite school. When we walked in, the students didn't react, and asked and answered questions naturally. They didn't have that exhaustion born of day-and-night striving to get into the best school at the next level, but rather were full of a healthy life-energy.

After that, we went to a seventh-grade class. When the students heard our footsteps, many of them ran out to take us by the hand and pull us over to sit by them; in China this would be called "liberalism," and would be dealt with sternly. They were in the middle of a Chinese class. There were some Han characters written on the blackboard, and when Wu Ga explained in fluent English why we had come, a the students immediately asked us a lot of questions. When they found out we were Yi people from China, one of them immediately asked, "Do Yi people have their own writing?" Wu Ga said they did, and right away they asked us to write some for them to see. The group nominated me to take care of this matter, so I wrote in Yi, *"Zzymu li va ma nge"* and *"Nowo tida Nuosu qubo mo"* (The world is beautiful; Here you can see Yi friends). At that point, one of the students asked what sort of writing system that was. For first-year middle-school students to have that kind of broad knowledge was no easy thing; it depended on the lively nature of the teaching methods. The advantage of this kind of progressive teaching method—what the Chinese call "quality education"—lies in the fact that, although students don't understand many things on the surface, in fact they understand a lot. Education based on testing, on the other hand, produces students who appear to understand a lot, but in reality don't understand much. It would be very rare for a middle-school student in China to inquire about the nature of a writing system.

After we had visited the two American schools, some questions came up. American classrooms appeared to allow broad freedom, with the teachers and the students mixing like milk and water, and the students acquiring knowledge in a happy, or low-pressure environment. But in regard to behavior in the school grounds the schools are very strict, and use detailed legislation to ensure the preservation of order. For example, we were not allowed to give the schools any implements used for drinking alcohol, such as our Nuosu lacquer cups, or any tapes or publications that involved drinking songs.

In Chinese classrooms, students must follow teachers' instructions, and are not allowed to express any opinions or thoughts of their own. Relations between teachers and students in elementary and secondary schools appear to be well integrated, but in fact they are more like cats and mice. But regulation of order within school grounds is in fact very loose. For example, teachers collect illegal private fees. In school you can teach students to sing "Come drink some barley beer; come drink some *kumiss*; come drink some of our Yi liquor," and to dance drinking dances at times of celebration, or even ask students to bring glasses of liquor to welcome officials and other important people. Whether either system is right or wrong shouldn't be discussed without first removing the hats of "capitalism" or "socialism," because in striving

15.3 Ayi and Lunzy
on the beach at the
Harrells' vacation
home near Shelton,
Washington, 1995.

toward an excellent education system, an excellent society, or an excellent tomorrow, we move beyond the difference between "capitalism" and "socialism."

On the twenty-third of March, we went to the Harrells' seaside vacation home, which was built on a quiet bay, facing a long narrow marine inlet, with dense forest on both sides, and eagles soaring in the sky, sometimes mingling with a distant airplane. We saw dogs sniffing wild deer, and every color of wild duck and seagull floating on the green saltwater; every once in a while, the surface of the water would be disturbed by one of them taking off to fly off somewhere far away. Following the tides, we, who came from southwest China, where, in Wang Ningsheng's words, *Wanli gaoshan zhi shi po, Yi piao sishui bian shi hai* (A thousand miles of high mountains are nothing but slopes; a dipper of stagnant water is an ocean) gleefully rolled up our pant legs and experienced the marine flats; this was life as if in a poem or a painting (fig. 15.3).

I finally experienced the degree to which the life of my field companion, dressed in his sturdy leather boots, denim jeans, and casual shirt, was different from mine. I didn't envy his salary, nor did his wealth make me feel small in front of him. But I suddenly realized his respect for his anthropological profession. Wherever his spirit of pursuit through hardship came from, when he left his comfortable life to float around in the poor, dirty Nuosu areas, when he warmed himself by the fire with his objects of study, not thinking about the fine life he had left behind, I was absolutely right to have helped him out with his fieldwork.

In their comfortable vacation home, Barbara took out a picture album and used nonlinguistic methods to explain the pictures to me, even imitating the animals shown. I can't say whether it was true of Muga and I that *Hai nei cun zhi ji, tian yai ruo bi lin* (Wherever within the seas there exist people that know one, then the farthest reaches of heaven are like one's own neighborhood), but I did experience something like this in his family's enthusiastic warmth. And I felt that Muga's firm anthropological footprints had Barbara's strong support.

After an afternoon meal, we left the Harrells' vacation home and arrived at the Tacoma Dome around twilight to watch an NBA basketball game, between the Seattle SuperSonics and the Washington Bullets. The game was fiercely played, each team gaining points alternately. The whole arena didn't have an empty seat, and all the spectators were in a state of excitement, with cheering for the home team coming from all around us. I excitedly yelled for the Seattle team, too, and explained the game to some of my companions who didn't know much about basketball. Harrell was even more restless than I was, cheering loudly for Seattle. When the final whistle blew, Seattle had eked out a victory by three points.

Ever since I was little, I have liked basketball; in the monotony of a school, I had but to hear the sounds of basketball and I would feel an unusual affinity for the school; amid the bitterness of village life, I had but to see a court and I would feel that life was satisfyingly happy. Later on, when I was alone trying to make a living in a Han area, it was the companionship of basketball that took away my homesickness. I'm not a particularly talented player, but my love for the game has lasted a long time, and when I got the opportunity to see a professional game in America, I felt it was no small harvest; in a way, it even surpassed taking part in the academic conference. It's not an exaggeration to say that it will be a one of the moments I'll remember all my life.

Muga's days of "leading the horse" for us were over, and on the twenty-fourth of March he put us on a plane to San Francisco, where he had arranged for us to look around with Professor Peggy Swain. She took us to the California Museum, the Center for Chinese Studies at Berkeley, the anthropology library, and, in the afternoon, to a nature park.

The next day, we went to the Golden Gate Bridge, a forest park, a seaside park, and other places, plucking the string of tourism really hard.
Perhaps spending a little over ten days looking at the flowers from horseback didn't give us a basis for evaluating America from head to toe, but
still, from our direct observation we could comprehend the profundity
of the Yi saying *Zze li kur zze, bburma li hie jjox ddur* (Digestion goes
on in the intestines; the health results are visible in the muscles and
skin). One can't help saying that America's good social ethics, habits
of cleanliness, urban construction, and environmental preservation all
stem from the deeper levels of her culture.

After the conclusion of the International Yi Studies Conference in
Seattle, Muga's and my relationship continued to strengthen, and our
interest in cooperation continued to increase. At the end of 1994, we
made a preliminary decision on two plans for cooperation. One was to
conduct comprehensive research on the ethnic groups in the southern
part of the Yalong River watershed; the second was to prepare to mount
an exhibit in Seattle of Liangshan Yi clothing, lacquerware, and other
materials. The first project never got funded; the second, through Muga's
efforts, came to realization.

16

SEATTLE FIRST FREE METHODIST CHURCH, 1996–97

BAMO AYI

"**N**ow we're going to Queen Anne, to see a landlady called Amber. Amber is a single woman, a member of a Protestant church." It was the third day after my arrival in Seattle. Professor Harrell was explaining things to me while driving the van he had purchased especially to take his Chinese friends around. We were looking at rooms for rent.

In September 1996, through Professor Harrell's nomination, I had been fortunate to receive support from the Committee on Scholarly Communication with the People's Republic of China and the China Studies Program of the University of Washington to come to the anthropology department at the University, then chaired by Professor Harrell, as a visiting scholar for one year. Even though my primary motive for coming to America was to conduct research with Professor Harrell on bilingual education and Nuosu-language textbooks used in Liangshan Prefecture in Sichuan and to audit Chinese culture and comparative religion classes at the UW, part of my goal was to better understand American churches and their members. Of course, the best way to understand religion would be to live in a church member's home. So two months before I came to America, I asked Steve to help me find a landlord who was a church member.

A few days later I moved to Queen Anne and became Amber's tenant. My American home was the attic room of a gray house, a spacious bedroom with an entryway. On the windowsill, a flowering plant whose name I couldn't recall gave off a sweet fragrance. On the wall next to the window hung an old Chinese landscape painting. There was a finely worked paperweight on the desk, whose design resembled an old Chinese "hundred child picture," showing children in Chinese-style silk clothing playing. I felt a ripple of warmth, and also a bit of puzzlement: Where had Amber gotten ahold of these Chinese things? It looked like the landlady had put some real thought toward welcoming her tenant from China.

"Ayi, dinner!" came Amber's voice from the corridor.

"Let's say a prayer," Amber said, after her son Jason and I sat down at the table. Watching Amber beside me out of the corner of my eye, I could see her sitting up straight, both eyes closed, saying grace before the meal. I sat as if fixed in place by the somber atmosphere, and didn't dare move, didn't even dare exhale, but inside I was completely satisfied, inwardly celebrating my choice of landlady and my choice not only to live in one of her rooms and eat the food she cooked but also to become her companion. Even eating had its religious aspect. I perked up my ears and listened to Amber's soft but clear recitation. She was thanking God, thanking God for bringing Ayi into her life, thanking God for the abundant food.

I peeked at Jason across the table; he appeared wooden, unmoving. I guessed that he might be saying a silent prayer. There are many kinds of prayers, some spoken and some silent. On my first day in Amber's house, I had already begun my American fieldwork.

Amber was fifty-three years old, and had been divorced from her husband for five years. She had a pair of children. Her son Jason was thirty-three, unmarried, and worked in an old car restoration shop; he paid monthly rent just like me. Her daughter Gwendolyn, not yet thirty, was a construction worker and a single mother; she lived with her twelve-year-old daughter Katrina in a rented house. Amber worked two jobs: She cooked and found shelter for the homeless at Operation Night-watch, and cooked lunch in a public elementary school cafeteria. Her earnings from the two jobs were still not sufficient for her, and rent was undoubtedly an important part of her monthly income. I hadn't been living at Amber's very long when her old friend Cheryl also moved in and became another paying tenant.

Before I had moved into Amber's house, Steve had spoken to her about his hope that she would help me to learn about religion, but wouldn't try to get me to join her church; he had told her that my interest was strictly in research. Steve had shown considerable foresight in announcing this publicly and bringing everyone into agreement at the beginning. Amber had already consulted with her pastor, Mark, about letting a non-believing Chinese scholar participate in church activities and do research, but I didn't learn that until later. I had never imagined that Amber would be so earnest about my research, and that a church member could have such self-discipline as to ask for such permission.

On the first Sunday, I impatiently asked if I could go to church with Amber. Her church was called the Seattle First Free Methodist Church (FFMC). The church was at the foot of Queen Anne Hill, one street away from and facing Seattle Pacific University (SPU), a church-supported college, and many of the FFMC members came from the faculty, students, and staff of the University, so that the relationship between the University and the church was particularly close.

From where we lived, it was only five minutes by car, along steep streets, to the church. First we attended Sunday school in the SPU music department auditorium. We went to the old folks' class, called the Home-builder Class. As we entered, the chair of the meeting was leading everyone in a prayer. After that, he asked if there were any announcements. Amber pulled me to my feet and introduced her new tenant, making sure to announce that I was interested in religion and was conducting fieldwork, and wittily pointing out to group, "We are her field."

The speaker that day was Eugene Lemicio, a professor of religious studies at SPU, who gave a lecture entitled "The nature and characteristics of the early church," one of a series of lectures on church history. What was surprising to me was that he had to say a prayer before the talk. He asked God to help everyone to understand the content of the talk, to help everyone to grow in their spiritual life. How could God help people understand a lecture? I, who had spent half a lifetime as a teacher and student, couldn't make any sense of it at all.

Coming out of the auditorium, I went with the flow of people into the church. The worship program began with beautiful music. There is a proverb that says "Those who know observe how something is done; those who don't know observe the fun." In the beginning, because of the language and cultural barriers, I was honestly just observing the fun. After the hour-long worship service, I was most interested in two things: the music and the offering. At least half of the service was conducted against the background of beautiful music and the singing of hymns. If someone like me with poor English rushed in and didn't think for a minute, she would certainly think she was in a concert. With music played that well, I thought, people might come to the church service just to hear the music. Later on, I learned that the First Free Methodist Church of Seattle was known up and down the West Coast for its music—because they were seriously interested in the musical education of their members, and because of the help of the excellent music department at SPU. Amber was extremely proud of her church choir.

The other thing that had attracted my attention during the service had been the passing of the bamboo offering basket. Because it was my first time attending church, I kept my eyes wide open and my ears alert, fearing that I might miss something or do something wrong. When I discovered that people were passing a little bamboo basket and putting envelopes or cash into it, I suddenly realized that it was the offering, and nervously reached for my purse. At that point Amber had softly said to me, "No, you're not a church member; you don't have to give money." I had known that a church's existence depended on its members' contributions, but I hadn't known that they were collected in that way. In Chinese Buddhist or Daoist temples, the contribution box is fixed in one place, and people decide for themselves whether or not to contribute. But at Amber's church, the collection is conducted in public, the basket passes through everybody's hands, and it seems as if it would be very hard to pass it on without adding a little bit.

The first few times I went to church, the offering basket troubled me. Making an offering wouldn't do, because I wasn't a church member, and not making an offering wouldn't do either, because I came to church almost every Sunday, and I benefited from the service of the church, in both senses of the word. Every time the basket came around,

I felt nervous. After about two months, however, I decided that I would put in a few dollars every time the basket came by, since I had come to like the church, the service, the music, and the sermons, as well as the new friends I had made there. I not only thought that I ought to make offerings, I wanted to make offerings. When Amber saw me putting bills into the offering basket, I could tell from her pleased expression that she was thinking that I was beginning to accept her God. Amber never tried to persuade me to join the church, even though I had the feeling that she was trying to covertly. I never dared to ask Amber about the offerings or the way they were used; I didn't want her to think that I was investigating church secrets.

On Sunday, January 19, 1997, the topic of the sermon was "money." Pastor Mark and two other members conducted a dialogue that was almost a skit on the Protestant Church's ideas about money. The Order of Worship announced the financial figures for the church for the preceding year, and the projected budget for the following year. Every member was advised to go home and make his or her own budget and to plan the use of income wisely, and was urged to make offerings to God and the church.

When we got back from church, Amber curled up on the couch and figured her budget according to the church's teachings. In a half year of contact, Amber had seldom avoided any subject with me. Her earnings from Operation Nightwatch, the school cafeteria, and the three rented rooms added up to $28,000. Amber planned to give $280 per month ($70 per week) to Methodist missionary activities in South Africa and to Operation Nightwatch, and $20 per month to a girl in South Africa whose education she was sponsoring. Amber explained that when one wrote a check to the church, one had only to indicate a program, and the church would put the money into the budget for that program, according to the member's wishes. Out of curiosity, I asked Amber if the church leaders might use the money for private purposes or waste it. Amber said, "On this point, you can rest assured." She used Pastor Mark as an example. Pastor Mark kept only a portion of the salary the church paid him to live on, and returned the rest to the church. He lived in a small house and drove a small car. He was trustworthy, and intelligent and wise, and capable of spending money where it ought to be

16.1 Ayi with Bible teachers Hugh and Frid Nutley (left), English teachers Ken and Bonnie Peterson (right), and international students, Seattle First Free Methodist Church, 1996.

spent. I always thought of tithes as taxes, but Amber held to the idea that offerings were completely voluntary. Later, her son Jason said that, on the contrary, a tithe of 10 percent was the unwritten rule of every church; that was one reason he did not believe or to go to church.

In addition to attending Sunday school and church services, I also went to an English class and a Bible class for international students held by the church. We had classes every Friday evening from 7:00 to 9:00 p.m.; we studied English the first hour, and the Bible the second hour. Ken and Bonnie, the English teachers, taught English at several colleges in Tianjin and Beijing, and could speak a little Chinese (fig. 16.1). (When they later took positions teaching English at a college in Xuzhou in 1998–99, I entertained them in Beijing.) The teachers of the Bible class were called Hugh and Frid. Hugh was very conscientious in his teaching. In order to get us to understand the relationship between God and humans, he used the analogy of a father and his children, which I thought was very interesting. If the children were obedient, it was a reward for the father; if they were rebellious, it was a reprimand and a punishment for the father. When I told Amber that I thought that Hugh's Christianity had an obvious tendency toward paterfamilias, she said that Hugh would certainly talk about God's forgiveness and mercy. One time, Hugh asked everybody in the class, "If you unexpectedly received a million dollars, how would you spend it?" The students' answers were all over the place: some would buy a big house, some would travel around the world, some would contribute it all to the church. At the time, I thought that Hugh would certainly have a lofty, inspiring answer to his question; when I heard him say that he would give the money to his grandson to go to the best university, I was at first disappointed, and then I felt that he was honest and lovable. Through this experience, I discovered that I myself had unknowingly begun to conform to the Christian mold—in fact, church members lived in the real world, and there were all different kinds of them.

In China, when I had gone to observe a Buddhist or Daoist temple, I had imitated others and clasped my hands and closed my eyes to pray for something I wanted, but I had never believed it, and didn't count it as real prayer. I had never imagined that a preacher in an American church would pray for me, with the entire congregation as witnesses, all helping with the prayer. It happened on Sunday, February 2, 1997. A few days earlier, I had gotten a phone call saying that my daughter had gone into the hospital and was about to have surgery; since then, I had been constantly disturbed and uneasy. During the service that Sunday, Amber passed me a note: "Would you mind putting Asa's hospital stay into the program for prayers today?" According to the order of worship, at a time near the final benediction, the minister would lead the congregation in praying for a few people who had special needs. Perhaps because I didn't want to refuse Amber's good intentions, or because I wanted to have the experience myself, or because I really hoped the prayer would have an effect, I nodded to Amber. At prayer time, Amber and I walked to the front of the church and knelt together with seven or eight others who had requested prayers on a bench for that purpose next to the altar. When it was my turn, I told the assistant pastor, Bonnie, simply, "My daughter's name is Asa; she is six years old; she has already gone into the hospital, and is about to be operated on." "Ayi's daughter and husband are in Beijing," Amber added. The newly hired assistant minister, David, put his hands on my shoulders, and Bonnie put her hands on my head and led everyone in a prayer for Asa, asking God to protect Asa's safety during the surgery and to give her a quick recovery. From behind me came a chorus of believers' prayers. I was deeply moved, and my eyes filled with tears. The prayers expressed good wishes, and I so hoped that those good wishes would become reality. After the service was over, believers whom I knew and some whom I didn't know surrounded me and comforted me, one after another, saying that they would continue to pray for Asa. Hugh and Frid, and Bonnie and Ken telephoned to ask how Asa was doing, and Bonnie put Asa's name on her list of people to pray for.

Of all of the activities I took part in at the First Free Methodist Church, the most casual, the most unstructured, the most fun was the women's group. The group's meetings took place every Thursday evening at the house of the organizer, Soph. There were eight or nine women at the most, and sometimes only four or five. The main topics in the discussions were children, husbands, and friends; books, movies, clothes and cooking were also discussed. The activities ranged from telling stories or jokes to doing handicrafts to exchanging presents to having birthday parties. When we got together, we shared joys and happiness and also troubles and sadness. I remember one woman, Gene, talking about her eldest son's return from the Vietnam War; he was mired in self-deprecation, self-accusation, and self-hate. Relatives didn't dare mention the war in his presence, but recently her son had told her that during the war, he had killed unarmed peasants while they were working in the fields. Gene was very worried and sad about her son's mental state. Upon hearing Gene's story, Becky, a nurse who worked in a hospital, said that she wanted to take Gene's son to a specialized psychiatric clinic at the University of Washington hospital to have him looked at. Soph suggested that Gene should encourage her son to take part in church activities, and thus help him to solve his problems through faith.

One thing that surprised me about the group was that these American women were extremely interested in cultures that they knew nothing about; as soon as I joined the group, China and the Yi became frequent topics of conversation. One time, when I was talking about the traditional Yi ways of dealing with those who broke clan rules, one woman, Cindy, simply couldn't understand why Yi society didn't have forgiveness or tolerance. I told her that if Yi society was forgiving and tolerant, the society would be shaken, it would fall apart. Cindy's culture shock was a result of using Christian ideas to look at the rest of the world.

At the farewell party that the group organized for me before I went back to China, Soph spoke, saying that my stay had been a new experience for the group, not only because I had shared the joy of stories about China and about the Yi, thereby ridding the group of many misconceptions and adding to their knowledge, but also because of the time I led the group on an adventure to a black church. "Adventure" was her word. It happened like this: I once suggested to Soph and Amber that they should organize a trip to a prayer meeting for the recovery of drug addicts at a black church. Even though Soph and Amber were enlightened believers, organizing group members to go to another church, particularly a black church, was something they had never done before. I thought I would just try, and didn't really expect we would do it, but I soon received a notice that they had decided to do it as a group activity.

On March 20, 1997, group leader Soph took Amber, Cindy, Cheryl, and me—five of us in all—to the Mt. Zion Baptist Church. As soon as I walked into the black church, I felt a new and unfamiliar feeling. I felt quite excited, and leapt to the front of the group, all the way to the second row (the first row being occupied by seven or eight young black people, the recovering addicts who were being prayed for) because I wanted to get the best seat so I could observe better. I pulled Soph over to the front without saying anything. The prayer meeting began; that day's preacher was a famous black author and missionary, the Reverend Dr. Arlene Churn. Her preaching was very lively; in contrast to Pastor Mark, with his set delivery and relatively calm voice, she waved her arms and strode about the podium, sometimes with her eyes closed, beseeching the Lord, sometimes looking heavenward, thanking Jesus. The believers in the audience responded excitedly, calling out "Yes!" "Right!" and "Amen!" A large number of people sang the hymns (there were probably seventy or eighty people in the choir), accompanied only by a few simple percussion and electronic instruments. In addition to having a strong rock-and-roll flavor, the hymn singing there also had an African rhythm to it. The black congregation all seemed to be unself-consciously joining in the music, clapping, adding extra parts, joining in with the choir. In the choir loft, in the pulpit, and in the audience, the entire church was rocking and soaring with the music, and the music and the singing were extraordinarily contagious. When the prayer meeting was over, the tearful youngsters in the first row came back and greeted and shook hands with those of us sitting in the second.

In the car on the way home, I discovered that everyone was deep in thought. Cindy, quite moved, said "That prayer meeting was great; I wish I were a black person—if I were, I would definitely belong to that church." I pursued her thought. "Why do you have to be black to go there; we went, didn't we?" Cindy said, "But I still felt unnatural." Soph complained about my dragging everyone to the front, saying, "You just about took us to the front row." They had been meaning to sit at the very back. Soph said that the thing that had scared her the most was when the young black people in the front row had turned around and faced us four white ladies (leaving me out) and made us particularly uncomfortable with ourselves. "But I didn't think about color," I said. "It would be great if we could get that black Ph.D. preacher to come to 'our' church sometime." Amber immediately replied, "Even though Dr. Churn's preaching really moved people, and her sermon was rich in emotion, it lacked depth. Faith is the head plus the heart. Otherwise, once the emotion is gone, the faith would just wither. Today the recovering addicts were overcome with tears, but if they don't have rational belief to hold on to, just wait and see, their recovery will be temporary." Cheryl didn't agree; she said that she really liked that kind of preaching, and the lively and warm atmosphere of the black people's prayer meeting. Some sermons needed to be simple, others incisive; some needed to be lively, others profound; it depended on the audience; Mark's sermons were suited to the believers of the First Free Methodist Church, because most of them were intellectuals; if he took his sermons to that black church, they wouldn't necessarily be welcomed.

I remember the first time I called the church "our church." When I spoke to Steve and to friends at the university, I would call it "my land-lady Amber's church." After half a year, at the time of our "adventure" to the black church, I blurted out "our church," indicating my change in identity; it had been an unconscious process. From that time on, I began to use "our church" with Amber and friends from the church, but as a matter of participating in the church's activities, having friends in the church, and liking the preaching and the music. It had nothing to do with believing in Jesus or God. "If the speaker doesn't mean it, then it's nonsense to the listener." On the twenty-third of March, Cheryl and I were chatting. "I was really happy when I heard you say 'our church,'" she told me. "Are you planning to become a church member before you go back to China?" I curtly replied, "No, I don't plan on joining the church." She said, "This is a hope of mine, that you will be able to join the church before you leave America." I was quiet for a minute, pondering how I could explain myself to Cheryl, but I quickly gave up the effort. I knew that she wanted to "save" me, and I had already answered her. Cheryl was sad, and went to the living room to speak with Amber.

Upstairs by myself, I guessed that they were discussing whether or not I would become a believer. This made me somewhat confused. Cheryl knew my attitude toward joining the church. Even though she had never discussed it with me directly, she had frequently broached the subject indirectly. One time, during a deep discussion about salvation, the hereafter, and eternal life, she talked about faith being the core question, and asked me, "Do you believe in Jesus? Do you believe in God?" I changed the direction of the conversation, and said instead, "In our homeland, Yi people worship ancestors, and believe in ghosts and spirits; they have never heard that there's a God, or of Jesus, so they can't even talk about believing or not believing—will they ever be able to be saved? Will they ever be able to go to Heaven?" Without pausing at all, Cheryl answered, "If you don't believe in God and don't believe in Jesus, then of course you can't be saved." "Your God is unfair," I replied. "Not knowing is not a sin." This seemed to stump her. Several days later, Cheryl came upstairs specifically to tell me, "If God's gospel has never been transmitted to your homeland, God couldn't, just because of that, not care about your Yi people; even though they worship idols and believe in many gods, they can still get God's forgiveness and salvation, and after they die, they can go to heaven and be together with God and have eternal life. But those who heard God's gospel and refused his message would forever be unable to enter heaven

and have eternal life." Right then, I understood the cleverness and sharp-
ness of Cheryl's discourse.

Shortly after Cheryl had moved to Queen Anne, she took the church's
membership class. I wanted to go with her, but she said that it was impossible; the membership class was for those who were already believers
and had decided to become church members. But I never gave up. The
membership class did not run on a regular schedule; whenever there
were people who wanted to join, a class could be organized. On the third
of March, 1997, the Order of Worship gave notice that the church was
about to run another membership class. The theme of the training was
"How to be a member of the Free Methodist Church and a Christian."
I immediately told Amber that the membership training class was very
important for understanding the church, and that I would really like to
audit it. When the service was over, Amber said that she would ask Mark
whether he would allow me to join in. She was probably afraid that if
I had gone directly to ask Mark publicly, it would have put him in a
difficult position. Not five minutes later, Amber came back all sunny
and told me that Mark had agreed. I jumped up happily, thanking Amber
and sighing to her that Mark really was an open-minded pastor.

Amber said that she was thinking of reviewing her religious knowledge, so we went to the class together. It began with self-introductions.
From these, I learned that Mark's parents had both been missionaries,
and that in 1940 they had been ready to go to China to proselytize, but
that it had not happened, and they had ended up going to India. Mark
had been born in India, and was baptized into the Baptist Church at
the age of twelve. In India he had attended a boarding school run by
British people, but had returned to America for higher education. He
had joined the Methodist Church in 1982. Mark's class was divided into
two time periods, in which he discussed four main subjects: the conditions for being a Christian, the history of the Methodist Church, the
basic beliefs of the Methodist Church, and the structure and function
of the church. To accompany his explanations, Mark passed out materials. The one I liked best was "Our Family Tree," a historical record of
the Methodist Church, which used an anthropological genealogy chart
to trace the important people and events of that church, from its found-
ing by John Wesley (1703–1791) up through 1977.

A lot of the things that Mark explained were things that I would not have been able to learn in my year of observation and experience. For example, in his talks, Mark compared the Protestant Church (of which the Methodists are a denomination) with the Catholic Church, arguing with the Catholic doctrine of placing the pope's authority on par with that of the Bible, and disapproving of the Catholic Church's determination of the special powers and roles of priests. I'm afraid that the detail and strength of his impressions of the factional struggles within Christianity were difficult for an outsider to understand. I asked Mark about a few of these questions, such as the difference between Baptists and Methodists. His answer was that the Baptists place more emphasis on emotion and faith, while the Methodists place more emphasis on rationality and wisdom. I regret that Mark was so busy with his church affairs, and that I didn't have more time to discuss religion with him. But, in all honesty, no matter how much Amber and Soph said he was fair-minded and egalitarian, not stern and distant like some ministers, and however much he encouraged me to speak with him, deep down I was always a little bit afraid of him.

I'm sure that Amber joined the membership class to review her knowledge of the church, and not just to accompany me. Amber is a believer who never gives up her religious quest. Her grandfather was a missionary, and her father was a professor of economics at Seattle Pacific University and a devout believer. According to Amber, they were "God's men." But Amber had been a religious rebel in her youth; she had investigated Buddhism from Asia and the Mormon Church from her native America. After flitting about for over ten years, in 1985 she returned to her original church, the First Free Methodist Church. Amber told me that even though she had come full circle, and had established her belief in Jesus and in God, she still had questions, and she was still looking for answers; spiritual growth was a lifelong project. Daily morning prayer was something that she would not be budged from. Reading the Bible, praying, reading religious books, keeping personal notes—Amber was diligent and determined. I once kidded her, "Amber, if you were writing a doctoral dissertation, it would have come out a long time ago." Actually, when talking with her, I felt that she was not a blind believer; she had done rigorous research.

I remember attending a dinner at the Seventh-day Adventist Church one Saturday. I was a little bit bothered by the fact that the Adventists paid so much attention to the diet and were so picky about nutrition, and when I returned, I discussed it with Amber. This began one of Amber's "comparative religion" sessions. According to Amber the Seventh-day Adventist Church placed its focus on bodily nourishment and thus lost sight of something more important: the growth and elevation of the spirit. The Baptist Church placed its focus on the rite of baptism, but in reality baptism is only a form, and to place too much emphasis on form was not the same as having firm belief in and sincere loyalty to God. Catholics were always going to worship the Blessed Mother, and how could there be any good in approaching God and Jesus through the Blessed Mother? God had a calling for everybody. It was impossible that Mary was different from everyone else just because she had given birth to Jesus. Amber felt that her own church could understand God from all angles, and didn't "select the sesame seed and lose the watermelon." This made her feel very fortunate.

After I had lived with Amber for two or three months, I gradually realized that, except when she invited guests to a formal dinner on Sunday, she didn't pray to thank God for food. During the first few months of my stay she had prayed—perhaps to proclaim that she was a believer or to let the woman who had come to research religion feel what it was like—but after we began to understand each other, saying grace had become unimportant. She didn't need to keep up appearances. After I realized that, I gradually left off basing my research on such external manifestations as saying grace before meals.

In comparison to Amber, Cheryl was much more open to other religions. She accompanied me to Greek and Finnish churches, a mosque, and a Tibetan Buddhist temple. I remember that Greek Orthodox church, whose interior was filled with icons of Jesus, Mary, and the saints. Cheryl commented that Christians are always criticizing other religions' worship of idols, but that Christians also have idols. I could see that she was speaking critically, but her loyalty was still clear. Unlike Amber, Cheryl identified with Christianity in general, but was also curious about other religions.

Our visit to the mosque was not terribly happy for Cheryl. At breakfast on Saturday, July 19, I told Cheryl that I would like to see a mosque. Cheryl suggested that we call first. She said that Islamic mosques didn't welcome visitors as Christian churches did, which allowed you to just go in. So I called the Islamic mosque. I got an answering machine. Luckily, I called a second number, the Evergreen Islamic Institute. They told me that I was welcome to visit at 2:00 p.m. I looked up the address, and it was far away. Cheryl volunteered to drive me, and told me to put on something long-sleeved, since women were not allowed to go into the mosque uncovered.

At 1:50 p.m., Cheryl and I drove up in front of a simple little mosque, a gray building with a basketball court outside the front door. We were received by a middle-aged man named Khalid Ridha, who spoke with us on a bench outside the mosque. Khalid Ridha was very articulate; he introduced himself as a Kurd who had emigrated from Kurdistan to America seventeen years earlier. I asked him if he was used to America, and if he felt that there was religious freedom here. He said that America was a good place to live, and that although the people were prejudiced against Islam as a religion (for example, it was difficult for a woman wearing a headscarf to find a job), compared to where he had come from, it was much freer. He drew the analogy that American religious freedom was sweet water, but that the water still had a bitter taste. He said that there are 1.2 billion Muslims in the world, 6 million of them in America. But he felt the figure was not accurate, because American society was prejudiced against Muslims, so that many believers did not publicly admit their religion. Because Muslims had a high fertility rate and a lot of children, the number of believers was rising rapidly; he guessed that there were probably 10 million Muslims in the United States. In the Seattle area, there were seven mosques and 27,000 believers, including not only Middle Easterners but also quite a few blacks and a few American whites. What he was saying was that Muslims are a diverse community.

I asked about seeing the mosque. As we were walking toward the mosque, I took out my camera, thinking to ask Cheryl to take a picture of me and Khalid Ridha with the mosque as background. He cleverly deflected my interest, pointing to a one-story building next to the basketball court and saying that that was their daycare. Khalid Ridha led a group of cute four- and five-year-old children from the building; most

16.2 Bamo Ayi and preschool girls, Evergreen Islamic Institute, Seattle, 1997.

of the girls were wearing headscarves (fig. 16.2). As they were lining up for a picture, a little girl turned around and asked innocently, "Why do you want to have your picture taken with us?" I said, "Because you are so pretty and so cute."

Cheryl and I did as Khalid Ridha did, and took off our shoes when we entered the mosque. He said that a mosque is a sacred place, and one cannot bring in the dirt from outside; it appeared that taking off one's shoes was more than good hygiene. The inside of the mosque was divided by a wooden door, separating the men's and women's worshipping places. Khalid Ridha told us that that was a tradition, a custom, and not, as people thought, a prejudice against women. He said that the mosque had formerly been a church; it had been bought by the Islamic congregation because it faced precisely toward Mecca. I picked up a Qur'an from a rack next to me, and noticed that it had Arabic and English on facing pages. I asked Khalid Ridha what language they used in their prayer services. He said that they used only Arabic for prayers, but that the sermons were in English. I'm pretty sure that Khalid Ridha did not know that Cheryl was a Christian; if he had, he may not have made the following comparison between Islam and Christianity:

> The Bible was not put together until 300 years after Jesus died. How many of the apostles' recollections and memories were accurate? How much of it really came from Jesus' sayings? How much of it really accords with God's will? It is difficult to say. Also, with so many editions of the Bible, which ones are real? But our Qur'an only has one edition, the word of God as recorded by Muhammad, so it is the most reliable. All Muslims in the world read out of one Qur'an.

I looked at Cheryl, who was standing there silently. I thought, luckily it's Cheryl who came with me today, and not Amber, or else there would definitely be a shouting match. Khalid Ridha continued, comparing Jesus and Muhammad. I wanted to hear it. He said:

> We recognize Jesus, but not as the Son of God, like the Christians do; he was the son of people, the son of Mary; he was nothing but a prophet. Islam believes in only one God, one true spirit, and even though Muhammad was the greatest of the prophets, he was only a prophet. Christians, who believe in Jesus in addition to God, are actually polytheists.

After listening this far, I felt that what he was saying must have been trying Cheryl's patience, so I quickly told Khalid Ridha that we had to leave, and thanked him for his hospitality and his explanations.

But Khalid Ridha was deep in his discourse, and as we walked out of the mosque, he accompanied us to our car, continuing, "The contributions of Muslims to American society are greater than Americans can conceive—particularly in the area of social ethics, in the area of rescuing people from lives of crime, we have done a lot of work." I immediately saw a point that I could make, and said that Cheryl and I were also helping the homeless; in fact, we needed to leave right then to go downtown to Operation Nightwatch, since it was already time to cook soup. "But you need to be careful. . . . there are drugs and alcohol there; it's very dangerous," he said with concern, closing the conversation. Cheryl started the car, I said "good-bye" and "thank you" one more time,

16.3 Cheryl Lee, Bamo Ayi, and Amber Joy at Operation Night-watch, Seattle, 1997.

and we drove off (fig. 16.3). Cheryl drove without saying anything. I felt a little sorry to have put her through a difficult hour and a half. I decided not to have her go with me to any more mosques.

The next afternoon, Jamil from the Islamic mosque returned my call, and arranged to meet me on Tuesday. I noticed that Islamic believers really weren't as difficult to approach as Cheryl had thought; as soon as we made contact, we had an appointment. On Tuesday afternoon I took the bus to the mosque and waited by the front door for a half hour without seeing anyone. Then an Arabic-looking man walked by, and I approached him for help. He said there was someone named Jamil, and asked me to come to his house to wait; his house was right next door. His wife, Monica, enthusiastically poured tea, and we easily struck up a conversation. Monica had eight children, the oldest was twenty-one, and the youngest, four; they had come to Seattle five years earlier because of her husband's business. In heavily South-Asian-accented English she told me that because there were so many children in the family, she needed to do housework and watch the children, so she had not learned English well. But in order to get American citizenship, she had to study English so that she could take the naturalization test. Her brother was married recently, but she hadn't been able to attend; without U.S. citizenship, she might have had trouble coming back. She brought out the book that she was studying for me to look at: *Voices of Freedom: English and Civics for the U.S. Citizenship Exam.* There was a picture of the Statue of Liberty on the cover, and the contents included U.S. maps, U.S. geography, states and capitals, religion, the flag, government organizations, Congress, the president, the Supreme Court, and so on. She said that she went to citizenship class twice every week; the students in the class came from all over the world, including some from China.

After a little while, three of her daughters and two of her sons came home; the daughters were all wearing scarves. The beautiful, twenty-one-year-old oldest daughter was a first-year student at a community college; she was studying computers. She said that she had begun to like America, because, in comparison with women in Pakistan, the women there had a much easier life, without such strict restrictions. With regard to fertility, she told us that her mother was one of eight children, and her father one of eleven; her mother had given birth to ten, of whom two had died and eight were left. She explained that abortion was strictly forbidden in Pakistan, so women gave birth to children until they couldn't give birth anymore; their burden was very heavy. The reasons were, first, that Allah did not allow the murder of living things, and a fetus was a living thing, and, second, that Pakistan had been fighting wars since the 1940s, and had lost a lot of people, so they needed to increase their population. Her eight-year-old little brother told me that he didn't like America, and when I asked him why, he said he just didn't like it. This little boy had come to America when he was only three, and should not have had any memory of Pakistan, I thought. I told Monica that I couldn't wait for Jamil to arrive, but that I would be back for prayers on Friday. She warned me that I couldn't go in by the main door, but needed to use the side door to go upstairs to the women's worship hall.

On Friday afternoon, I put on a scarf that I had borrowed from Amber and went to the mosque; using the side door, I went upstairs to the women's worship hall, which was full of women and children. They were mostly Arabs, with a few blacks and whites. I had arrived half an hour late, and the prayers had already started. I sat in the front row, hoping to be able to see what was going on in the big room below. Through the square-patterned grate, I noticed that I could see only the clergy who were leading the service; the other men were not in my field of view, but I could hear the resonant voices of the worshippers. The mullah leading the service was wearing a turban, and looked a little bit like Yasir Arafat. I performed the complicated bodily motions of praying according to what the women beside me were doing; when I first started, I didn't have the order right, and was a bit clumsy of hand and foot. There was a cacophony upstairs, a mixture of prayers, crying, and the admonitions of mothers. But I could distinguish that the language being used for prayers below was Arabic, and that the English translation was given section by section, unlike the sentence-by-sentence translation given at the Sakya Tibetan Monastery in Seattle. The translator was an Arab with a heavy accent. I could not hear clearly or understand. The service at the Islamic mosque, like that at the Tibetan monastery, was very simple— nothing more than prostrations, prayers, and a sermon.

When the service was over, I met Jamil, wearing a white cap and robe, and his American wife, wearing a scarf. Jamil was about sixty, and very enthusiastic. As soon as he saw me, he told me that he had been to China, and that the white cap he was wearing had been given to him by a Chinese Muslim. I asked him if he were the imam, and he said that I could call him that. Anyone who was knowledgeable and could lead prayers could be an imam. He explained that a mosque of that size had only one full-time caretaker; everyone else was a volunteer. Jamil proudly told me that the mosque was Seattle's largest, built in 1981. He said that Seattle had eight mosques (which didn't agree with Khalid Ridha), of which two were converted churches and six had been built as mosques. There were believers of every race, not just Arab, because Allah was the God of all races, all over the world. With regard to the language used for the prayers, Jamil said that it was required to use Arabic to read the Qur'an, because it was originally written in Arabic, and so one could not use any other language in its place. But in exegesis, one could use an English translation. The mosque was a Sunni mosque. Jamil said that the Qur'an was one book, and that Muslims were one family. I asked him how many people had been at prayers that day, and he said that it was difficult to count, but that he guessed there had been more than 600. Jamil had come to the United States in 1947, and before retiring had been an engineer at Boeing; he had six children. He had prepared for me two books that he had written: one was on the Hajj, or Pilgrimage to Mecca. It was a guide to the route of the pilgrimage, the

16.4 Bamo Ayi with Imam Jamil and his wife, Islamic Mosque, Seattle, 1997.

process, the clothing, the restrictions, the places, and so on. The other book was entitled *Islam: The Perfect Way of Life*. Before saying good-bye, I had my picture taken next to the mosque with Jamil and his wife. In the heat of summer, his wife and I were both wearing scarves (fig. 16.4).

At the end of 1996, Amber and Gwendolyn had hatched a plan to buy a house together, and, after many prayer sessions and a half-year of busyness, on May 1, 1997, everybody finally moved to Shoreline, a sub-urb of Seattle. The new home was a long way from the university, and I had to change buses twice; it took three hours for a round-trip. But I had become fond of Amber, and I didn't want to look for another land-lady. I also still needed to go to church and understand religion. Cheryl and Jason also moved with us, but this time Jason became a tenant of his sister Gwendolyn downstairs. Catty-corner from the house was a lit-tle gray church, with a sign saying that it was the Seattle Christian Assem-bly. When I went past, I saw a lot of Chinese-speaking people going in and out, which tempted me to do something I had long wanted to do— visit a Chinese people's church. Because I was away on two trips, it wasn't until Sunday, July 7, that I got Amber to go to church there with me.

The church was small, but it was packed with people. A tall, middle-aged woman, seeing that we were new faces, helped us find two places in the crowd. I thought that we had been lucky to come during communion, but after I had gone a few times, I discovered that the church emphasized communion, which was the first event in the service each Sunday. The entire service was focused on Jesus—thanking Jesus for washing away the sins of humanity with his own blood, thanking Jesus for interceding between people and God. The service was conducted in Standard Chinese, with the sermon being translated into English. There was no choir, only a piano accompanist and someone at the side leading the singing.

Because it was just after Independence Day, the title of the sermon was "Freedom and God." It began with the story of Grandfather Zeng, a member who had just passed his citizenship test at the age of ninety-one, after many years of effort. The minister said,

> America is a free country, and God has opened the door of saving grace, allowing everyone to have the good fortune of becoming Americans. But this free country is full of materialism, sex, violence, and sin. If we use our freedom carelessly, we will encounter danger and be damaged, even to the point that we may exterminate ourselves. If we don't have God's love, if we leave God's embrace, the free country may become the most unfree of places. Only if you believe in God and allow God to be your protector can you achieve true freedom, only the Gospel is an eternally free country.

The English translation of the service was very well done. Amber praised the sermon, saying that the minister was able to take advantage of the timing of Independence Day, cleverly moving from Grandpa Zeng's citizenship to the main topic of the sermon; he was undoubtedly an experienced minister who had graduated from seminary. Actually, the minister, whose name was Zeng Jincai, had gotten a computer degree and had worked at a very influential computer company in Washington State. Later on, following God's call, he had given up his high-salaried position to become an impoverished minister. Pastor Zeng's wife was called Yingmei; it was she who had shown us to our seats. Yingmei had been a dominating basketball player, a famous member of the national team in Taiwan. She was now retired, taking care of her husband and children, and helping him run the church. I was invited to their house for dinner. I didn't think that the athlete Yingmei would cook an excellent meal; but it was the most elaborate and tasty Chinese dinner I had eaten since I arrived in America.

The year passed quickly, and it was time to go home. I went to church to say good-bye to Mark, and to thank him for letting me participate in church activities—particularly his church membership class—and to thank him and his parishioners for a year of caring. Mark said, "It seems like you are already a member of our church; when you leave, we will miss you." After Amber and I had said all our good-byes in the church offices and were ready to get in the car, Mark hurried out of the church with a book in his hand. He told me that it was a book he had just written, called *Spirituality in a Mixed-up Age*. It was an advance copy that he had just received; I was the first person to get a copy. On the way home from church, Amber and I went to Pastor Zeng's church to say good-bye to him and Yingmei.

On the morning of September 30, 1997, in the waiting room of Sea-Tac Airport, as I was saying a reluctant good-bye to Steve after the announcement came to board the plane, an out-of-breath Pastor Zeng suddenly appeared in front of us. He handed me several books on Christianity and a couple of presents for my daughter, and said a special prayer for my trip. He prayed to the Lord for my safe journey and to help me to come soon to believe in the Lord. Taking with me Pastor Zeng's blessing and Steve's friendship, I left Seattle and America.

17

COLLECTING MOUNTAIN PATTERNS, 1999

MA LUNZY

The exhibit wasn't conceived overnight. The subject came up in casual conversations on country paths or over meals or tea, after we had spent a long time with Stevan Harrell conducting fieldwork in Nuosu areas in Liangshan, after we had spent a long time creating friendship in the field. The purpose of the exhibit was not only to facilitate continued scholarly exchange but also to contribute to the mutual understanding of folkloric culture. Chinese and American fieldworkers of Liangshan Nuosu culture designed the exhibit together. We went through the process of applying for funding, and collecting clothing, lacquerware, *bimo* implements, and other artifacts to display and deposit permanently in the Burke Museum. A lot of people previously unacquainted with the culture of the Nuosu of Liangshan appreciated its particular aesthetic charm and joined in. The common good fortune of the Burke Museum and the participants was that, in the process of realizing this dream, we could present it as a gift to humanity at the beginning of the twenty-first century.

As soon as we got our $8000 funding in 1998, I began thinking of how best to use the limited funds, even though we did not actually begin the collecting work immediately; the exhibit was always floating around in my consciousness. As the Nuosu say, "If there's not much buckwheat, the pancakes won't be so thick." How would we collect things that were both inexpensive and beautiful? Frankly, at the time, when people were thinking in terms of commodities, with such a small amount of money in hand, we were like a couple of old, weak-winged eagles perched on a rock near a roost, unable to descend or ascend, able only to flip around, eyeing their potential prey: Every object would have to go through mentally and emotionally exhausting consideration before we would be able to have it in hand. That was the first important stage in mounting the exhibit.

Our collecting started in the beginning of May, 1999, when Bamo Qubumo and I arrived at the jutting peaks and crisscrossing river valleys of the concentrated Nuosu area of Meigu. As soon as we got to the county town, we sought out our many relatives and friends to get information, and on the following days went and mingled on the streets with Nuosu people, examining the clothing they were wearing. Whenever we heard of a remote place where there had been comparatively little outside influence on clothing or lifestyles, we trudged and sweated our way there.

Meigu has over 160,000 people, 98 percent of whom are Nuosu who speak the Yynuo dialect. In terms of language, customs, and clothing, traditional Nuosu culture is comparatively well preserved there, but my impressions were completely different from those I had gotten ten years earlier, when I had first collected there for the Liangshan Museum of Yi Slave Society. At that time, all of the young ladies wore Nuosu clothing, and all of the young men grew the traditional hair lock and wore various kinds of *vala* (capes). You could count on your fingers the number of people wearing sports jackets or Han-style clothing. It was very difficult to buy an object that had been passed down in a family, or to buy a used piece of clothing. It was said that family heirlooms reflected the faces of the ancestors, that clothing that had been worn retained the soul of the wearer, and that to buy the ritual tools or books of a *bimo* would be to ask the tiger to change his colors. The only way to acquire artifacts had been to rely on relatives, and to gradually approach the owner and talk about how important it was to display the piece in a museum; maybe then a few enlightened owners would let you have a piece. The interesting thing was, they would not only not bargain over the price, but would just give it to you.

One wouldn't have thought that ten years later, Nuosu people wearing sport jackets or Han-style clothing would constitute half the crowds on the Meigu streets. Whenever we arrived in a place with the intention of collecting, there would immediately be a big reaction, and everyone would come with big and small bundles of things for us to choose from. And as soon as we had chosen something, the owner would bargain bravely, talking about how generous the Japanese buyers had been, to the point that you didn't know whether to laugh or cry. After ten years of interaction with cultural workers, research teams, and private collectors and connoisseurs, people knew that the older an artifact was, the greater its value. Because of this, when one asked when something had been made, some people would give a very early date. One person who had a very finely worked silver drinking vessel told us that it had been handed down from an ancestor five generations back. When I looked at it carefully, I saw that the artisan had written, in crude Nuosu script, the 1992 date of manufacture; when we jokingly pointed this out, he, embarrassed, flattered our connoisseurship. The *bimo*, who previously were so innocent of market relations as to be able only to chant their texts by the light of pine resin, were now eagerly giving their yellowed, brittle ritual books to people to sell for them. This would have been inconceivable ten years earlier.

But although the "commodity" attitude was very strong, feelings of kinship had not diminished. Going through kin connections enabled us to avoid irresponsible talk and unfair prices. But the thing that gave us headaches was that relatives would turn over the purchasing arrangements entirely to us, so that we had to decide what would be a fair price. We stood between the Burke Museum and the people whose things were being collected, and this required us to set a fair price ceiling. So for many objects, we had to slowly figure out the labor involved and the cost of the raw materials, and carefully consult each other before we named a price. With relatives or close friends, all we needed to do was state a price, and they would say "fine"; but other sellers would not only overstate their own prices, they would remind us that "there are no relatives in business," and lay on us the responsibility for making our relatives suffer. There were times when we stood between the seller and our relatives, or when we stood between our close American friend Muga and our relatives, and we had to speak with indirection. Unavoidably, we often worried afterward whether we had bought too high or too low.

One day in late May, we were bumping along in a belching diesel bus on a dirt road in Puge, accompanied by the now-loud, now-soft groan of the engine and a tape of Nuosu pop music. We were tired, but joking around. We could see Luoji Mountain, inseparable from Nuosu mythology, on the side of the road, even if we could not hear the hoofbeats of Nzymo Gogo's horse or see the smoke beacons of the oppressive Cibu. We saw on the road the brilliant, free-flowing, delicate river of colors on the clothes worn by the young Nuosu women who speak the Suondi dialect. The luxuriant blooms of the buckwheat and rhododendrons were wrapped up in the patterns on the Nuosu women's clothing, like an accumulation and proclamation of the history of the Suondi people. Nuosu culture is not something that survives in a form of the past but something that surrounds and dissolves into the mountain patterns of life today. Even though the descendants of the divine seamstress Sihnishysse can appreciate the speed and cleverness of the modern spinning machine, their left hands still hold the puffy clouds of raw wool, and their right hands the lightly revolving spindle, as they slowly twist together the threads of the past and the present, making the ancient and youthful red wool skirts of the Suondi—a thousand years of red skirts attracting a thousand years of young men's glances. The descendants of the first ancestor, Apu Hmamu, have inherited who-knows-how-many millennia of the felting skills of Ayo Asi, lightly twanging the heirloom felting bow, wearing millennia of fringed capes, and prompting millennia of young women's charm and laughter.

From the bumping bus, we could see that we would need to collect a lot of materials there. We decided not to look for acquaintances to help out but to approach people purely as buyers. On the narrow lane to the hotel, we immediately ran into the county magistrate, whom we knew. In Nuosu culture voluntarily helping out a guest has long been a kind of duty. When he found out why we had come, he called upon Anyi Zzyrnzi, who was familiar with the local situation and who had written several works on local culture, to help us out. Mr. Anyi was unusually intelligent, and perceptive about people's thoughts. He did not intervene in the matter of price but occupied himself exclusively with promoting our collecting project. Going from village to village and house to house, we not only collected many satisfying examples of hand-made men's and women's clothes but did so comparatively inexpensively. When we got back to our hotel, women in groups of three or five offered us all sorts of clothing to choose from. There we were not worried about an insufficient variety or an excessive price but, with all the styles and patterns vying to be the most resplendent, we found it most difficult to choose the best flowers in the garden.

After we were finished in Puge, we proceeded to the Adur district in Butuo County, famous for its celebration of the Fire Festival. Nuosu fashions in this area have been interesting for a long time. Most of the women wore black wool "sun hats" with broad-shouldered capes and pleated skirts. The men wore Western- or Han-style shirts with the "small-legged" pants peculiar to the area. Their particular fashions not only preserved a local flavor but also incorporated cross-ethnic features to create a multi-origin variegation that became a unique local style. Seeing the young women walking single-file on the country roads, each with a red skirt and a yellow oilcloth umbrella, and seeing the young men in their conical straw hats with embroidered shoulder bags and narrow-cuffed pants, one easily understands just why Butuo seems like such a magical place. Feasting one's eyes on the silver jewelry that has captured the imagination of Butuo people, and always seeing a few women on the street wearing a kilogram or two of silver apiece, one begins to understand how determined and extravagant the Nuosu people's pursuit of beauty is. It seems that poor families would have had to spend a good portion of their money in pursuit of beauty, and that women would have to put on a decorative facade of heavy, expensive silver jewelry just to seem normal there.

Bamo Qubumo and I spent a week in that cultural atmosphere, and, after we collected exhibit materials we thought representative of a rich area, we left Butuo. As we sat on the return bus, looking at what we had collected, I wondered if the pieces would be appreciated as much after they had gone through customs as they were here in Butuo. How much were they really worth to the Burke Museum, to Seattle audiences, to us three scholars who had pursued them all over with little compensation, to the Nuosu of Butuo themselves? An answer would require close consideration; better to drop such thoughts, look out the bus window, and proceed on the road toward the Shama District in Jinyang to continue collecting.

Jinyang is called Muhnitenzy in Nuosu; on the road east from Zhaojue County, practically every place name on the way to Jinyang carries a close connection with Nuosu popular mythology. Today on the steep slopes one can no longer see the lush primeval forests described in the Nuosu classics, or hunters with bows and arrows stealing into the mountain forests in pursuit of bears and leopards. But the rhododendrons of June were at the height of their bloom on mountain after mountain, and nature absorbed one's attention. Looking at the ribbons of flowers on both sides of the road, and seeing the loss of protection of the forest canopy, the rhododendrons blooming on the impoverished hillsides seemed less like "directing one's gaze downward as the colors of spring fill the eyes" and more like a forced laughter under the searing solar rays. But so many geographic names that connected with the world of ghosts had rooted themselves in our Nuosu people's memory, that told us not to go there, that shocked us to our bones.

The bus crawled slowly up the mountain, and I looked up and saw Zzehxalomo, the home of the ghost beauty Zyzyhninra. The sight struck a chord in me; when I saw the little streams on Zzehxalomo, I thought of a story I had heard from my elders in my childhood and which is written in so many of the *bimos'* books. The story tells of the silvery-white musk deer that turned into Zyzyhninra—her soft black hair, her slender nose and white teeth, her long graceful neck, her soft white face, her fine and delicate hands. As soon as she united with her husband, Awo Nyiku, she became fierce and hostile and had no feelings for him— with her eyes to the front, looking at the path where she was walking; with her eyes to the back, looking jealously at people; with her mouth to the front, eating rice; with her mouth to the back, eating people; with her hands to the front, burning firewood; with her hands to the back, digging people's hearts. Just as I was thinking of Zyzyhninra and the origin of all Nuosu ghosts, thinking of the sequence of her transformations from silvery white river deer to woman to goat to ghost to origin of all ghosts, we had entered the former territory of the Shama *nzymo*. When I saw the display of clothing and jewelry on the Nuosu women, I returned from my reverie to the business at hand. Looking down from the road winding around the mountaintops, I saw the turbulent Jinsha River. We reason that if the mountains are high and the emperor is far away, the inaccessibility of a place ought to make its people conservative and provincial. But this area also set in motion the recent change in the history of the Nuosu of Liangshan. The Shama and Ali *nzymo* both forced the submission of the Nuosu people there, and the powerful Chinese warlord Long Yun was also born and raised there.

Because the mountains are high and the roads are narrow, because the slopes on both sides of the road are steep, and because there were landslides everywhere, there were very few vehicles on the road. About forty kilometers from Jinyang Town, a boulder had slid down and blocked the road. Two road maintenance workers, after hitting the rock with sledges for a while, had decided that there was no way it could be broken and that they would have to use explosives to blow it apart; That would cause a large part of the mountain to come sliding down, so we would have to wait quite a while. I had worked breaking up rocks in the countryside, and knew something about the grain patterns of rocks, and that even though a rock was big, it could be split rather quickly. I had a lucky feeling, and so I went to take a look. I took up a sledge and began slowly whacking at it, and it worked—within twenty minutes, the bus could drive gently across. Bamo Qubumo happily took several tens of yuan and, according to Nuosu custom, bought some liquor for the people who had helped out. They asked who she was. Jokingly, I offered, "She couldn't say clearly herself. Does the family of your Shama *nzymo* have any forgotten descendants?" They broke out laughing. We said goodbye and proceeded on down the mountain.

After twelve hours on the bus, we arrived at Jinyang Town at 8:00 in the evening. When the cultural elites of Jinyang heard the news that Qubumo and I had arrived, several of them gathered to treat us to dinner. Before we ate, the two of us agreed that we should accept their invitation politely, but then leave and get some rest. But we were inspired by their hospitality, humor, and knowledge. They all seemed to know a lot about Nuosu customs, classical texts, religion, and philosophy. They also discussed early and recent research on Liangshan Nuosu, from head to tail, bringing up many well-known points. They also brought up several sharp points about our published articles, and discussed them with us there. In a place known to outsiders as a poor and backward nook, to run into so many deeply learned literati who could happily talk of ancient and modern times and point accurately to the problems of present-day society was totally unexpected. No wonder that the Nuosu of Jinyang have produced so many famous people. We felt that the people we encountered there were *ndeggu*, wise Nuosu mediators with true knowledge, and that we were partaking of a meal whose main course was cultural discussion. Many of them had participated in exhibits of folk customs, representing Jinyang. One by one they listed the material objects that were representative of the Nuosu of Jinyang. From the second day on, they not only took turns as unpaid guides for us but also entertained us in turn. They were not completely impoverished scholars, but none of them was in easy economic circumstances, and because it was difficult to refuse such heartfelt help, we felt indebted to them in our hearts. Because of their help and support, we completed the whole collecting process in a few days, satisfied with our Shama-style clothing and related articles, all fine goods obtained at fair prices.

That just about finished up the majority of our collecting. After that we went to a few counties to fill in the gaps. Xichang is the capital of Liangshan Prefecture, and Nuosu of all branches have established clothing stores there, but authentic, handmade clothing is relatively scarce. Most of the clothing there conforms to current fashions, and we collected quite a few miscellaneous pieces.

Two months of frantic collecting was over, and we both felt very tired. From the time we started, there was one thing that weighed on us and made us very unhappy: Many of our friends were sure that because we were working with an "old foreign," we must have been getting excellent compensation. We often ran into people who asked us how many American dollars we had been paid, and if we answered that in the whole process we hadn't earned a copper cash, and moreover didn't want one, then they acted very surprised, and some of them replied, "Well, then why did you run around the countryside doing the work, anyway?" I don't know what my two colleagues think about this question, but my answer is very simple: I just wanted to tell the rest of the world that there are still Nuosu people in China, that there are still exquisite artistic patterns of mountain life, and that there are still people like us who want to display artistic skills without figuring the profit; this is where our motivation to work for this exhibit came from.

18

CONCEPTUALIZING MOUNTAIN PATTERNS, 2000

BAMO QUBUMO

W hen he saw me carry our exhibit "baby," the yak head, though the final customs line at Seattle, "American Muga" gave me a thumbs-up through the glass. I had not only brought that thing, with its long, sharp horns, all the way from the mountains of Liangshan to the city on the West Coast of America, I had brought upon myself the inspections of customs, the suspicious eyes of stewardesses, and the curious questions of fellow passengers—and it had nearly been carried off by someone on the way. I had fidgeted nervously at the airport, wondering if it would be confiscated under some endangered animal act or animal quarantine regulation. I didn't crack a relieved smile until Muga happily took it out of my hands.

Afterward, as Muga took me from my new home in the Fremont District to the University of Washington campus, I saw the eye-opening sign for the Burke Museum. We could have taken a shortcut to his office through the employee entrance in the back, but Muga took me around to the front, saying as we walked, "The first time, you should go in through the front door, and experience the museum from the visitor's perspective." When we saw the Burke director, Karl Hutterer, Muga held up the yak head in front of his face, and I suddenly realized that what Muga was most anxious to introduce was the lacquered yak head done by the hand of a herdsman. "Amazing!" Karl was equally delighted. After a short exchange of greetings, Muga took me to see our gallery.

From the time that we had first conceived the exhibit, all through the process of collecting, I had thought many times about "our" gallery on the other side of the Pacific, and had turned the floor plans over and over in my mind. Nevertheless, when I first saw it, I was a little surprised. "Isn't it a little small?" I asked Muga quietly, even though he had long ago given Ma Lunzy and me the exact dimensions. "Whatever the size, this is the Burke temporary exhibit gallery." His answer had a little flavor of "There is no choice in the matter." The huge space I had vaguely imagined shrank to a hallway in the shape of a fish's gullet, perhaps because the exhibit in the gallery at that time was Scary Fishes. It was very different from my original idea of a "magnificent gallery." "Good that our yak from Luoji Mountain isn't looking for pasture here," I joked, "but don't we need to find a place for him to stay?" Turning around and exiting the gallery, Muga and I said just about in unison, "Over the main entrance," as he held up the yak head to try out the idea. Clearly Muga knew something about domestic Nuosu customs, because we do hang sheep and cattle skulls over the main doorways to our houses, in order to "suppress evil influences" and provide "peace in entering and leaving"; we could borrow Liangshan's influence and use the yak head to ensure the success of our Nuosu cultural exhibit in Seattle.

Early the next day, I took the four keys I received from the Burke public programs director, Erin Younger (something that would have been inconceivable in China, and that gave me a sense of responsibility toward the Burke), and began in earnest my three months as a curator there (a title for which I have still not been able to come up with a good Chinese translation). I opened the gate to the ethnology storage area, and immediately recognized the Nuosu objects there; suddenly the Burke became much more familiar to me. Most of the objects had already arrived by air freight, but it was still unknown when the remaining large things and pieces of domestic architecture would arrive courtesy of the China Overseas Steam Navigation Company. My main task was to figure out how to display the objects. Each object we had collected had a story that was familiar to me, but how would we organize the stories anew and link them together into an "ethnic narrative" that would make sense to an American audience that wasn't familiar with them?

At that time, the position of exhibit designer at the Burke was temporarily empty, so for me and Steve, and also for the museum professionals, putting together the exhibit was a new experience. After serving for six years as chair of the UW anthropology department, two months earlier Muga had taken a new position as curator of Asian ethnology at the Burke. I had been involved in the design of the Yi village exhibit at the Chinese Nationalities Park in Beijing, but that was a commercial tourist park rather than a museum. And the "Son of the Horse,"[1] Ma Lunzy, who did have actual museum experience, was having visa problems and was absorbing the sunlight in distant Southwest China, so we couldn't look to him.

That morning, Erin called a meeting of Arn Slettebak, the Burke exhibit builder; Jeanine Ipsen, the specially hired preparator; Ruth Pelz, the education planner; Susan Libonati-Barnes, the editor; and others to discuss the plans and schedule for the exhibit. Everyone recognized that it was a new kind of exhibit for the Burke: there was no designer, and there were three curators without museum experience: an American anthropologist and two native scholars. Erin set out twenty tasks for us to accomplish. I don't remember how many times we met to redesign the exhibit; I only remember that every time Erin opened her 2000 date planner, I was gripped with fear, and that every time she used her pen to point to a work deadline and asked for ideas, there was a debate. Because there was no designer, everyone became a designer, and with all the opinions floating around, there were bound to be conflicts among us—over placing a case, over the use of a platform, over the wording of a label, over what colors to use—each would engender divergent opinions, and sometimes quite heated ones.

The directness with which the Americans were willing to express their opinions brought sighs to this Easterner, accustomed to using soft methods and indirect suggestions, and also caused me to gradually change

---

1. Changing 马尔子 to 马儿子 (pronounced exactly the same) makes "Ma Lunzy" into "Son of the Horse," a pun often used by the Bamo sisters.

my original decision not to join in the debates. For example, in a meeting early on, Erin decided against the idea of using clothing to demonstrate caste differences. I had had my own idea on the matter, but didn't say anything, restrained perhaps because I had difficulty expressing myself in English, but probably more because I had not yet recognized my own role as a curator. Later on, when Muga and I were being interviewed, I said something to the reporter about my own idea concerning this matter. Muga reported to Erin the opinion of the "native scholar" on the matter, and the caste display ended up in the gallery. Such a resolution illustrated to me my role and responsibility as a curator. I was expected not only to participate in making decisions about the display, presentation, illustrations, translations, and interpretations of the Liangshan that had borne and nurtured me and of the culture with which I was so familiar, but, even more, I was expected to display my culture in a museumified space far removed from any local context, without twisting, distorting, or wrongly representing it, to "defend" the essence of my culture to a culture with which it hadn't the slightest link, with the minimum possible loss of cultural meaning.

Muga soon realized that his own anthropological viewpoint could be used to serve a communicative function, and we gradually developed a pact: Whenever there was a difference of opinion between the natives and the Americans, Muga would stand on the side of the natives and undertake liaison—particularly when there was a conflict between scholarly ideas and museological principles. This was a clever way to operate. Actually, Muga and I never stopped debating, while the relatively easygoing Ma Lunzy stood between us, either saying nothing or chuckling, to the point that I scolded him for indecision. I have always liked to chew over words and to deliberate phrasing, and more than once Muga and I "looked at each other with knives and spears" in front of our museum colleagues over the use of a single word or technical term. I remember that when we were trying to decide between using the word "myth" or "legend," our dispute turned white-hot, and Muga stormed out of the room angrily. I thought that I would quickly gather up my things from the work table and go home. Five minutes later, however, Muga was back, and his "You win!" quickly revived my enthusiasm for my work.

In this way, the display plans emerged from our discussions and debates, were overturned, and reached a consensus once again. Sometimes our debates would carry to Muga's museology seminar, "Exhibiting Culture," where Muga gave the students sixteen topics, touching on every aspect of the exhibit; the students engaged the topics enthusiastically, and in fact did come out with quite a few good suggestions. The pieces of Arn's Styrofoam model got moved around, and the bright yellow Post-it notes that represented pictures and storyboards were repeatedly taken down and put somewhere else by different people's fingers. It was like a yellow traffic light, suspending us between red and green. But we couldn't just "hang"; the plan changed almost every day as we encountered new questions and had new debates.

When the Scary Fishes exhibit was dismantled, and we switched from Arn's model to real objects in the real gallery, the objects began to move around restlessly. The installation took two months, and proceeded from chaos to order, from unending debates to gradual consensus, under considerable pressure. The "mountain pattern" that the exhibition presented to the audience was conceptualized in such fighting and debating, but the collective spirit and the individual wisdom of the collaborators ended up surpassing my expectations. Everybody pulled together to construct the late-arriving architectural pieces, even though the carpenter from Yuexi County in Liangshan, whose arrival everyone eagerly awaited, never appeared under the Seattle sky. One day, practically on the eve of opening, we were still looking for the elusive space to display the heirloom *bimo* saddle that Steve had bought for not a little cash. In the end, it seemed best to leave the elegant piece, which had once ridden the mountains, in our imaginations. Out of Muga's bald cranium there would always emerge a new idea to resolve every dispute. After the opening ceremony was over, Muga invited all of the main participants in the planning and construction to dinner at a nearby Chinese restaurant. Erin took the floor to present him with a little keychain that read, "I just had another idea"; before she was done, everybody was laughing riotously, because everybody knew that the mantra that was always hanging on Muga's lips, and which was often the lead-in to one more debate.

I hadn't known a thing about museology, although I had been to all kinds of museums, including the Musée de l'Homme in Paris and the

Kokuritsu Minzoku Hakubutsukan in Japan, and the transition from visitor to curator had not been an easy one. Because both Muga and I had come to exhibiting from a scholarly perspective, we didn't have much of a museological framework to refer to in our work. In conceptualizing the exhibit, we were not constrained by preexisting models; and this may have been why we as curators continued to have differences of opinion with the museum staff, and also why the exhibit emerged from a process of arguing and consensus with a rather unusual design. So conceptualizing Mountain Patterns from start to finish was a fluid process, changing from beginning to end, embroiled in debate from conception to completion, full of strategy and rich in creativity.

Maybe I understand Nuosu conceptions of time in terms of "ritual process." How was this understanding embodied in Mountain Patterns? Let's go together into the Burke Museum, and stand under the introductory panel, with the Nuosu and English signs "Gguhxo Jjojju" and "Mountain Patterns." There are three colored pictures on the panel, from left to right: sheepfolds on a snowy day, a mountain scene from late spring or early summer, and fields in autumn. In his years of fieldwork in Liangshan, Muga has photographed who knows how many scenes. His professional-quality photos certainly added not a little color to Mountain Patterns, and also filled the gaps between the exhibited objects. Nevertheless, we put a lot of consideration into selecting those three photos. In the end, we decided to lead off the exhibit with the seasons, to think of time as a cycle leading back to a new beginning. These pictures aren't simply pretty landscapes; they have a deep cultural background. Visitors used to the order "spring, summer, fall, winter" might ask, "Why should the first picture be one of *winter*?" The decision to put those three seasonal photos together on a panel was influenced by a set of four Han shell-inlaid panels in Muga's house, representing the four amusements—the zither, the chessboard, the book, and the painting. But the time conceptions embodied in our panels came from my familiarity with the Yi calendar year and calendrical rituals.

The traditional calendar of the Nuosu was the ten-month solar calendar. According to it, the new year started with the blowing snows of the tenth month of the Chinese lunar calendar, so we started our exhibit with winter snows. Nuosu divide the year into winter, spring, and fall, in accordance with the mountain climate, and in rhythm with the changing of the seasons, they carry out the three important calendrical religious festivals: the *yyrci naba* (calling of the souls) in the winter, the *xio bbur* (counterspell) in the spring, and the *jijuo* (turning back of spells) in the fall. The seasons and their rituals are always turning and coming back to the beginning, reflecting the perpetual Nuosu concerns about production and reproduction, human longevity and agricultural productivity, and at the same time giving rise to a series of folk phenomena dealing with the agricultural cycle, plowing and herding, astronomy, and divination. These three pictures portray the changes in the course of a year, using the cycle of time to draw visitors into a vividly nature-oriented mountain society.

Detailed cultural concepts such as the ten-month solar calendar and the calendrical rituals can only be hinted at in a museum exhibit. Only a limited amount of prose would fit on the labels. I suppose this is unavoidable. Whenever we considered introducing the cultural meaning behind an object or a picture, the museum specialists would all be afraid of "confusing the audience." In particular, it seemed that the more scholarly a display, the more it deviated from the Burke's orientation toward children. We debated whether the exhibit was "scholarly" or "educational," and in the end we achieved a kind of synthesis, both educational and scholarly—the scholarly part found almost entirely in the *bimo* culture displays at the end of the exhibit, allowing those visitors who really had an academic interest to digest the material slowly.

The problems we had ordering the presentation were numerous and complex. We needed to choose photographs that connected with the main topics being exhibited. For example, we used photographs to explain some of the processes used in the manufacture of lacquer and silverware that could not be demonstrated by the objects themselves, and to illustrate important life events such as funerals and the summertime Fire Festival.

We also had to decide which colors to use for the different kinds of labels. Even though everybody leaned toward using the three primary colors of Nuosu lacquerware—red, yellow, and black—when we saw the number of choices presented by the publications office, the only thing we could do was to take a reasonably representative piece of lac-querware and hold it up for comparison.

Another thing that caused us trouble was choosing the color for the gallery walls. At first, Arn and Muga both advocated using a color close to that of Liangshan's mud; Arn spent a considerable amount of time turning the pages of *The Yi of Liangshan* and examining Muga's slides, looking for the right mud color. Erin and I wanted to use a "cool color" in order to give visitors the feeling of having entered the Cool Moun-tains. Both proposals were to the same purpose: to try to visually create the feeling of "Liangshan" for the visitors. Finally, Arn painted stripes of the many possible colors on the walls of his exhibit shop, and every-body gradually came around to a cool gray. After the exhibit opened, one old woman told us that she felt cold in the gallery, making us feel that we really had achieved our goal of bodily bringing the visitor into the environment—"Labor is not a burden to the believer." So we led into the exhibit with the snow scene, creating the "cold of the Cool Mountains."

Another way that time is intimately connected with the lives of moun-tain people is their use of the life cycle to construct an account of human existence and life experience. Nuosu people have a birth ceremony in which naming, horoscope casting, and feasting are used to pray for the smooth growth of the newborn. There is an adolescence ceremony that involves changing a girl's skirt to indicate that she is an adult and can interact socially as an adult. There is a boisterous marriage ritual that includes carrying the bride, and the bride and the groom splashing each other with water and smearing pot soot on each other's faces. And there is a solemn, serious funeral ritual that involves cremating the corpse on a wood pyre. Birth, adulthood, marriage, and cremation—each rit-ual has important cultural meaning and social significance in the lives of the mountain people.

For our exhibit, Steve brought the anthropological concept of the life cycle into our display of women's clothing, incorporating folkloristic ideas explaining the form of rites of passage. We attempted to illustrate the simple Nuosu life-cycle concepts using the changes in Nuosu women's clothing with age, marital status, and social rank, from the fern patterns of children's hats, symbolizing the flourishing of life, to the different styles of girls' and women's skirts before and after the skirt-changing ceremony; from the silver-saturated bridal outfit to the sober, heavy old woman's skirt. The clothing we collected was mostly women's, reflecting the fact that women's clothing has changed less than men's under the influence of Han culture.

By using clothing in the life-cycle section, embodying serious content in the concrete, from head to toe, thoroughly stimulates deep reflection, vivifies the covert and symbolic nature of beauty, and stimulates the audience's understanding of Nuosu ideas of life and death. Nevertheless, the life-cycle section was almost truncated in a debate. Only a few days before the exhibit opening, the life-cycle section was complete except for the last scene, the funeral clothes. In order to display a traditional Nuosu cremation ceremony though a combination of objects and photographs, Muga and Ma Lunzy had built a seven-tiered pyre in the gallery (there are nine tiers for a man, seven for a woman), while I had busied myself with preparing the section labels on Muga's computer. Suddenly, Ma Lunzy appeared in the doorway and said, "Qubumo, Muga wants you to go right upstairs to have a look." I said, "What this time?" and he answered, "Abbe, it's too terrifying. As soon as we built that pile of firewood, the effect was really realistic, but it scared everybody. I think the best thing would be to get rid of it." I thought of how Ma Lunzy had been muttering throughout the planning of the exhibit, saying that displaying a certain piece of women's clothing or a ghost board violated a Nuosu taboo, or that looking through *bimos'* spell books made him vomit blood. Generally when he was afraid of something like that, I would just forge ahead without regard for my own safety, even when I harbored internal fears. But at that moment, seeing him blanch, I hurried upstairs with him.

I don't know where Muga had gone. The only person in the gallery was Karl, the director. He was standing over by the rather startling funeral pyre; he looked as though he were mulling something over. As soon as he saw me, he said, with an air of concern, "If we display it this way, it's sure to scare some of the audience, especially the children. Should we think about getting rid of this part?" I immediately disagreed. Eliminating the funeral pyre would render the life cycle incomplete; the whole clothing section would lose its thread of coherence and become random, and, more importantly, Nuosu ideas of life and death would have no place to be expressed.

I briefly explained to Karl about common Nuosu ideas of death and cremation. When one's parent dies of natural causes in old age, the Nuosu commission a *bimo* to conduct a solemn cremation ceremony; the mood is serious, but the atmosphere is not lacking in warmth. Except for the children and grandchildren of the deceased, who wear signs of mourning in their clothing, the young people of the village all dress up in their best clothing to go to the funeral—the girls in new jackets and colorful skirts, with pretty headdresses, and yellow sashes tied to their head cloths and trailing down their backs, and the boys in their most formal clothes, with a yellow sash around their waists and the studded "hero's belt" over one shoulder. When the ceremonies are over people begin singing traditional funeral songs, which are about astronomy, geography, customs, and human nature, or they chant the mythical-historical epic *Hnewo teyy* or the long instructional poem *Hmamu teyy*, amplifying and embellishing with their lively and quaint language. Or they sing somber, tragic tunes about the lives of the deceased, fitting them into a commonly recognized pattern of social morality. When the funeral ceremonies are over, there is a big meeting in the village, where the young men each wear a long white yak tail, carry a sword in one hand, and do ancient warrior dances to open the way for the deceased to go back to the ancestors. At the same time, there are beauty contests, horse races, wrestling matches, and other traditional sports, all of which give an air of even greater gravity and warmth to the funeral ceremonies. All of this demonstrates Yi people's positive attitude toward death, in which cremation embodies an optimistic and accepting life-orientation. I have gone to cremations since I was a child, and never felt them to be scary.

Maybe my words made sense; Karl told me to create an appropriate explanation for the label, and to think of a way to make the pyre a little smaller, so that it would not be quite so obvious or frightening—in short, to make the audience understand and accept it. In the end, Muga and Ma Lunzy stood on my side, so that in my stressed-out state I could let out my breath (even though Muga said that if Ma Lunzy continued to oppose it, he would respect his wishes and consider taking it out). We

18.1 *The controversial funeral pyre in the Mountain Patterns exhibit, Burke Museum, Seattle, 2000.*

came to a perfect resolution: We took out the platform, moved the pyre away from the central position in the gallery, and covered the "dead" mannequin with fake pine branches—a "cremation" half hidden and half visible diluted the "death" flavor and made the pyre more mysterious, more grave, and more solemn (fig. 18.1).The "dead lady" on the pyre really did trouble everybody's thoughts, and the decision as to whether the audience ought to be subjected to such a realistic depiction of death caused divisions that we hadn't had before. But I really believe that attitudes toward death constitute an important element of the psychological structure of a people, and the question of whether attitudes can be adequately expressed in an exhibit is a separate question from whether such an exhibit might induce "terror of death" in the audience. I think life and death are things that everyone worries about; they are part of everyone's experience, no matter what a person believes or what kind of funeral they have. From the audience's reaction to the exhibit, we could tell that displaying the "cremation" was the right thing to do, that visitors were able to see in it the positive Nuosu attitude toward

18.2 Stevan Harrell, Zhong Jingwen, and Bamo Qubumo, Beijing, 1999.

dying and the psychological structure that derives from that. Keeping
the funeral clothes in the life cycle section had real public educational
value. Attending my friend Amber's mother's memorial service in Seattle and seeing a tape of my landlady Soph's late husband Jack's funeral
both expressed cultural attitudes toward life and death.

A space influences and limits a display in ways that go without saying, but the natural correspondence between the spatial and temporal
aspects of the exhibit that emerged during the design process was something we had not counted on. As one of the Burke's curators, I played
the role of "native scholar," but perhaps I should have played the role
of "folklorist" instead. I had studied ethnic literature from early on in
my schooling, and I had recently been working on a Ph.D. in folklore
under the famous scholar Zhong Jingwen at Beijing Normal University
(fig. 18.2). The study of material folklore—including clothing, utensils,
and vernacular architecture—has traditionally been an important topic
of folklore research. Due to the continuous influence of Japanese folklore studies on Chinese folklore studies, the latter has historically concentrated on "time" and relatively ignored "space." As a result, the customs
of every ethnic group have been explained in a temporal sequence that
neglects the spatial logic of ethnic folk customs in many places. Even
the studies that attempt to explain local differences in folk customs tend

to temporalize matters of spatial significance. For example, research on local Yi cultures does not explore the particular nature of the cultures of different areas but rather uses local cultural differences to explain the origin and development of Yi culture as a whole. When scholars go to a Yi area to carry out research, what is most often neglected is attention to folk phenomena that bear on spatial arrangements—borders, landscapes, districts, and environments.

From the time Muga began considering the presentation of Nuosu culture, his idea had been to encompass it in a scheme of regional subcultures of the "big and little Cool Mountains," including Ninglang County of Yunnan—the Yynuo, Shynra, and Suondi local variants. This idea received its most concentrated expression in the clothing and textiles section. This was simply using cultural geography as an organizing principle; the more difficult problem was deciding how to use tangible space to display intangible borders.

When we first laid out a plan for the Mountain Patterns exhibit, our choice of topics had been constrained by the raw materials, because the only Nuosu cultural things we could bring into the museum were tangible objects. Spatial and monetary constraints precluded us from collecting and bringing into the museum many Nuosu cultural objects; for example, interesting bamboo implements and wooden farming and herding equipment were excluded. So our collection plan had three major categories: body ornamentation (including clothing and jewelry), objects of use (including lacquerware, silverware, and musical instruments), and objects of religious culture. Wooden architectural pieces were added to the exhibit later as a framing device, since it would have been impossible to ship an actual house to America (though we did consider it).

In this way, Mountain Patterns could be divided into three major zones. When it came to installation, the two concrete pillars in the middle of the exhibit area became a kind of "natural wall" that divided the gallery into a larger and a smaller space. The traditional Nuosu house door that Muga had ordered was originally going to be placed at the entrance to the gallery, giving relatively tall Americans the experience of having to duck their heads to enter a Nuosu house. But in the end, the door became a "mysterious gate" erected between the large and small sections of the gallery; , a hearth with a burning fire could be seen deep within, in a photograph of the interior of a Nuosu house that was hung on one side of the doorway. So the doorway became a boundary line. Outside was the "apparent world" of ordinary Nuosu life, somewhat like the courtyard of any dwelling, where the family would hang clothes, make felt, or weave; inside was the "hidden world" of Nuosu spiritual life, somewhat like the *gaku*, or hearth, inside the house, which fewer outsiders would see, with an altar where offerings were made to the ancestral spirits.

We had many things to consider in positioning the objects in the large and small spaces. One consideration was the receptivity of the audience. We laid out the exhibit so that the religious element, the esoteric *bimo* culture, was at the very end, to be seen after the audience was somewhat familiar with more accessible aspects of the culture. Another consideration was the wall color. We chose two different shades of gray for the inner and outer portions of the exhibit, with the inner color a shade darker to indicate both the interior location and the "deeper" nature of the cultural objects displayed there. A third consideration was that the presence of the freestanding door between the outer and inner galleries further restricted the already rather cramped space of the inner gallery, and partially blocked the ceiling lights there, creating an obscure, somber atmosphere that was different from that of the outer gallery. The solution to this problem was purely serendipitous. When we moved the original seven units of the house frame into the gallery, we discovered that they wouldn't all fit. We set up only three units, but the result was not ideal, so we expanded it to five units (fig. 18.3). And Muga, in another inspired move, decided not to put the shingles on top, thereby limiting the oppressive feeling of a too-narrow space and allowing the lights from the ceiling to filter indirectly through the dense structure of posts and beams. As the saying goes, "Deliberately prune the flowers, and they don't bloom; accidentally plant the willow, and it gives shade." The strong contrast between the inner and outer spaces produced an interplay of light and shade, an atmosphere of rapidly shifting rhythms.

This door—which was itself a folk object made by a Nuosu carpenter (who had given up a once-in-a-lifetime chance to travel abroad because he was afraid of the complex visa application procedures)—became the

18.3 *Ma Lunzy assembling the Nuosu architectural structure for the Mountain Patterns exhibit, Burke Museum, Seattle, 2000.*

18.4 *Bamo Qubumo, Bamo Ayi, and Stevan Harrell assembling the arena for the leprosy ghost exorcism in the Mountain Patterns exhibit, Burke Museum, Seattle, 2000.*

key to understanding the exhibit: the exterior revealed the extant material world of the Nuosu—manifestations of clothing, food, residence, and travel—while the interior contained the belief realm of the spirit (fig. 18.4). This doorway offered a vantage point that embodied a deep perspective; through it, we attempted to explain the intangible culture behind the tangible objects, to covertly display the multilayered mountain pattern that pulls together Nuosu spiritual beliefs, systems of knowledge, rituals, and rites of passage into one embodiment. A visitor passing through the doorway could move from the superficial to the interior, from the shallow to the profound, from the apparent to the hidden, understanding and connecting with a culture rich in its uniqueness, and being stimulated, surprised, and delighted.

Our practical solution to the dictates of the exhibition space allowed us to display a cultural concept, which was validated by the reactions of the visitors. When Dr. Ralph Litzinger, an anthropologist come to write a review of the exhibit, had walked around the exhibit for only a short time, he understood the exhibit as an attempt to present two worlds to the visitor: one of tangible material customs, and one of intangible spiritual customs. When one bent one's head to go through the wooden doorway, one moved from the multicolored world of everyday Nuosu life into a profound and somber spiritual world. I remember that upon hearing one evaluation of the exhibit, Muga and I exchanged looks, recognized each other's meanings, and smiled ("At this time, the unspoken prevailed over the spoken")—"We did it!"

During the process of installing the exhibit, we were doing as Deng Xiaoping said of China's "reform and opening": "crossing the river by feeling the stones"—or maybe "following our feelings." The hidden "pattern" of the exhibit which evolved gradually, day by day, was somewhat abstract and academic, but as long as it could be detected by sensitive visitors, who thereby gained a deeper understanding of Nuosu culture, we individual scholars could enjoy the realization of a scholarly idea.

After the exhibit had been open for a month, I had to say good-bye to Seattle. Walking out the front door of the Burke and turning around to look at "our" gallery, guarded by the yak head that I had transported there, protecting those Nuosu cultural objects that would stay forever in the Burke, I couldn't suppress a reluctance to part. When Ma Lunzy and I hugged Muga good-bye at the airport, Muga said, "When you two leave, I won't be able to get used to the office with just me in it." I said to myself, "After I leave I won't be able to 'fight' with you any more, Muga." In fact, the thing that would be hardest for me to forget would be our debates; from them I learned very, very much, and the benefits I derived from them were not shallow. As my American friend, Aaron Tate, wrote me in an e-mail:

> Thank you for the updates on your work in Washington; they were very interesting. It was fascinating to read about the disputes between you and Dr. Harrell; it became clear to me that he is trained as an anthropologist and you as a folklorist! It is great that you are "standing your ground," so to speak. I am sure that you are both learning a tremendous amount from the experience, and that is a very valuable thing. I also always love to read about your improvement with English—you sound like quite a fast learner.

It was true: Muga's anthropological perspective contributed not only the temporal concept of the Nuosu life process but also the idea of the two kinds of spaces in which ordinary Nuosu moved: the outer world of living and the inner world of the spirit. And I, from my background as a folklorist, had been able to transmit what I understand as the patterns of Nuosu culture extracted from the concrete phenomena of customs. Different perspectives, different scholarly backgrounds—the process of conceptualizing Mountain Patterns had been one of reciprocal complementation and mutual advantage. Speaking frankly, the reason why I had dared to "fight" with this respected anthropologist was because Mountain Patterns had transformed us from collaborators into friends, between whom there was nothing we couldn't say, who were completely open with each other. When I went back to Beijing, Muga and I started calling each other "sister" and "brother" on e-mail, and I am happy to have this kind of "big-brother" senior colleague, because Muga will always be my private anthropology tutor.

Not long after my return, Chinese Central TV repeatedly broadcast two documentaries, one about my career and one about Muga's scholarly work in Liangshan. Immediately, the telephone which had lain silent on my desk for a long time began ringing unceasingly. Beijing class-mates and friends, fellow students and fellow workers, Liangshan kin and hometown relatives, friends and neighbors from all over, all con-gratulated us on the success of the exhibit. Some asked how we possi-bly could have shipped such a heavy "wooden house" to America. When friends heard Muga's good wishes spoken on TV in the Nuosu language, when they saw the objects collected from their own houses, even pic-tures of themselves and their relatives, appearing in America, and, even more, Nuosu qobo (friends), one told ten, and ten told a hundred about Nuosu culture having reached American Muga's country. But what did they think about it? In September 2000, my sister Ayi and I would be returning to America as visiting fellows at Harvard. Before that, we would return to Liangshan to visit our parents, so at that time, I found a few days to return to Meigu and interview a few families.

19

CELEBRATING MOUNTAIN PATTERNS

STEVAN HARRELL

O pening night was glittering. The gallery reflected and rereflected light from the overhead tracks to the buffed-shiny wood floors, and in between, in the polished glass cases, the silver jewelry scintillated, the variegated needlework sparkled, the glossy lacquerware shone. We three curators practically floated about the audience, Bamo Qubumo positively incandescent in her red wool skirt, mirrored jacket, and profusion of silver jewelry, Ma Lunzy and I merely resplendent, he in his elaborately embroidered black *vala* and I in my undyed wool one, worn over a Yynuo-style velvet jacket with multicolored couched designs (fig. 19.1). Ma Lunzy and Bamo Ayi sang "Azzibaddi," a Nuosu duet in which a child asks her mother where to find beautiful things such as capes, bowls, and hearthstones, and the answers, at least that evening, were "Seattle," "University of Washington," and "Burke Museum" (fig. 19.2) We held a book signing, something that made us all feel elevated above our customary stations, and congratulations and hugs rained upon us from a multitude of well-wishers, ranging from regents of the University of Washington to old friends not seen in years to the only Nuosu emigrée resident in Western Washington.

After that, we waited nervously for the reviews in the local media.

19.1 Erin Younger, director of public programs at the Burke Museum, with Bamo Qubumo, Stevan Harrell, and Ma Lunzy at the opening of the Mountain Patterns exhibit, Burke Museum, Seattle, March 1, 2000.

19.2 Bamo Ayi and Ma Lunzy sing the Nuosu duet "Azzibaddi" at the opening ceremony for the Mountain Patterns exhibit, Burke Museum, Seattle, March 1, 2000.

They all turned out to be favorable, and probably brought in a few extra viewers, but the *Seattle Weekly*, a fairly respected arts-and-politics tabloid, was the one that gladdened our hearts. "A remarkably beautiful exhibit," it said in its short feature blurb on the local events page, "not for anthropologists only." When Father Benoît Vermander, an expert on Nuosu religion, came to visit and give a lecture, I worried. He had told me not to make the exhibit too pretty, not to leave out the realities of life in today's Liangshan. After he had seen it, he told me not to worry: "It's not pretty; it's beautiful." Pierre van den Berghe, best known for his sociobiological approach and second-best known for his brutal honesty, sent me an e-mail saying, "The combination of the photos, the artifacts and the carpentry was stunning."

So everyone agreed: It was beautiful. The question was, why had we chosen to make it beautiful, and what did that beauty say about the realities of life in one of China's poorest regions, about the relationship between the Chinese government and the disadvantaged minorities? How should one present the life, the culture, and the arts of an ethnic group to an audience previously ignorant of that group's existence?

Life in Liangshan is hard. In the high mountains where most people live, the climate is too cold and the slopes are too steep to grow rice, so people must content themselves with potatoes and coarse grains such as buckwheat, corn, and oats. There is nothing green to eat most of the year, and meat is available only on holidays or when someone is entertaining important guests. Most villages are still not reachable by road, so getting from one place to another requires hours of walking over steep, slippery trails. The houses may have decorated wooden beams and eaves, but the walls are mud and the floors are dirt, and soft chairs or beds are practically unknown. People have to haul water from streams; very few have access even to wells, let alone piped water. Medical care, never very good, has declined since the marketization of society in the 1980s and '90s, and infant mortality, as well as adult morbidity from infectious diseases, remains high. In the winter, when the *shuohly*, the "Han wind," comes howling out of the north, it is impossible to keep warm even in the sunshine, so the only retreat is to the smoky hearth to sit on a mat on the hard ground. None of this harsh reality is reflected in Mountain Patterns.

Society in Liangshan is undergoing wrenching changes. There is often not enough livelihood from the land, so people are driven to migrate, and when they migrate to the cities, urbanites despise them as dirty, dishonest, and uneducated, and often refuse them work. The temptation to commit crime is great, and not everyone resists; those who are caught are often without legal recourse and are punished severely. The temptation to drink is even greater, and the streets of many market towns, and sometimes even the county highways, are punctuated by passed-out drunks. Other drugs, including heroin, are increasingly available, and the temptation there, too, is great; everyone knows someone who is addicted. Educational opportunities are few; probably only about 40 to 50 percent of Nuosu children in the mountain areas even begin school, and only a small proportion of those finish. None of these signs of despair is shown in Mountain Patterns.

The Nuosu arts, though experiencing a renaissance after their near-extermination during the Great Proletarian Cultural Revolution, are now under attack from the even more powerful forces of the global economy. This is particularly true of the textile arts. In Zhaojue City, in one of the core counties of Old Liangshan, one looks in vain for a woman wearing a skirt; even in Meigu, the deepest font of cultural traditionalism, many women have given up wearing skirts, except on special occasions, and almost nobody wears the traditional head covering. The market at Niuniuba in Meigu (fig. 19.3), once the site of a famous slave market, now has tens of stalls selling cheap warm-up suits, synthetic blouses, and stretch pants for every one or two stalls selling brightly colored, banded skirts. One rarely sees a man younger than fifty wearing the traditional wide-legged pants, and pink floral-patterned towels have replaced black turbans as the favored headgear of young men in Meigu. None of this change is apparent in the textile cases of Mountain Patterns.

Our portrait of Liangshan is thus very idealized; nowhere except in a museum or at a cultural performance or perhaps on a major holiday would one find a scene so full of intricate, neatly sewn patterns or of shining lacquerware or glittering silver. We have, in a certain sense, repeated the portrait of minority life that adorns so many official media: that minority peoples make and wear colorful costumes and fine jew-

19.3 *Selling skirts and wool at the market in Niuniuba, Meigu, 1999.*

elry, like those in the Mountain Patterns cases; that they play haunting folk tunes on quaint instruments like those that visitors can listen to in the Mountain Patterns music display. Poverty, underdevelopment, hard work, and lack of social services are not emphasized in official portrayals of minority life, especially not those intended for tourists or other casual observers. Museums and cultural displays, such as those at the many ethnic culture parks in Chinese cities, do not show the mixing of hand-tailored clothes with cheap things off the rack or the introduction of chopsticks and porcelain bowls into a world of lacquered spoons and wooden tureens; neither does our exhibit.

Our exhibit is not, of course, confined to the things that an official museum or cultural show would present. We have, for one thing, quite a large section on the religious texts and rituals of the *bimo*. It is true that their official status was changed in the late 1980s from "superstitious practitioners" to "popular intellectuals," and that their activities by the late 1990s were hardly restricted anymore by local governments. And some government tourist agencies have even explored the possibility of displaying *bimo wenhua*, or culture, along with the activities of the *sunyi* or shamans, as an attraction for visitors, in the same way that the "Dongba culture" of the Naxi priests in northwestern Yunnan has become a tourist attraction. But *bimo* as potential tourist attractions are not the same as *bimo* as active ritual healers and specialists, and in their latter, more important role, officials are still suspicious of them, making sure, for example, that elementary school textbooks include lessons demonstrating the ineffectiveness of their healing rituals.

But even our portrayal of *bimo* culture and activities might be seen as somewhat idealistic. Probably none of us curators would trust a *bimo* to perform an exorcism if we were afflicted by leprosy or some other serious skin disease, or call on a *bimo* to treat a severe and chronic health problem of one of our children. At least, we would not do so without also consulting a physician. And while Mountain Patterns presents an elaborate mock-up of a ritual arena for expelling leprosy ghosts from a village, and explains in some detail the nature and function of many different kinds of ghosts and spirits, we never consider that living under the power of so many kinds of demons might create worries for ordinary people, render undue power into the hands of the priests, or prevent people from seeking elementary medical care that might be more effective in some conditions than are the rituals.

In short, Mountain Patterns celebrates Nuosu culture; it does not analyze it. Many of the aspects we celebrate are those same aspects that are celebrated in the official vision of multicultural China; others are not, but they certainly do not contradict that vision. Why did we not take an alternate approach?

For example, we could have tried to present Nuosu culture in its realistic, everyday, mixed reality. We might have shown mannequins dressed in the ordinary cheap clothing available in local markets, perhaps intermixed with other mannequins in traditional dress. We might have included a nice print blouse on a mannequin, like the striped one worn by the young woman in one of the portraits (fig. 19.4). We might have included a little disorder in our domestic architecture, hanging a ripped skirt from a beam or chalking Chinese characters on the big wooden door. We might even (and we considered it) have included some of the roughly turned, crudely painted lacquerware I purchased in the

19.4 Jjihni Molur spinning by the side of the trail, Meigu, 1998.

Butuo market. Instead, we almost entirely chose to buy fine examples of each craft, and when we had lesser samples, we left them on the storage shelves.

Or, as some visitors suggested in response to a survey, we might have presented a more complete cultural or ethnographic exhibit, showing not just the arts but the daily life of Liangshan. We might have created a domestic environment or diorama showing people around a fire, or devoted space to some of the more mundane aspects of life, such as the agricultural cycle or the patterns of animal husbandry. Instead, we decided to ignore the prosaic and concentrate on the artistic, to dispense with the everyday in favor of the holiday, to place "culture," in the old anthropological sense, in the background, while bringing "culture," in the even older artistic sense, to the fore. We chose not only to celebrate the culture but to do so through its most visually striking elements.

We certainly could have treated less savory aspects of the traditional society. Our labels devoted only one sentence to the sensitive topic of slavery (it seemed wrong to leave it out altogether, but to put in more than that would risk ruining the celebration), and only one sentence directly to the practices of raiding and warfare, though the latter were mentioned in the explanation of the suit of buffalo-hide armor. We might have mounted an informative display about the elaborate system of social ranks and obligations, or about the inequalities between men and women. But we chose to brush over these things lightly, illustrating the difference between aristocratic and commoner castes with a pair of differently colored jackets, and hinting at the subordination of women in some of the material on weddings and in the remark that the respected status of *bimo* was available only to men.

We were careful, all the same, not to present an absolutely essentialized version of Nuosu culture, or an atemporal one. Every object whose maker is known is labeled with that maker's name, and the subject of every portrait is clearly identified. We were careful to treat the seamstress, the silversmith, and the carpenter as individual artists, not as representatives of some unvarying cultural tradition. And the dates on the labels indicate that almost all of the material on exhibit is new, most of it manufactured between 1995 and 2000. We devoted two cases specifically to recent artistic trends and outside influences. One platform was occupied by three mannequins, the outfit of one showing Qing influences and those of the other two demonstrating the special kind of creativity that comes when techniques that have been around for a long time are applied to modern materials—in this case, brightly colored, shiny synthetic fabrics. A nearby vitrine was filled with lacquerware from two factories established in the 1980s, in Zhaojue and Xide counties; among the objects displayed were a bookcase, a telephone stand, and a drinking vessel in the shape of a little boy on a water buffalo, a Han Chinese motif if there ever was one. In sum, we did not essentialize or atemporalize Nuosu culture, but in some senses we idealized it, or we chose to demonstrate its most attractive and artistic aspects. And, as I said, the main thing was to celebrate it.

Why did we, who have written so critically about minority policy and so sympathetically about poverty and underdevelopment, choose to present such a celebratory vision in Mountain Patterns? There are two sorts of reasons. I explained the first sort of reason to several museology students before the exhibit opened, and to newly hired Burke designer Andrew Whiteman on the day of the opening. All these people had asked me personally what I hoped that visitors to the Burke would take away from the exhibit. What I told them were my own personal goals, but we three curators had discussed these issues repeatedly, and I knew that my partners shared at least the outline of my objectives. I answered that I had five primary goals, in order from the easiest and most general to the most difficult and specific:

1. I wanted people to know that there were, in fact, autonomous minority peoples in China, who had distinctive cultural and historical traditions.

Most Americans, I have judged, have little idea of China as a multicultural country. They know, of course, about Tibet, and many of them have heard of the situations in Xinjiang and Inner Mongolia. But they do not consider these, especially Tibet, to be part of China at all; they rather look upon them as occupied territories. Liangshan, as culturally separate as it has often been, is unambiguously part of China, and its culture is one of China's cultures. To show this, we needed to contrast Nuosu culture with Han Chinese culture in every possible way, which meant displaying those objects that were most characteristically Nuosu, even when Han influence was shown (because we weren't about to essentialize), illustrating the particularly Nuosu way of adapting Han elements.

2. I wanted people to understand the very anthropological point (though my co-curator Bamo Qubumo might think of it as a folkloric point) of the significance of clothing and social status—including gender, caste, and particularly region and stage—in the life cycle. In the modern, everyday world, younger men almost never wear the traditional regional styles of pants, big, middle, or small, and although women's clothing retains many distinctive regional elements, these are easiest to see in a completely "traditional" outfit—that is, one without any purchased elements.

3. I wanted visitors to be able to see the recovery of a local culture after the homogenizing efforts of the Great Proletarian Cultural Revolution. During that time, as we said in the introductory labels to the exhibit, many aspects of local culture were repressed. Those included, of course, such things as clan solidarity and all expressions of ethnic pride, but those things are difficult to display in a gallery. What one could display were the arts, because they, too, were suppressed; neither silversmiths nor lacquermakers, according to current reports, were allowed to ply their trades, and were denounced for pandering to feudal or bourgeois tastes. That they have survived is testimony to the fact that the authorities have now given not just latitude but encouragement to these aspects of local culture.

4. I wanted visitors to be able to get some hint of the less superficial, more profound aspects of the culture, contained in the ritual life and the religious texts. In a context in which people's attention spans are notoriously short, I wanted visitors to at least be aware that these deeper aspects of knowledge and belief existed, and I hoped, in addition, that visitors would begin to appreciate the knowledge embodied in Nuosu ritual and phi-

losophy. This meant displaying the texts, translating the inscriptions on religious paintings, and even constructing a mock-up of the ritual arena.

5. Finally, I wanted viewers of the exhibit to come away thinking about a paradox. Life in Nuosu country is harsh, and people have responded with what Americans would consider a remarkable lack of concern for creature comforts. Beds are hard; floors are bumpy; it is difficult to keep clothes or skin clean; sanitation is not a major concern in everyday life. Amidst such hardship, people create things that are, as the *Seattle Weekly* so aptly put it, "remarkably beautiful." Skilled and creative people such as seamstress Molie Ago, silversmith Shama Qubi (fig. 19.5), lacquer painter Jjivo Vuqie, and carpenter Ayu Mujy are artists whose work deserves to be recognized in its own right, and the fact that they can create such beauty in such harsh surroundings adds to the interest of an exhibit of Nuosu arts.

The second sort of reason for mounting this kind of show is less specific, less philosophical, and more emotional and aesthetic. It has to do with the nature of cultural celebration. Two of the three of us curators grew up in Liangshan; one spent his entire life there, and the other lived there for many years. I have visited regularly since 1987. We know about the contradictions, the tragedies, the inequality, the poverty. In some contexts, such as academic articles and cadre conferences, these are appropriate things to concentrate on. But Nuosu culture is not just heartbreak and despair. It is also a long and proud tradition of creativity and artistic skill, and a deep aesthetic appreciation for all sorts of arts, many of which—such as buffalo-hide lacquer, painted beams under the eaves, or certain kinds of silver filigree—are unique not only in the uplands of Southwest China and northern Southeast Asia but in the world. Nuosu scholars and cadres, and Nuosu people in general, particularly Nuosu artists, are justifiably proud of this tradition. To take a critical, academic attitude toward the arts, to contextualize too much, to remind people constantly of poverty and inequality, would be to give the victory to hardship and sickness.

A Nuosu proverb tells how each linguistic/cultural region of Liangshan emphasizes one particular kind of celebration. In the most populous, central Shynra region, this is the *kushy*, or New Year, and in the southern, or Suondi, region it is the *duzi*, or Fire Festival; both cele-

19.5 Silversmith Shama Qubi at his forge, Meigu, 1998.

brations involve dressing up, eating, and drinking. In the northern, or Yynuo, region, the biggest celebration is the *cobi*, the ritual in which the *bimo*, using myriad chants and sacrifices, sends the soul of the dead along the road that leads back to the land of the ancestors and the peaceful afterlife. At the end of the *cobi*, the young men of the deceased's clan, along with their close affines, put on their best clothes, including leather armor if they have any, and take up whatever weapons their households possess. The young women of the host and affinal clans dress to the nines, and the young people of both sexes meet each other other on a flat space near the village. They parade, clan by clan, showing off their bravery and beauty, and then they stage horse races and wrestling matches. The elder has died, the clan lives on; they celebrate. In the same way, the magnificent arts of the Nuosu live on, enduring first the Cultural Revolution and now globalization. In Mountain Patterns we, too, celebrate.

And so this story of our field research and collaboration comes to an artificial end, a cutoff point, because we want to get this book out. Since the events described here, we have continued to work together on a variety of projects. Most notably, Lunzy and I, together with many other friends, collaborated on building an elementary school in his home village of Yangjuan and conducting a multidisciplinary ecological study of the watershed in which it lies. Qubumo and I, along with many colleagues, held the fourth International Yi Studies Conference in Meigu in August 2005, and planned an edited volume of some of our papers. So cutting off the story in March 2000 is arbitrary, as all ends are. The fabric of our work together continues to be woven.

EPILOGUE

FIELDWORK CONNECTIONS
AND THE PROCESS OF ETHNOGRAPHY

STEVAN HARRELL

The process of anthropological research has undergone an enormous amount of self-examination since the 1970s. At first glance, it is difficult to see the reason for this. If we look at accounts from former times, beginning with Bronislaw Malinowski's *Argonauts of the Western Pacific* (1922) and including such classics as Raymond Firth's *We, the Tikopia: A Sociological Study of Kinship in Primitive Polynesia* (1936), E. E. Evans-Pritchard's *The Nuer: A Description of the Modes of Livelihood and Political Institutions of a Nilotic People* (1940) and Margaret Mead's *Blackberry Winter: My Earlier Years* (1975), and compare them with the much more highly theorized recent accounts (some of my own favorites are E. Valentine Daniel's *Fluid Signs: Being a Person the Tamil Way* [1984], Smadar Lavie's *The Poetics of Military Occupation: Mzeina Allegorias of Bedouin Identity under Israeli and Egyptian Rule* [1990], and Margaret Trawick's *Notes on Love in a Tamil Family* [1990], but there are hundreds), it appears that fieldwork itself has not changed much. A researcher, with the help of one or more natives, goes to one or more communities for a while, and gathers data by means of observation, questioning, and, sometimes, more formal techniques, such as projective tests, text taking, and various questionnaires. The researcher, sometimes with the acknowledged collaboration of one or

287

more of the natives, then translates the information gathered in the field research, along with other material from written sources, into academic prose, and occasionally into a different kind of prose for a popular audience.

What has changed radically since the days of Malinowski and Mead is not the process of anthropological field research but the conscious, self-reflexive attention given to the epistemological, rhetorical, emotional, and ethical aspects of such research. Early accounts of fieldwork are plenty, but they present the anthropologist as a more or less heroic figure overcoming the harshness of the physical environment and the initial suspicion or hostility of the natives (Evans-Pritchard 1940, 7–15; and Chagnon 1968, 1–17). More recently, along with the critique that anthropological research was long motivated by colonial projects of domination (Fabian 1983; Asad 1973), there has been a much closer examination of several aspects of the process of fieldwork and the process by which fieldwork is translated into documentary form. These include the epistemological problem of coming to know the subject, the rhetorical problem of formulating arguments, the emotional problem of personal relationships between researchers, collaborators, and subjects, and the ethical problem of potentially intrusive research into sensitive topics. Each of these four problems is examined below.

THE EPISTEMOLOGICAL PROBLEM: COMING TO KNOW THE SUBJECT

It is no longer assumed, as it once was, that there is a single truth to be extracted from the ethnographic encounter. This idea is not necessarily rooted in the disputed philosophical point that human subjects are harder to know than inanimate objects (Roscoe 1995). It is simply the realization that all ethnographers are enmeshed in a web composed of the anthropologist's desire for knowledge and professional recognition; the subjects' help, accommodation, resistance, and sometimes purposeful deceit; and the requirements of institutions external to the field encounter, such as colonial officials, postindependence governments, funding agencies, institutional review boards, doctoral committees, journal editors, and academic presses.

In this ethnographic matrix, a research agenda, formulated at the beginning of the process, develops and changes as the research proceeds. The subject of the study, as well as the attitudes, interests, and desires of the ethnographer, often shift in the course of the research. In a clearly narrated example of such a process, Trawick went to Tamil Nadu to study conceptions of the body, but ended up writing a dissertation on theories of life process (1990, 8–9). Dissatisfied, and believing that she had contributed little more than one outsider's construction of a part of a way of life, she then apprenticed herself to an unusual guru and ended up doing a study (informed by Western theories) of love and human interaction in the guru's family. When she visited the family a few years later, all of the patterns she had so painstakingly observed and analyzed had changed in completely unpredictable ways (1990, 259–60). Trawick wrote a brilliant book about her findings, but even though the book is crammed with indisputable facts, it reveals more about the process of knowing than about the thing known. Other recent ethnographies describe the same evanescence of knowledge, something that is not found in classic accounts such as Evans-Pritchard's *The Nuer*, for example. But when we read of Evans-Pritchard's own difficulties in his field situation, and realize that he, too, constructed a model out of fragmentary, shifting data, we realize that his was only one out of many possible accounts of the "modes of livelihood of a Nilotic people" (Rosaldo 1986; Geertz 1988, 49–72).

Another epistemological problem involves the persons through whom one knows. Trawick's analyses of Tamil family life, as she herself admits, are derived primarily from a single family, and her cultural concepts from a single eccentric, if brilliant, guru. Victor Turner's analyses of Ndembu ritual seem almost entirely filtered through the knowledge of Muchona, an intellectually gifted Ndembu elder (Turner 1960). Even if we discard the notion of cultures as bounded entities (Abu-Lughod 1991), and realize that different individuals in any time and place have differing approaches to life, we may be frustrated, as I was in 1993, by the realization that we have little choice but to present the views we learn from—or, at least, through—particular individuals. My knowledge of ethnic identity and ethnic relationships in Liangshan is filtered through my own position as Professor Hao Rui, as Meigui Muga, or even as Hxielie Muga, as well as through the theoretical lens of my style of anthropology and the conceptual lens of my original research design, however much I modified the incredibly naïve original 1987 proposal. Perhaps more importantly, my view is colored by the years of collaboration described in the narratives in this book.

THE RHETORICAL PROBLEM: FORMULATING ARGUMENTS

Knowing what we know, or choose to know, or happen to know, the next problem that confronts the anthropologist is how to present it to the reading public. Why, we ask (as do they), should they believe us? Unlike the results of experimental laboratory and field science, our results are rarely readily or precisely replicable. What gives us the authority to represent Trobriand trading patterns, the Tamil family, or the basis of Nuosu ethnic identity? Both James Clifford's *The Predicament of Culture: Twentieth-Century Ethnography, Literature, and Art* (1988) and Clifford Geertz's *Works and Lives: The Anthropologist as Author* (1988) have presented typologies of ethnographic authority, the means by which ethnographers assume the mantle of authority for their reading public. Clifford, for example, suggests that in the twentieth century, ethnographic authority has expanded from experiential to interpretive to dialogic to polyphonic modes (1988, 21–54).

The experiential mode of authority is what Geertz (1988) calls "being there." Ethnographers assume authority because they have (a) experience in the place being written about, participant observation of native life, and (b) the scientific tools to take observations, which by themselves constitute only a small portion of life in a particular place, and synecdochically represent them as a broader picture, be it the culture under study or some comparative aspect of human behavior. In a sense, the ethnographic writer is a messenger, bringing knowledge from there to here. In this mode of authority, the majority of ethnographers are "from here," and only a minority are "from there." When the ethnographer is "from here," the claim of authority is "let me tell you, my compatriots, about an exotic place I have been." When the ethnographer is "from there," a much less common case, the message becomes "let me, a native, tell you, my hosts, about my country." Either way, the reader has to take

the ethnographer largely on faith; there are seldom any means of checking the accuracy of the facts reported.

In ethnography written after 1950, however, Clifford discerns a second mode of authority—the interpretive. No longer are observations
and conversations from the field to be taken as objective fact; ethnography becomes instead an interpretive exercise in the hermeneutic sense,
and transferring observations into writings involves finding meaning
in the acts observed—interpreting them. Observations become a text,
which the ethnographer interprets, much as one would interpret a literary or dramatic text. The ethnographic writer is no longer merely a
messenger, but an active and acknowledged author of the material, even
if the material was originally gathered elsewhere and created by others.
The centrality of the interpretive enterprise becomes obvious through
examples in which two ethnographers gave radically different interpretations of the same community, the most famous example being the
wildly different accounts of political power in the Mexican village of
Tepoztlán by Robert Redfield (*Tepotzlán, A Mexican Village: A Study of
Folk Life,* 1930) and Oscar Lewis (*Life in a Mexican Village: Tepoztlán
Restudied,* 1951).

Beginning in the 1970s, however, even interpretation became subject to the critique that the fieldwork process itself was a colonial (or,
at best, postcolonial) encounter, in which the anthropologist approached
the culture studied as a representative of a superior and often repressive power; whether the anthropologist's interpretation consciously portrayed this or not did not change this fact. Frankly, anthropologists felt
guilty for being implicated in such projects of inequality (see below),
and sought to mitigate the idea of truth authority based on political
authority. Some of them thus began to enter the dialogic mode, in which
the field encounter is portrayed as a conversation between the ethnographer and one or a series of people from the culture studied, in which
all contributed to the construction of the account.

In this dialogic mode, however, the ethnographer still held the final
authority; however much consultation went on, it was almost always
the ethnographer who actually wrote the study, who selected which of
the natives' utterances would be included. So some recent works have
experimented with a fourth mode, which Clifford calls "polyphony," in

which the only distinction between the ethnographer and the other participants is that the ethnographer is from "here" and the others are from "there." All are listed as authors, and all of the participants' words enter directly into the formation of the text.

The present work is, in a sense, a chronological series of reflections on an incomplete journey from an interpretive or dialogic to a polyphonic mode. The journey begins with works of which I am sole author, which bump uneasily between the interpretive and dialogic modes. This is because in China, given the ethnological tradition there, there exists an overlapping series of social roles that blur the distinction between "here" and "there." I have at least three kinds of Chinese interlocutors (which are not rigidly separated from each other) in my field research. First, there are the formulators of the standard discourse: the ethnological establishment. Some of these people are my good friends. But they have a very different view of the natives and of the enterprise than I do. Many of them consider themselves superior to the people being written about, because of their higher level of formal education, and the elder among them, at least, still believe in the Marxist-Leninist idea of social macroevolution. Second, there are my active scientific collaborators, those with whom I have spent time in the field, with whom I have engaged in weeks- and months-long dialogues of observation and interpretation, swerving back and forth between the minutiae of local society and the questions of what it all means. Bamo Ayi and Ma Lunzy, and, to a lesser extent, Bamo Qubumo, are representatives of this group. Finally, there are the "informants," those who had no formal role as researchers, but who contributed most of the material.

The material in my own works is a result of this uneasy mixing, but what of articles or books written together with native scholars (Harrell and Ma 1999; Harrell and Bamo Ayi 1998; Harrell, Bamo Qubumo, and Ma 2000)? What about this book? Is it polyphonic ethnography? Does collaboration constitute polyphony? Do scholars from native backgrounds count as "natives"? Is much of this material even ethnography? Is it ethnographic critique? Does it matter what genre we assign this book to? I leave these for readers to decide. I am more concerned about the ways in which collaboration has shaped the content and arguments of the work.

In the first place, the contributors to this book don't all think alike. Bamo Ayi is passionately committed to the idea of the Yi as a *minzu*, and to their social and economic advancement. I am always worrying about whether the category of Yi is constructed or not, and if so, how. Ma Lunzy's knowledge of Nuosu society, the result of a lifetime of speaking Nuohxo as his native language and living in and out of rural comsmunities, is much more organic than that of the Bamo sisters, who grew up in various parts of urban China, speak Chinese as their native language rather than Nuohxo, and have pursued comparative religion and folklore studies, respectively, as ways of finding their own roots. I know more about anthropology than they do, and speak more languages. But my knowledge of Nuosu society is a lot more superficial, and my Nuohxo language skills are embarrassingly poor. So we are different people, and do not speak alike. Perhaps the least refutable sense in which this book is polyphonic is the literal one; readers of my drafts all commented that I had managed, even through translation, to preserve three very distinct voices.

At the same time, we are all each other's creatures in some sense. My view of Nuosu ssociety is filtered through Ma Lunzy's, and his view is sometimes considered rather quirky, if brilliant, in the Yi studies establishment. His refusal to consider pre-1957 Liangshan to be a "slave society," for example, and his fluid view of the relationships between the various social strata in that society, put him at odds with much of orthodox interpretation (Ma 1993). The fact that he and the Bamos are members of the *quho*, or commoner stratum, influences their view and mine; the much more rigid view of hierarchical relations put forward by Martin Schoenhals, for example (Schoenhals 2001, 2003), may have a lot to do with his close association with a collaborator from the Nuoho aristocracy.

And my position has also influenced Yi scholars in their own work on their own society. The translation and publication of a collection of my essays by Bamo Ayi and her husband, Qumo Tiexi (Harrell 2000), meant that my analyses were available to people with no or limited knowledge of English; my interpretations have been cited by Yi scholars both favorably and critically (see Li Shaoming 2002). I am now regularly mentioned in the literature as "the founder of international Yi studies," and as such given a prominent position at international conferences on the topic. And my views, so strongly influenced by fieldwork and collaboration with Ma, the Bamos, and others (particularly my Yunnanese Yi student, Li Yongxiang; see Harrell and Li 2003), have in some ways thus circulated the views of my Yi collaborators back to their own scholarly world.

THE EMOTIONAL PROBLEM: PERSONAL RELATIONSHIPS

I remember going to hear James Clifford talk to an audience of literary critics at the University of Washington in April 1993, when I was only a few weeks back from Liangshan. Everything he said about fieldwork, about the epistemology and the rhetoric and the intellectual history, rang true; I had "been there." But having just recently been there, I was taken aback by his critical stance. I remained polite during the talk (I liked Clifford and agreed with much of what he said), but when I walked outside afterwards to talk to some of my graduate students, I spewed forth a torrent of puzzlement and frustration, more bemused than angry. Clifford's approach was so bloodless. In his critique were no purple fingers from washing clothes in cold water while standing on ice-covered ground, no diarrheal midnight trips in the snow to the unspeakably filthy outhouse, no involuntary three-day binges on cheap white lightning, no longing homesickness in a dingy hotel room, no anguished and later embarrassing sleepless 4:00-a.m. self-revelations in the diary (even though we know that Malinowski was given to these, too, and that his revelations were a lot more embarrassing than mine; see Malinowski 1967; Young 2004). And there were no rushes of warmth when ducking through the door into the firelit house, with grown men shouting "Oooooh!"; no wrenching farewells from dear friends who could be seen again only occasionally; no tastes of freshly caught carp in pepper sauce that surge through head and body with satisfaction, making one long for more; no reassuring arm around the shoulder from people who understood me and my frustrations at the time far better than I understood myself.

When I think of fieldwork, I think more immediately of these things than I do of the key interview in which I finally understood the genealogy of the local rulers, the precious sheet of local statistics that would allow me to reconstruct the process of agricultural development, or the volunteered tidbit about someone who had once proclaimed himself emperor in a village so high on the mountainside we could only point to it, having no time to go there. The chapters in this book by Ma Lunzy and Bamo Ayi, and even the short contribution by Bamo Qubumo, all contain similar reflections. Lunzy is irritated, impatient, wondering, and by degrees warm and generous. Ayi is nervous and nurturing. What is difficult to know is the extent to which emotional ups and downs influence the end product of the experience; perhaps the only possible analysis is psychoanalysis. Maybe a fieldworker is too close to his or her subject, and only a critical reader can judge what the influence might be.

THE ETHICAL PROBLEM: INTRUSIVE RESEARCH

An enormous amount has been written on fieldwork ethics, usually from a polemical stance. I think the two best that I have ever read are Robert Borofksy's *Yanomami: The Fierce Controversy and What We Can Learn from It* (2005), a truly polyphonic collection on the controversies surrounding the fieldwork ethics of James Neel and Napoleon Chagnon and the journalistic ethics and reliability of Patrick Tierney's exposé on the two fieldworkers, *Darkness in El Dorado: How Scientists and Journalists Devastated the Amazon* (2000); and Hsieh Shih-chung's brief article "Minzuzhi daode yu renleixue jia de kunjing" or "Ethnographic Ethics and the Predicament of the Anthropologist" (1987). In *Yanomami*, Borovsky and seven interlocutors debate the morality of various ethnographic practices in both fieldwork and writing, and broadly consider what the moral and ethical obligations of an ethnographer might be. Hsieh observes that anthropologists conducting field research have conflicting obligations to four groups of people: the people studied, their local scholarly collaborators, the scholarly and professional community to which they belong, and the university "human subjects" bureaucracy. To me, the last is the least compelling ethically, but it is a good entry point into a discussion of the larger issues. The university's "human subjects" guidelines permit our Liangshan research only if we stretch the letter of the regulations in what we all hope is the spirit of ethical

oversight. For one thing, informed consent is a concept not easily transferred to either a semiliterate society or a context in which almost all
knowledge is acquired publicly. It is also nearly impossible to make
people anonymous, in spite of the cheap and transparent trick of
changing personal and place names. And the canons of professional
ethics in Chinese ethnology, which, after all, contributed most of the
material for this book, give little thought to the protection and welfare
of the communities studied, and are not well codified—if they were
codified, they would probably be at odds in some areas with their U.S.
counterparts. The bureaucratic procedures of institutional review boards
have only recently begun to take special account of how ethnography
happens and how it is different from biomedical or social-survey
research; at the time our fieldwork connections were established,
Americans had to make things up—numbers of subjects, oral consent
scripts, procedures for dealing with unintended adverse effects of
research—to meet their guidelines, and the Chinese effectively had no
guidelines.

A much more serious ethical problem is anthropologists' obligation
to the local people of the research area. The American Anthropological
Association statement on "Principles of Professional Responsibility,"
adopted in the aftermath of accusations against anthropologists allegedly
working for the Central Intelligence Agency and the U.S. military, adopts
a version of the famous provision in the Hippocratic oath: "First, do
no harm." In this case, it means no harm to the people being written
about:

> In research, an anthropologist's paramount responsibility is to those he stud-
> ies. When there is a conflict of interest, these individuals must come first.
> The anthropologist must do everything within his power to protect their phys-
> ical, social, and psychological welfare and to honor their dignity and privacy
> (AAA 1971).

But what is "protection" and what is "harm"? Certainly, writing anything or acting in any way that will bring a people undesired attention
from repressive or extractive state bureaucracies is harm, as is raising
false expectations or promising the undeliverable or conducting ques-

tioning that is in any way coerced or uncomfortable for them. Indeed, the long and bitter Yanomami controversy described by Borovsky centers around questions of whether certain fieldworkers violated these ethical principles. At present, however, many villagers in Liangshan do not clearly understand the purpose of fieldwork, and even if they did understand it and approve of it now, what will they think in twenty years or the next generation? Would they feel better if they were anonymous, or would they rather see their names in print, especially if the latter caused the writer to be more careful about what he wrote?

One's obligation to the subjects of study is complicated by, and entangled with, the obligation to one's local scholarly colleagues, who are operating in a tradition that is less reflective of "informants' rights." They would be startled by some of our concerns, as one of my collaborators was when he found out that I hadn't written down actual names in one of my censuses for fear of violating subjects' anonymity—how could I tell later who I was talking about? Long-term fieldwork would seem like unnecessary hardship to many of them; they are much more interested in extensive than intensive research. At the same time, Ma Lunzy and scholars like him, who are still organically part of the village society of which they write, see fieldwork ethics from both sides of the looking glass. Ma Lunzy was visibly offended, for example, by the Han scholar who questioned the safety of his homeland; at the same time, he makes little effort to create anonymity for the people of whom he writes.

I think that a work like the present one goes beyond the parameters set by the discussion of ethics in Borovsky's *Yanomami*. In that work, the arguments take place among outside scholars, and concern the welfare of native subjects, whose views are sometimes invoked, refuted, or patronized by outsiders who are party to the controversy. In our book, however, the categories of native and scholar are blurred, as one scholar is a native and another a seminative. This raises the possibility of there being more than one set of ethical criteria for ethnography; these different criteria may not only conflict but may cross-fertilize each other as we develop an ethnographic ethics free of condescension.

The epistemological and ethical problematics which have so knotted the brains of cosmopolitan anthropologists in the last two decades have barely begun to intrude on the Chinese discipline, partly because in China there has been a fairly clear separation between the ethnographer as scholar (and thus morally superior being) and the subject as ignorant (albeit sometimes admirably innocent because of this ignorance). But this will change as more and more subjects enter the ethnographic process, first as readers and then as writers. Perhaps the international dialogue recounted in this book will give Chinese anthropology a head start in formulating what we can hope is a more thoughtful and less tangled ethical system than that possessed by its Western counterpart.

The ethical obligation to the scholarly community seems to me less serious, but this is because I sit at the Olympian height of full professorship, and could not be fired, only ostracized. This ostracism, of course, could come in the form of denial of subsequent grant applications, which would make it very difficult to conduct future research. But that would hurt me more than anybody else, and is thus not really an ethical concern. My main obligation is to tell some version of the truth, and to be open about how this version was arrived at.

Emerging from these four kinds of obligations are three concrete ethical issues that are apparent in the chapters of this book: issues of implication, exploitation, and reciprocation. The most obvious issue is that of implication. In conducting our research, we have all been complicit with local and regional bureaucrats, with the establishment and practice of Chinese ethnology, and with the project of Nuosu and Yi propaganda. We can (and do, to various degrees) criticize state projects that lead to disempowerment and assimilation of ethnic minorities, as well as the simple-minded epistemological assumptions of Chinese ethnology and orthodox Marxist social science in general. But we all work together; we could not work with the villagers except through each other and through the bureaucrats and the ethnological establishment. And, anyway, the bureaucrats and scholars are as much a part of the story as the villagers.

The issue of exploitation is significant on two levels: that of the villagers, and that of the local cadres and scholars. At present, exploitation is not much of a problem with the villagers. We usually talk to them in the slack farming season, and, true to their stereotype as minorities, they really are "fond of guests" or "hospitable." Only once was I made to feel unwelcome—at the Han wedding described by Ma in chapter 13—and we left after ten or fifteen minutes. The only possible threat of exploitation of the villagers might be from their own hospitality—they serve expensive food (whole animals) that they would not eat otherwise. Since they have always fed us enthusiastically, however, I have usually not felt exploitative in that situation. As Ma pointed out, Yi scholars feel pride rather than shame when animals are slaughtered for the benefit of them or their foreign hosts and collaborators. With the scholars and bureaucrats, however, the question of exploitation seems more serious—they have put themselves at personal risk and spent a lot of time and money facilitating my research.

This last brings us to the final ethical issue, reciprocation. Many times—especially in the 1980s and 1990s, when Chinese government offices were strapped for cash and when hard currency was literally worth far more than gold—I heard American scholars say that they had been "ripped off" by Chinese universities or research institutes who had charged them high fees and requested impossible favors, and still hadn't provided "good access" to whatever the object of research was, be it archives or villages. I sometimes sympathize, but not always. I ask myself what's in it for the Chinese collaborators, other than hard currency fees. What foreigners going to China have to realize is that by entering into any kind of research collaboration, they enter into a Maussian web of obligation and counterobligation, of debt and prestation, that requires something of a commitment. Often, however, the commitment of time or resources required is no greater than that which Chinese colleagues have made to facilitate the research in the first place.

What are the ethical implications of this Maussian web? Does the fact that I helped raise money to build a school in Ma Lunzy's home village mean that the local villagers need to cooperate willingly in all the research conducted by me and my students? Does bringing all three coauthors to the United States to work on a collaborative project give me a kind of credit account that I can draw on to do research that they are not particularly interested in, especially since my own work increasingly consists of ecological surveys and supervising undergraduate research projects whose main contribution is to the students' own training and not to the welfare of the local community? To what degree is quid pro quo the right way to think about obligations between researchers and subjects, or between researchers and researchers?

The present work does not attempt to analyze any of these questions in detail, or to present definitive answers to any of them. But we hope, at least, that our story will give food for thought to our friends and colleagues in the United States and in China, in the anthropological community and in the village communities.

CAST OF CHARACTERS

Abbott, Mark (b. 1944). Pastor of Seattle First Free Methodist Church.

Aga Bimo. *See* Yyhxo Aga.

Amber. *See* Joy, Amber.

Arn. *See* Slettebak, Arn.

Arnold, Solveig (Soph; b. 1921). Member of the Women's Group at Seattle First Free Methodist Church; later landlady of Bamo Qubumo in Seattle.

Asa. *See* Qumo Asa.

Azhe Bimo. *See* Jjike Azhe.

Bamo Ayi 巴莫阿依 (Ngan Lan 安兰; b. 1961). Anthropologist and comparative religion scholar. Elder sister of Bamo Qubumo. Now deputy director of the Foreign Affairs Department, State Nationalities Commission (Guojia Minwei), and professor of philosophy at Central University for Nationalities, Beijing.

Bamo Erha 巴莫尔哈 (Bamo Lurhxa; b. 1933). Father of Bamo Ayi and Bamo Qubumo. Former mayor and Party Secretary of Xichang. Later vice-prefect of Liangshan.

Bamo Qubumo 巴莫曲布嫫 (b. 1964). Folklorist, author, and curator. Younger sister of Bamo Ayi. Now professor of folklore at the Institute for Ethnic Literature, Chinese Academy of Social Sciences, Beijing.

Bamo Vusamo 巴莫巫撒嫫 (b. 1969). Youngest sister of Bamo Ayi and Bamo

Qubumo. Married to youngest son of Yang Zipo. Now reporter for Sichuan Radio in Xichang.

Cheryl Lee. Amber Joy's friend and tenant in Seattle.

Cindy. Member of the Women's Group at Seattle First Free Methodist Church.

Dai Wanping 戴万平 (b. 1945). Driver for the Panzhihua City Artifacts Preservation Office.

Deng Yaozong 邓耀宗 (Lao Deng; 1936–2003). Mentor of Stevan Harrell. Classmate of Tong Enzheng at Sichuan University. Director of the Panzhihua City Artifacts Preservation Office, Panzhihua City Government.

Director Zhou. *See* Zhou Xiyin.

Driver Dai. *See* Dai Wanping.

Erin. *See* Younger, Erin.

Father (Ayi). *See* Bamo Erha.

Father (Lunzy). *See* Mgebbu Ashy.

Gaga Erri. *See* Gaga Lyssyr.

Gaga Lyssyr (Gaga Erri 呷呷而日; b. 1949). Researcher at the Liangshan Nationalities Research Institute. Native of Ganluo County. Research collaborator of Steve and Lunzy in 1993.

Gladney, Dru C. (b. 1957) Ph.D. student of Stevan Harrell. Now professor of anthropology at the University of Hawai'i. Author of several books on ethnicity in China and on Chinese Muslims.

Gwendolyn. Daughter of Amber Joy.

Hao Rui 郝瑞. Chinese name of Stevan Harrell.

Harrell, Barbara Blain (b. 1949). Wife of Stevan Harrell. Now retired physician in Seattle.

Harrell, Stevan (Hao Rui 郝瑞; Meigui Muga; Muga; b. 1947). Anthropologist and translator. Now professor of anthropology at the University of Washington.

Hoqie. *See* Jjike Hoqie.

Hsieh Jiann 谢剑 (b. ca. 1935): Anthropologist. Participant in the first Yi conference. Now professor of sociology at Fo Guang University, Taiwan.

Hu Jin'ao 胡金鳌 (Luoho Tuha; b. 1940). Nuosu scholar in Yanyuan. Teacher and confidant of Lunzy.

Huojy. *See* Nuobu Huojy.

Hutterer, Karl (b. 1940). Archaeologist and museum director. Director of the Burke Museum, 1990–2000. Now executive director of the Santa Barbara Museum of Natural History.

Jason. Son of Amber Joy.

Jjike Azhe (1951–1999). *Bimo* in Meigu. Fluent in Chinese, with progressive ideas. Interviewed by Ayi in 1995.

Jjike Hoqie (b. 1953). Education cadre and former apprentice *bimo*. Field collaborator of Bamo Ayi in Yinchang.

Jjike Nyieddu (Nyieddu Bimo; 1923–1996). Prominent *bimo* in Yanyuan, famous for curing tuberculosis. Consultant for Ayi's research.

Jjike Sadda (Sadda Bimo; 1914–1998). Prominent *bimo* in Ganluo County. Chief consultant for Bamo sisters' Ganluo research.

Jjike Vudda (Vudda Bimo; 1926–1990). *Bimo* in Yinchang. Father of Jjike Hoqie.

Jjike Yuoga Hlumo (Yuoga Hlumo; 1904–1997). One of Liangshan's most prominent *bimo*. Interviewed by Ayi in 1994.

Joy, Amber (b. 1943). Ayi's and later Li Yongxiang's landlady in Seattle. Active in the Seattle First Free Methodist Church.

Karl. *See* Hutterer, Karl.

Lamo. Ayi's research assistant in Zhaojue and Meigu, 1994–95.

Lan Mingchun 兰明春 (b. 1964). Graduate student in sociology at Sichuan University. Member of the 1988 Panzhihua research team. Later an editor at several presses in Chengdu.

Lao Deng. *See* Deng Yaozong.

Lao Xiang. *See* Xiang Dexin.

Lao Yan. *See* Yan Dezong.

Leng Guangdian 岭光电 (1913–1989). Nuosu educator, reformer, and scholar. Born into a *tusi* family in Ganluo; attended Whampoa Military Academy; returned to Liangshan to found the first modern elementary school in his native Ganluo. Later taught Yi studies in Beijing.

Li Chaoshen 李朝申 (b. ca. 1942). Head of the Panzhihua Municipality *minwei* in 1988.

Li Mingxi 黎明曦 (b. 1945). Researcher at the Panzhihua City Artifacts Preservation Office; "elder sister" of the 1988 Panzhihua research team.

Li Yongxiang 李永祥 (b. 1966). Nisu Yi anthropologist from Xinping, Yunnan. Participant in the first Yi conference. Later Ph.D. student of Steve. Now researcher at the Yunnan Academy of Social Sciences.

Liu Xin 刘欣 (b. 1962). Graduate student in sociology at Sichuan University. Member of the 1988 Panzhihua research team. Now professor of sociology at Fudan University in Shanghai.

Liu Yulan 刘玉兰 (b. 1940). Mother of Bamo Ayi and Bamo Qubumo. Mixed Mongolian and Han ethnicity, originally from Inner Mongolia. Formerly head of the Foreign Affairs Department, Xichang City government.

Long Yun 龙云 (1884–1962). Chinese warlord. Originally from a Nuosu family in Jinyang. Governor of Yunnan, 1927–45.

Ma Erzi. *See* Ma Lunzy.

Ma Lunzy 马尔子 (Mgebbu Lunzy; Mgebbu Vurryr; Vurryr; b. 1957). Ethnologist, historian, author, and curator. Native of Yangjuan, Yanyuan. Now deputy director of Liangshan Minorities Research Institute.

Ma Xueliang 马学良 (1913–1999). Chinese ethnologist, philologist, and historian; author of numerous books on Yi and related languages and peoples. Bamo Ayi's Ph.D. advisor at the Central Nationalities Institute in Beijing.

Mama (Ayi). *See* Liu Yulan.

Mark. *See* Abbott, Mark.

Meigui Muga. Yi-language name of Stevan Harrell.

Mgebbu Ashy (b. 1933). Father of Lunzy. Son of prominent *qunuo* clan leader in Yanyuan. Now farmer and herder in Yangjuan Village, Yanyuan.

Mgebbu Lalyr. Nephew of Lunzy. Truck driver and transport entrepreneur. Drove Lunzy and Steve to Lugu Lake, 1994.

Mgebbu Lunzy. *See* Ma Lunzy.

Mgebbu Vurryr. *See* Ma Lunzy.

Muga. Nuosu-language name of Stevan Harrell.

Ngan Lan 安兰. Han-language name of Bamo Ayi.

Nuobie Yopuo (Yopuo Bimo; b. 1941). *Bimo* specialized in cursing rituals; interviewed by Ayi in 1994.

Nuobu Huojy. Researcher at the Liangshan Nationalities Research Institute. Native of Xide County. Companion of Ayi and Steve in Mishi, 1994.

Nyieddu Bimo. *See* Jjike Nyieddu.

Pastor Mark. *See* Abbott, Mark.

Qubi Shimei 曲比石美 (b. 1936). Former head of the Liangshan *minwei* and the Liangshan Nationalities Research Institute. Also trained as a *bimo*.

Qumo Asa (b. 1990). Daughter of Bamo Ayi.

Ren Hai 任海 (b. 1965). Anthropologist. Former research assistant of Tong Enzheng. Participant in Harrell's 1988 fieldwork. Later M.A. and Ph.D. student at the University of Washington. Now faculty member at the University of Arizona.

Rock, Joseph (1884–1962). Austrian-American classicist, botanist, ethnologist, and historian. Lived in Lijiang for many years, and made many expeditions to Lugu Lake and other areas mentioned in this book, between 1926 and 1950.

Sadda Bimo. *See* Jjike Sadda.

Schoenhals, Martin (b. 1961). Anthropologist specializing in education. Now associate professor of anthropology, Dowling College.

Secretary Yang. *See* Yang Zipo.

Shi Shuqing (b. 1923). Archaeologist. Deputy head of the State Relics Appraisal Committee, Beijing.

Skinner, G. William (b. 1925). Anthropologist. Senior professor at Stanford University 1966–85. Stevan Harrell's Ph.D. advisor and doctoral committee member. Now at UC Davis.

Slettebak, Arn (b. 1947). Exhibit curator and exhibit builder, Burke Museum.

Soph. *See* Arnold, Solveig.

Swain, Margaret Byrne (Peggy; b. 1948). Anthropologist and tourism researcher. Works with the Sani, a group of Yi in Yunnan. Now associate professor at UC Davis.

Tao Xingzhi (1891–1946). Educator and reformer in late Qing and Republican China.

Tomlonovic, Kathleen. Former Ph.D. student of Tong Enzheng. Now professor of Chinese at Western Washington University.

Tong Enzheng (1935–1997). Mentor of Stevan Harrell and Ren Hai. Professor of history and director of the Sichuan University Museum. Author of numerous scholarly and popular works in archaeology, art history, anthropology, and science fiction. Later visiting professor at Wesleyan University in Connecticut.

Vudda Bimo. *See* Jjike Vudda.

Vurryr. *See* Ma Lunzy.

Wang Chengxiao 王成孝 (b. 1950). Calligrapher and researcher in the Panzhihua Artifacts Preservation Office. Member of the 1988 Panzhihua research team.

Wu Ga 伍呷 (Luovu Vugashynyumo; b. 1957). Nuosu scholar and anthropologist. Daughter of former Tibet Party Secretary Wu Jinghua. Now researcher at Yunnan Academy of Social Sciences, Kunming.

Wu Gu 伍谷 (Luoxi Wuge 罗西吾戈; b. ca. 1935). Yi Scholar from Yunnan. Participant in the first Yi conference.

Wu Jingzhong 伍精忠 (b. 1940). Nuosu scholar. Former head of the Sichuan Nationalities Research Institute. Participant in the first Yi conference. Uncle of Wu Ga.

Xiang Dexin 向德馨 (Lao Xiang; b. ca. 1930). Deputy director of the Panzhihua Culture Bureau. Deng Yaozong's nominal boss.

Yan Dezong 晏德宗 (Lao Yan; b. ca. 1946). Deputy director of the Panzhihua Artifacts Preservation Office. Field companion of Steve in Futian, 1994.

Yang Ziha 杨子哈 (b. ca. 1960). Party Secretary of Mishi Township in 1994.

Yang Zipo 杨子坡 (b. 1947) (Atu Nzypo). Party Secretary of Yanyuan County. Later vice-chair of Liangshan Prefecture People's Congress. Former teacher of Lunzy. Father of Ayi's youngest sister's husband.

Yopuo Bimo. *See* Nuobie Yopuo.

Younger, Erin (b. 1952). Director of public programs at the Burke Museum, in charge of all exhibits and other public activities.

Yu Hongmo 余宏漠 (b. ca. 1935). Yi historian from Guizhou. Participant in the first Yi conference.

Yuoga Hlumo. *See* Jjike Yuoga Hlumo.

Yyhxo Aga (b. 1962). *Bimo* from Yanyuan, working in the translation office of the Yanyuan County Government. Research assistant to Ayi in Yanyuan.

Zeng Qiansu 曾乾素 (Zeng Saosao; 1936–2004). Wife of Deng Yaozong.

Zeng Saosao. *See* Zeng Qiansu.

Zhang Boxi 张伯西 (b. ca. 1935). Second Party Secretary of Panzhihua in 1988; classmate of Tong Enzheng.

Zhang Yong 张勇. Researcher at the Miyi County *minwei*.

Zhong Jingwen 钟敬文 (1903–2002). Folklorist. Longtime professor at Beijing Normal University. Bamo Qubumo's Ph.D. advisor.

Zhou Xiyin 周锡银 (b. 1936). Ethnologist. Former director of the Sichuan Nationalities Research Institute.

CHINESE AND NUOSU GLOSSARY

Chinese terms (C) are romanized in the pinyin system, and are given in (simplified) Chinese characters as well. Nuosu terms (N) are romanized according to the standard system used in the PRC, omitting letters used as tone markers (t, x, and p) at the end of syllables for ease of pronunciation.

Adur. A subdialect of the Suondi dialect of the Nuosu language. Spoken in parts of Puge and Butuo counties.

ama (N). Grandmother.

bainian 拜年 (C). To pay respects at the new year.

bimo (N). A priest of the Nuosu people.

bisse (N). An apprentice *bimo*.

Black Yi. See *nuoho*.

Chuanda 川大 (C). Short for Sichuan Daxue 四川大学, or Sichuan University, the most prestigious university in Sichuan Province.

Democratic Reforms (C; *minzhu gaige* 民主改革, usually shortened to *mingai* 民改). The Communist Party's program to revolutionize the societies of minority peoples, begun in 1956.

diaocha (C). "Investigation," or field research.

Fire Festival (Nuosu duzi). The midsummer festival shared by all the Yi and related peoples in Southwest China, celebrated on the twenty-fourth day of the sixth lunar month. Called *houbajie*

火把节 or "torch festival" in Chinese.

gefi (N). A woman's "birthing" or fertility spirit.

Guomindang 国民党 (C). Also Kuomintang or KMT. The Chinese nationalist party, in power on the Chinese Mainland 1927–49, and in Taiwan 1945–87 as a one-party dictatorship. Now a democratic political party in Taiwan.

Han or Hanzu 汉族 (C). The dominant ethnic group in China; "ethnic Chinese."

Hnewo abu or *Hnewo teyy* (N). A compilation of Nuosu myths about the creation of the world and the origins of humans and society.

huajiao 花椒 (C). Sichuan peppercorn (*Zanthoxylem sp.*), the spice that gives the characteristic *ma* 麻 or "numbing" taste to Sichuanese food.

Hui or Huizu 回族. China's largest Muslim nationality. Chinese-speaking. Living in almost every county in China.

kerre (N). Diaphonic rhythmic chanting done at Nuosu weddings, funerals, and other ritual occasions.

Lipuo. A subgroup of the Yi living in north-central Yunnan and Panzhihua. Inhabitants of Yishala.

luoluo 倮罗 (C). Pejorative Han-language term for Yi peoples. Often Anglicized as Lolo.

lurby (N). Nuosu proverbs, often in couplet form.

manzi 蛮子 (C). Barbarian. Pejorative Han term for Nuosu and other minorities.

Menggu or Mengguzu 蒙古族. One of China's fifty-six officially recognized *minzu*. The Na in Yanyuan and Muli are classified as part of this *minzu*.

minwei 民委 (C). Short for *minzu shiwu weiyuanhui* 民族事物委员会, or Central Nationalities Affairs Commission. The branch of government in charge of affairs involving *shaoshu minzu*, or officially designated ethnic minorities.

minzu 民族 (C). One of the fifty-six officially recognized "nationalities" in China. Han, Yi, and Zang are the three *minzu* that are most frequently mentioned in this book.

Mosuo. *See* Na.

Na. Also Naze or Mosuo. An ethnic group, famous for its matrilineal social system, living around Lugu Lake and in nearby parts of Yanyuan, Muli, and Ninglang. In

Sichuan, usually grouped with the Meng, or "Mongolian" *minzu*.

Nationalities Institutes 民族学院. Institutions of higher education operated especially for members of China's minority nationalities, or *shaoshu minzu*. Some of them later Nationalities Universities 民族大学.

Naxi. An ethnic group or *minzu* living in northwest Yunnan.

nimu cobi (N). The seven-day-long ritual of sending off the soul of and worshipping the ancestor.

nuoho (N). A high-ranking, aristocratic stratum of Nuosu society. Called *heiyi* 黑彝 or "Black Yi" in Chinese.

Nuosu (N). An ethnic group of about two million members; part of the Yi *minzu*.

nzymo (N). A high-ranking stratum of Nuosu society, from which the *tusi* were appointed by successive imperial governments.

Operation Nightwatch. A Christian ministry to the homeless in Seattle, where Ayi volunteered in 1996–97.

Ozzu (N). A name for Na, Prmi, and other non-Yi peoples who speak Tibeto-Burman languages and are classified by the Chinese government as Zangzu or "Tibetan Nationality."

Panzhihua 攀枝花 (C). Local dialect word for the kapok tree (*Bombax sp.*), also called *mumian* 木棉. The city of Panzhihua is named after this large tree that flowers red in the spring.

People's Congress (C; *renmin daibiao dahui* 人民代表大会, usually shortened to *renda* 人大). Nominal legislature of Chinese governments at each administrative level.

People's Consultative Conference (C; *renmin zhengzhi xieshang hui* 人民政治协商会, usually shortened to *zhengxie* 政协). An advisory arm of the Chinese State, whose members are usually non-Party figures of importance in society, but whose leaders are often senior Party members. In Liangshan, *zhengxie* representatives are often drawn from the leadership of traditional local Nuosu society.

Prmi. Also Premi or Pumi. An ethnic group speaking a Qiangic language, living in the Sichuan-Yunnan border area. In Sichuan they belong to the Zang ("Tibetan") nationality; in Yunnan they are classified as their own nationality, Pumi Zu (普米族).

quho (N). A middle-ranking, or commoner stratum of Nuosu society, called 白彝 or "White Yi" in Chinese.

saosao 嫂嫂 (C). Older brother's wife.

Shama. The realm of the Shama *tusi* in Jinyang, whose cultural styles are distinctive and display considerable Han influence. Also the Shama Qubi clan, from which Shama (Mgebbu) Lunzy and his relatives derive their Han surname, Ma.

Shuitian 水田 (C). A small ethnic group, also called Laluo, within the larger Yi *minzu*. The population of Zhuangshang in 1988 was over 80 percent Shuitian.

shuo (N). "Slave, clanless person." A pejorative Nuosu name for Han.

Shynra. The central and standard dialect of the Nuosu language.

soft sleeper (C; *ruanwo* 软卧). The most expensive and comfortable class on an overnight train in China. In the 1980s, only high-ranking officials and foreigners and their companions were allowed to travel soft sleeper.

SPU. Seattle Pacific University. A Church-affiliated university in Seattle.

Suondi. The southeastern dialect of the Nuosu Language, spoken in Butuo, Puge, Ningnan, Huili, etc.

tusi 土司 (C). A local native official of the Ming or Qing dynasty government.

uoqie hxie (N). Ritual of pacification.

vala (N). A woven wool or yak-hair cape, often fringed, worn by Nuosu people in cold weather.

White Yi. See *quho*.

xiaoyou 校友 (C). "School friend." Alumnus or fellow alumnus.

xiucai 秀才 (C). Colloquial designation for the holder of the lowest degree in the Qing dynasty examination system, formally known as *shengyuan* 生员.

Yala or **Niluo.** A small ethnic group in Malong and Hengshan townships, Miyi County. Involuntarily classified as Yi.

Yi or Yizu 彝族 (C). The Nuosu, Lipuo, Shuitian, Yala, etc., are ethnic groups within the broader category of Yi.

Yynuo. The northern dialect of the Nuosu language, spoken in Meigu and environs.

Zang or **Zangzu** 藏族 (C). One of China's fifty-six officially recognized "nationalities," or *minzu*. Includes Tibetans and other related peoples such as Prmi.

BIBLIOGRAPHY

Abu-Lughod, Lila. 1991. "Writing Against Culture." In Richard G. Fox, ed., *Recapturing Anthropology*, 137–62. Santa Fe: School of American Research Press.

American Anthropological Association. 1971. "Statement on Principles of Professional Responsibility." American Anthropological Association: Washington, D.C.

Asad, Talal, ed. 1973. *Anthropology and the Colonial Encounter*. London: Ithaca Press.

Bamo Ayi. 1994. *Yi zu zu ling xin yang yan jiu: Yi wen gu ji tan tao yu Yi zu zong jiao yi shi kao cha* [Yi Ancestral Spirit Beliefs: A Discussion of Yi Language Scriptures and an Investigation of Yi People's Ancestral Rituals]. Chengdu: Sichuan Minzu Chuban She.

Borofsky, Robert, ed. 2005. *Yanomami: The Fierce Controversy and What We Can Learn From It*. Berkeley: University of California Press.

Bradley, David. 2001. "Language Policy for the Yi." In Stevan Harrell, ed., *Perspectives on the Yi of Southwest China*, 195–213. Berkeley: University of California Press.

Cai Hua. 2001. *A Society without Fathers or Husbands: The Na of China*. Translated by Asti Hustvedt. New York: Zone Books.

Chagnon, Napoleon A. 1968. *Yanomamö: The Fierce People*. New York: Holt, Rinehart and Winston.

Clifford, James. 1988. *The Predicament of Culture: Twentieth-Century Ethnography, Literature, and Art*. Cambridge, MA: Harvard University Press.

Daniel, E. Valentine. 1984. *Fluid Signs: Being a Person the Tamil Way*. Berkeley: University of California Press.

Evans-Pritchard, E. E. 1940. *The Nuer: A Description of the Modes of Livelihood and Political Institutions of a Nilotic People*. Oxford: Clarendon Press.

Fabian, Johannes. 1983. *Time and the Other: How Anthropology Makes Its Object*. New York: Columbia University Press.

Firth, Raymond. 1936. *We, the Tikopia: A Sociological Study of Kinship in Primitive Polynesia*. London: G. Allen & Unwin, Ltd.

Geertz, Clifford. 1988. *Works and Lives: The Anthropologist as Author*. Stanford: Stanford University Press.

Gladney, Dru C. 1991. *Muslim Chinese: Ethnic Nationalism in the People's Republic*. Cambridge, MA: Harvard University Press.

Harrell, Barbara B. 1981. "Lactation and Menstruation in Cultural Perspective." *American Anthropologist* 83, no. 4:796–823.

Harrell, Stevan. 1990. "Ethnicity, Local Interests, and the State: Yi Communities in Southwest China." *Comparative Studies in Society and History* 32, no. 3:515–48.

———. 1992. "Aspects of Marriage in Three Southwestern Villages." *China Quarterly* 130:323–37.

———. 1993. "Geography, Demography, and Family Structure in Three Southwestern Villages." In Deborah Davis and Stevan Harrell, eds., *Chinese Families in the Post-Mao Era*, 77–102. Berkeley: University of California Press.

———. 1995. "The History of the History of the Yi." In Stevan Harrell, ed., *Cultural Encounters on China's Ethnic Frontiers*, 63–91. Seattle: University of Washington Press.

———. 1996. "Jeeping Against Maoism." *Positions* 3, no. 3:728–58.

———. 2000. *Tianye Zhong de Zuqun Guanxi yu Minzu Rentong* [Ethnic Relations and Ethnic Identity in the Field]. Translated by Qumo Tiexi and Bamo Ayi. Nanning: Guangxi Minzu Chuban She.

———. 2001. *Ways of Being Ethnic in Southwest China*. Seattle: University of Washington Press.

Harrell, Stevan, and Bamo Ayi. 1998. "Chinese Nationalism in Minority Language Textbooks: The Case of the Nuosu (Yi) of Liangshan. *Bulletin of the Concerned Asian Scholars* 30, no. 2:62–71.

Harrell, Stevan, Bamo Qubumo, and Ma Erzi. 2000. *Mountain Patterns: The Survival of Nuosu Culture in China.* Seattle: University of Washington Press.

Harrell, Stevan, and Li Yongxiang. 2003. "The History of the History of the Yi, Part 2." *Modern China* 29, no. 3:1–38.

Harrell, Stevan, and Ma Erzi. 1999. "Folk Theories of Success Where Han Aren't Always the Best." In Gerard Postiglione, ed., *China's National Minority Education,* 213–42. New York: Falmer Press.

Hsieh Shih-chung. 1987. "Minzuxue daode yu renleixuejia de kunjing" [Ethnographic Ethics and the Predicament of the Anthropologist]. *Dangdai* 2:20–39.

Lavie, Smadar. 1990. *The Poetics of Military Occupation: Mzeina Allegories of Bedouin Identity under Israeli and Egyptian Rule.* Berkeley: University of California Press.

Lewis, Oscar. 1951. *Life in a Mexican Village: Tepoztlán Restudied.* Urbana: University of Illinois Press.

Li Shaoming. 2002. "Cong Zhongguo Yizu de rentong tan zuti lilun: Yu Hao Rui (Stevan Harrell) jiaoshou shangque" [Discussing the theory of ethnic groups through the identity of the Yi of China: Debating with Professor Stevan Harrell]. *Minzu yanjiu* 2:31–38.

Ma Erzi. 2003. "A New Understanding of the Old Liangshan Yi Social Structure and an Analysis of 'Black Yi' and 'White Yi.' *Chinese Sociology and Anthropology* 36(1):75–93.

Malinowski, Bronislaw. 1922. *Argonauts of the Western Pacific.* London: G. Routledge & Sons.

———. 1967. *A Diary in the Strict Sense of the Term.* Translated by Norbert Guterman. New York: Harcourt, Brace & World.

Mead, Margaret. 1975. *Blackberry Winter: My Earlier Years.* New York: Washington Square Press.

Mgebbu Lunzy. 2003. "Nuosu and Neighboring Ethnic Groups: Ethnic Groups and Ethnic Relations through the Eyes and Ears of Three Generations of the Mgebbu Clan." *Asian Ethnicity* 4, no. 1:129–45.

Potter, Sulamith Heins, and Jack Potter. 1990. *China's Peasants: The Anthropology of a Revolution.* Cambridge: Cambridge University Press.

Redfield, Robert. 1930. *Tepotzlán, A Mexican Village: A Study of Folk Life*. Chicago: University of Chicago Press.

Rosaldo, Renato. 1986. "From the Door of His Tent: The Fieldworker and the Inquisitor." In James Clifford and George E. Marcus, eds., *Writing Culture*, 77–97. Berkeley: University of California Press.

Roscoe, Paul B. 1995. "Perils of 'Positivism' in Cultural Anthropology." *American Anthropologist* 97, no. 3:492–504.

Schoenhals, Martin. 2001. "Education and Ethnicity among the Liangshan Yi." In Stevan Harrell, ed., *Perspectives on the Yi of Southwest China*, 238–55. Berkeley: University of California Press.

———. 2003. *Intimate Exclusion: Race and Caste Turned Inside Out*. Lanham, MD: University Press of America.

Shih, Chuan-kang. 2000. "Tisese and its anthropological significance: Issues around the visiting sexual system among the Moso." *L'Homme* 154–155: 697–712.

Siu, Helen F. 1989. *Agents and Victims in South China: Accomplices in Rural Revolution*. New Haven: Yale University Press.

Tierney, Patrick. 2000. *Darkness in El Dorado: How Scientists and Journalists Devastated the Amazon*. New York: Norton.

Trawick, Margaret. 1990. *Notes on Love in a Tamil Family*. Berkeley: University of California Press.

Turner, Victor W. 1960. "Muchona the Hornet, Interpreter of Religion." In Joseph B. Casagrande, ed., *In the Company of Man*. New York: Harper.

Wolf, Margery. 1985. *Revolution Postponed: Women in Contemporary China*. Stanford: Stanford University Press.

Young, Michael W. 2004. *Malinowski: Odyssey of an Anthropologist, 1884–1920*. New Haven: Yale University Press.

INDEX

Illustrations are indicated by page numbers in bold.

315

Baiwu Township, 93–95, 100: ethnic groups in, 94–95; fieldwork in, 103–8; schools in, 172

Bamo Erha: attitude toward fieldwork, 33; father in mixed household, 5, 8, **10**; and Manshuiwan, 136–37; as mayor and Party secretary, 11, 31, 34; meeting Steve, 164, 169; promoting education, 158; urging daughters to form research group, 72

Bamo Lurhxa. *See* Bamo Erha

Bamo Qubumo: fieldwork with Ayi, 72–78, **73**; as graduate student, 11; meeting Steve, 136, 163, 178; role of in Mountain Patterns exhibit, 248–74

Bamo Sisters' Yi Studies Research Group, 72, **167**

Bamo Vusamo, 146, 164, 166, **167**

banquets: in Panzhihua, 69–70; in Xide, 150; at Yang Erche's house, 195; on Yang Zipo's junket, 108, 131; in Yanyuan, 95, 100–101

baptism, 238

Baptist church. *See* Mt. Zion Baptist Church

bargaining for artifacts, 250–51

Baru District, 34

basketball, 20–21; Lunzy's love for, 223; minister's wife a star player, 246–47; NBA, 223; and social networks, 173, 195

baths: hot springs, 109, 132, 202; lack of, 42, 108

Bbaqie clan, 7

beauty: contests, 266; extravagant sense of, 252; and poverty, 284

"being there," 290–91, 294

bells, sound of, 171, 187

Bi Ashy Lazze, 36, 81

bimo: Ayi's fieldwork with, 72–88, 198–205; *bilu asa* protective spirit, 84; books of, 76, 249, 253; chants, 86–87; compensation to, 84; as curers, 50–51; cursing, 198–202; defined, 34n2, 35n3; dependency on, 203–4; and development, 203–4; and divination, 13n1, 76; efficacy of rituals of, 280; expulsion after ritual of, 85–86; income sources of, 201, 204; of the Jjike clan, 74–75, 80, 203–4; and modern communications, 205; in Mountain Patterns exhibit, 270–72, 279–80, 281; numbers of in Meigu, 205; place at a ritual, 36; relations with clients, 40, 82–83, 203; relations with state, 203–4, 279–80; ritual tools of not for sale, 249; role of in funeral, 266; romaniticization of, 280; and tourism, 280; types of, 81–82; woman studying to be, 35–36, 80–81, 83–84; and womanizing, 82

birthdays, Nuosu not celebrating, 13

birthing spirit (*gefi*), 39–40

Black Americans, 233–34

Bön religion, 173

book signing, 275

Borofsky, Robert, 295, 297

brideprice, 50

burial practices, 15, 145–46

Burke Museum, 217, 248, 250, 253, 258, 259; Qubumo's first sight of, 257

Butuo County, 252–53; laquerware from, 280–81

cadres: arrogance of, 132, 184; as asset to fieldwork, 150, 166, 176, 182; as *bimo* clients, 205; as impediment to fieldwork, 139, 187–88; loosening attitude to foreigners, 170; multiculturalism of, 109; suspicion of, 160

calendar, Nuosu, 263

calendrical animals, 5

canoes, ethnic, 109, **110**

Cantonese language, 24–25

caste system, Nuosu, 107–8, 130, 168–69, 260, 281

Catholic Church, 64–65, **66**, 237, 238

censuses, 104, 139–40, 151–53, 160, 171

Central Intelligence Agency, 296

Central Nationalities Institute, 53, 80; Bamo Ayi as student at, 9–12; ethnic relations at, 9–11

Chagnon, Napoleon, 295

Changma Village, 104

Chengdu, 56, 60–61, 103, 163

childhood: of Bamo Ayi, 5–8; of Ma Lunzy, 13–21

China-Japan Southwest Folklore Investigation Team, 136

China Overseas Steam Navigation Company, 258

China Studies Program, 162, 225

Chinese-American relations, 118–19, 123, 134, 209

Chinese Nationalities Park, 259

cholera, 136, 163, 179

churches. *See names of individual churches.*

Churn, Arlene, 233–34

circumambulation, 173

citizenship, U.S., 242

clan system: *bimo* and non-*bimo* clans, 81; expulsion from clan, 141; importance of, 74; and justice, 232–33

Clark, Dwight, 24

class labels: of Bamo family, 7–8; of Ma family, 20, 126; in Yangjuan Village, 16–17

class relations: in Baiwu, 107–8

class struggle, 19–20, 108, 126–27

Clifford, James, 290–94

clinics: in Mishi, 160; in Yinchang, 50–51

clothing styles, 15, 68–69; in Adur, 252–53; of American Muslims, 243–44; of *bimo*, 80; in Butuo, 252–53; changes in, 249–50, 278, 282; of curators, 275; displayed in Mountain Patterns exhibit, 260, 264–65, 269; as ethnic markers, 109, **132**, 157; at funerals, 266; life cycle and, 264–65; in Meigu, 249–50; in Puge, 251; regional, 269; of Shama, 253–55; and social status, 283; of Suondi, 251–52; of U.S. middle school students, 219; in Zhaojue, **199**

cobi ritual, 38, 205, 285

cold weather: in Baiwu, 105, 134; in Chengdu, 60; *shuohly* Han wind, 277; washing clothes in, 294; in Yinchang, 33, 40–42; in Zhaojue, 202

collecting, 248–56; commercialization/commodification of, 250; difficulties of in traditional society, 249–50; headaches of pricing, 250; Japanese collectors, 250; lack of compensation for, 255–56; local help with, 255; in Xichang stores, 255

colonialism, 288, 291

Committee on Scholarly Communication with the People's Republic of China: Ayi funded by, 225; Steve funded by, 55–56; Steve's 1992 proposal to, 95–97

grant applications: for comprehensive ethnology project, 224; Steve's 1986, 54–55; Steve's 1992, 95–97; Steve's conference, 162–63; tenuous relation of to final research results, 290

graves, worship at, 104, 145–46

Great Proletarian Cultural Revolution. *See* Cultural Revolution

Greek Orthodox Church, 238

Guabie Township, 170–72

guanxi. *See* connections

Hajj, 244–45

Han Guobin, 58

Han people: absorption into Nuosu clan system, 144; distrusted by Nuosu, 123; feared by Nuosu, 13–14; Nuosu becoming, 141–42; prejudice against Nuosu, 21–22, 67, 118, 128, 214, 278; resented by Shuitian, 65; as students, 15; as teachers, 14

Han roots (in Nuosu people), 154–55

Hanification (*han hua*): of clothing styles, 157, 160; degrees of among Nuosu, 113–14; fieldworkers' disappointment about, 61; lack of in Gaoping, 67; in Manshuiwan, 136, 143, 146

Harrell, Barbara Blain, 25–28, 216–17, **217**, 223

Harrell, Cynthia, 26

hats, in Butuo, 252

head-knocking ("kowtow"), 91–92, 145–46, **146**

Henry. *See* Wang Hao

hermeneutics, 291

heroin, 278

Heshang Village, 192–93

hiking, 114–15, 150, 156, 170, 180–

81, 183–84, 277; dangers of, 172, 185–86, 192–94

Hippocratic oath, 296

history, taught in school, 16

Hmamu teyy, 266

Hnewo abu (*Hnewo teyy*), 11, 266

Hnewo amo, 37

homelessness, 226

homicide: and *bimo* status, 81; penalty for, 141

Hong Kong, 24–25, 103

Hongxing Village (Baiwu), 126

horse-leading: by Lunzy, 99–101, 106–8, 127–28, 133, 180; by Steve, 197, 209, 214, 223

hospitality, 72, 95, 115, 118, 123–25, 151–53, 167–68; Barbara Harrell's, 216–17; from La Pinchu, 191; rejection of, 128; stereotype of minorities and, 299

households, matrilineal, 173, **175**, 192, 195

Housuo Township, 182

Hsieh Jiann, 214

Hsieh Shih-chung, 295–96

Hu Jin'ao, 106, 108–9, 129–30, **130**, 132–33

huajiao peppercorns, 160

Hui Muslims: Dru Gladney's research of, 50–51; in Miyi County, 95; in Ninglang County, 109; near Xichang, 166

human subjects, 295–300

Hutterer, Karl, 257–58, 265–67

hxe bbo mi ("go see, ah"), 79

hymns: at Mt. Zion Baptist, 233; at Seattle First Free Methodist, 228

icons, 238

illiteracy, 155

illness, of fieldworkers, 50, 60–61, 63, 67, 70

implication, in ethnographic research, 176–77, 298

income, household, in Yinchang, 50

Indian reservation, 215

informed consent, 296

interior decoration, 164

intermarriage: none between lowland and highland Yi, 144–45, 165; Yi-Han, 144–45, 147, 165; Yi-Na, 183

International Yi Studies Conference, 135, 209–14, 286

interpretation, in ethnographic writing, 291

interviewing, 62, 73–76, 106; convenience of in Manshuiwan, 136, 166; cursing *bimo*, 200–202; deception in, 121–22; distractions in, 123; refusal of requests for, 192; in Yanyuan, 129

Ipsen, Jeanine, 259

Jamil, Imam, 243–45, **245**

jeep travel, 58–59, 64, 93, 100, 103, 108–10, 114, 119–20, 173, 174, 180, 188–89

Jesus: belief in, 234–36; focus of Chinese church, 246; icons of, 238; as Islamic prophet, 241

jet lag, 215

jewelry: from Butuo, 252; and soul of wearer, 39; uniqueness of, 284

Ji family *tusi* (local rulers), 182

Jienuo (Wang) clan, 137, 139, 165; aristocratic origins of, 141–42; genealogy compiled for, 149

Jingtang Village, 64–65

Jinsha River, 254

Jinyang County, 253–55; cradle of famous Nuosu, 254; described in Nousu classics, 253; home of knowledgeable Nuosu scholars, 255

Jjihni Molur, **281**

Jjike Azhe Bimo, 202–3

Jjike clan, as *bimo*, 34

Jjike Hoqie, 31–52, **35**, 78–79

Jjike Nyieddu Bimo, 79–88, **83**

Jjike Sadda Bimo, 73–79

Jjike Vudda Bimo, 35–36, 38

Jjike Yuoga Hlumo Bimo, 198, 203–4, **203**

Jjivo Clan, 169

Jjivo Vuqie, 161, 284

Johnson, Lyndon, 119

Joint Committee on Chinese Studies, 162

journal entries: Lunzy's, 183, 212, 216; Malinowski's, 294; Steve's, 68–69, 105–8, 164–65, 294

Joy, Amber, 225–47, **242**; finances of, 226–27, 229; intellectual faith of, 234, 237–38; mother's funeral, 268; moves to Shoreline, 245; praises Chinese church, 246; prayers of, 226; religious biography of, 237–38

Joy, Gwendolyn, 226, 245

Joy, Jason, 226, 230, 245

June 4 massacres (at Tian'anmen), 69, 95

juren degree holder, 141

Kaiyuan Township, 31

Keyes, Charles, 55

Khalid Ridha, 239–42

La Pinchu, 190–91, **191**

labels, exhibit, 263, 282

lacquerware: buffalo-hide, 284; crude, 280; and ethnic identity, 165, 169;

factory-made, 169, 282; as gifts, 57–58, 156, 161; by Jjivo Vuqie, **158**, 161; manufacture of, 155–56, **156**, 169; in Mountain Patterns exhibit, 263, 284; purchase of for Burke Museum, 155, 160–61; uniqueness of, 284

lama, incarnate, 108

laments, bridal, 192

Lamo (Ayi's field assistant), 200–202.

Lan Mingchun, 60, 65, **66**, 70–71

language abilities: Ayi's, 7, 36–37, 293; of *bimo*, 202; Lunzy's, 14–15, 131, 293; Steve's, 23–24, 27, 60, 62, 69, 93, 100, 105–6, 108, 123, 142, 150–52, 165, 176, 210, 293; of Native Americans, 215; Qubumo's, 260, 273, 293; of urban Yi, 210; of Yi villagers, 6, 139, 141–42, 157, 160

language use: and ethnic identity, 142–44; in Liangshan schools, 6, 14–15; in Yinchang, 34

Lantern Festival (Yuanxiao), 64

Lao Deng. *See* Deng Yaozong

lathe, 156

Lavie, Smadar, 287

law, American attitudes toward, 218, 221–22

Lee, Cheryl, 227, 238–42, **242**

Lemicio, Eugene, 227

Leng Guangdian, 11, 40, 73

leprosy: afflicted families, 84; rituals to cure, 79, 81, 84, 86, 88; rituals in Mountain Patterns exhibit, 280; rituals for victims, 75; Steve suspected of having, 133

Lewis, Oscar, 291

Li Chaoshen, 57–58, 65

Li Miao, **59**, 60

Li Mingxi, 60, 62, 65, **66**, 70, 71, 111

Li Shaoming, 293

Li Wanxiu (Fifth Grandaunt), 138–39, 145–48, **148**

Li Yongxiang, 210, **217**, 294

Li Zhixia, 63

Liangshan Daily News (Liangshan Ribao), 210–11

Liangshan Minzu Yanjiu (journal), 178, 180

Liangshan Minzu Zhi (Liangshan Nationalities Annals), 178, 180, 181

Liangshan Nationalities Research Institute, 92–93, 98–99, 149, 163

Lianhe Village, Baiwu, 126

Libie language, 61–62

Libonati-Barnes, Susan, 259

life cycle, 264–68; clothing and, 264, death as part of, 265–68; rituals of, 264

Lijiang, 136

Lipuo (Yi) people, 61–63, 115

liquor: as gift, 114, 154, 168; as thank-you gift, 254. *See also* drunkenness

Litzinger, Ralph, 272

Liu Xin, 60, **64**, **66**, 70, 71

Liu Yulan, 46–47; and daughters' education, 6–7; opposes Ayi's fieldwork, 34, 198

logging, 127, 129

Long Yun, 254

Los Angeles, 23, 92

Lugu Lake, 108–9, **110**, 129–30, 173

Luoho Tuha. *See* Hu Jin'ao

Luoji Mountain, 251, 258

Ma Ming, 37

Ma Xueliang, 12

Ma Zhengfa, 31

museology: conflict with anthropology and folklore studies of, 261–63; seminar in, 261; students, 282

Museum of Yi Slave Society, 98, 213, 249

museums: and idealization of culture, 279; Kokuritsu Minzokugaku, 262; Liangshan Slave Society Museum, 98, 213, 249; Musée de l'Homme, 261. *See also* Burke Museum

music, in Mountain Patterns exhibit, 279. *See also* songs

Muslims: in America, 239; in Seattle, 238–44. *See also* Hui Muslims

Na (Mosuo) people, 109, 114; in Guabie, 171–72, 181–83; houses of, **175**, **191**, 190, 192, 194–95; identity as Mongols, 166, 172, 184, 187–88; matrilineal organization of, 166, 173, 192, 195; in Shuanghe, 187–88

names: Ayi's, 9, 140, 156; Lunzy's, 13, 104, 213, 259; Nuosu people's use of, 9; Steve's, 93–94, 100, 136, 146–47, 159, 289; woman who forgot her own, 144

Nasu (Yi) people, 111–12

National Science Foundation, 162, 170

Nationalities Affairs Commission: in Panzhihua, 61; visiting delegation, 53–55

Native Americans. *See* American Indians

Naxi people, 280

ndaba (priests), 171

ndeggu (mediators), 255

Ndembu, 289

Neel, James, 295

New Year, Han, 79, 103–4; gifts to

fictive kin at, 149, 165; knocking heads to elders at, 91–92; paying respects (*bai nian*) at, 63; tomb worship after, 104

New Year, Nuosu, 6, 13n, 44–45, 284

New Year's Eve gala, 46–47

news, spread of, 123, 154

nimu cobi ritual, 38, 205, 285

Niuniuba (Meigu), 278–79, **279**

Nixon, Richard, 119

Nuobie clan, 198–202

Nuobie Yopuo Bimo, 198–202

Nuobu Huojy, 149–54, 166–68, 172, 179–80

nuoho (aristocrats), 129, 130, 169, 200, 203, 293

Nuosu culture: Ayi's interest in, 5, 11–12, 38–40, 47–48; change of represented in exhibit, 282; conceptions of time in, 262–64; continuity in, 251; contrast with Han culture, 283; and death, 264–68; as described by ethnologists, 117–18; display in foreign museum of, 260; endurance of, 215; idealization of, 282; local variants of, 269; official conceptions of, 278–79; as target of reform, 17, 118

Nuosu language: retained in Manshuiwan, 142–44; Mishi as standard for, 149; perseverance of, 215

Nuosu writing: Ayi learns to write, 36–37; demonstrated at Seattle middle school, 221; modern standard Yi, 34, 37; relation to other Yi scripts, 37; spread of literacy in, 34, 155; Steve's ability in, 152; used by *bimo*, 34, 36–37; used in schools, 159, 172; village literacy campaigns, 155, 200

Nutley, Frid, 230–31, **230**
Nutley, Hugh, 230–31, **230**
Nyite (Gaoping Villager), 68, 174
nyu nimu ritual, 75
Nyundi Amo (cursing text), 76

Office for the Preservation of State
    Secrets, 61
officials. *See* cadres
Oksenberg, Michel, 25
Operation Nightwatch, 226, 241
opium, 138
origin texts, 45
Ozzu (Prmi and Na) people, 14, 19,
    122–23, 126. *See also* Na people;
    Prmi people

Pakistan, immigrants to United
    States from, 242–43
pants, narrow, 252
Panzhihua: fieldwork in 1974, 173–
    74; restudy in, 2005–6, 69; site of
    fieldwork 1988, 60–71; Steve's first
    visit to, 56–58
paper cutting, **87**
paperwork: human subjects of, 295;
    visa, 210, 259, 270
partings, 110, 135, 197, 198, 247, 272,
    294
Pelz, Ruth, 259
Peng Wenbin, 217–18
photography, 115, 121, 174, 195; as
    memory tactic, 119–20, 194; at
    mosques, 239–40; prohibition
    of, 192; use of in exhibit, 262–63
poetry, 105, 137
police, 61, 62
political campaigns: against Ameri-
    cans, 119; in schools, 7, 19–20, 184
pollution (air and water), 174

pollution (ritual), 40–42
polyphony, 291–94
postpartum confinement, 146
poverty, 50, 64, 67; conference on,
    93–95, 99–101; in contrast to cadre
    lifestyle, 130; and cultural represen-
    tation, 277–79; in Lunzy's youth,
    126–27; sympathetic treatment of,
    282
prayer: for Ayi's daughter, 231–32;
    Ayi's puzzlement at, 227; Friday,
    at mosque, 243–44; before meals,
    226, 238; by Pastor Zeng, 247
pregnancy, 39
Prmi people, 104, 110, 114, 126, 172,
    173, 181; weddings of, 122–23. *See
    also* Ozzu people
proposals. *See* grant applications
psychoanalysis, 295
Puge County, 251–52
Puwei Township, 95, 111–14
Puxiong, 137, 142
pyre, funeral, in exhibit, 265–68

Qubi Nuomo Bimo, **74**
Qubi Shimei, 92, 98–99, 117, 163,
    209, 210, **217**; articles by, 209,
    210–11, 217
Queen Anne Hill, 226–27
Qumo Asa (Ayi's daughter), 231–32
Quotations from Chairman Mao,
    16–17
Qur'an, 240–41

Radcliffe-Brown, A. R., 112
reciprocity: in ethnographic collabora-
    tion, 299; in international relations,
    162
Red Yi. *See* Nasu people
Redfield, Robert, 291